For my parents

General Editor's Introduction

Governments in recent years have used a variety of contractual techniques for the provision of services to the public. Dependence on contract has now reached the point where it can be said to be a major tool of governance. Such a shift raises important questions for lawyers and policy analysts about the appropriate mechanisms of accountability. Not only is it recognized that there is a lack of scrutiny of governmental contracting, there is, at the same time, little or no agreement as to whether some type of regulation is desirable, or what form it should take.

Anne Davies's book speaks to the problem of 'government by contract'. One of her aims is develop a better understanding of the idea of a public law of contract by exploring contracts internal to the government itself. This she does by way of an empirical analysis of contracting in the National Health Service. Another aim is to debate the merits of more extensive regulation of government contracting by public law; in doing so Dr Davies produces an agenda for further theoretical and empirical research.

The increasing reliance of government upon the provision of public services by contractual arrangements with private suppliers makes this careful and thorough socio-legal analysis by Dr Davies timely.

Keith Hawkins

Acknowledgements

This study would not have been possible without the assistance of the NHS staff who found time in their busy schedules to answer my questions. They have been promised anonymity and cannot therefore be named here, but I am grateful to them all for their patience and interest. This book is derived in part from my D.Phil. thesis, and I am indebted to my supervisor, Denis Galligan, and to my examiners, Mark Freedland and Tony Prosser, for their constructive comments. Mark Freedland also read a draft of the book, and I am grateful to him for helping to clarify my thinking on a number of points. I remain responsible for errors and omissions. It would be invidious to attempt a list of those friends and colleagues in Oxford, and at All Souls in particular, who have helped me in various ways—I am grateful to them all—but Stephen Cretney and Peregrine Horden deserve particular mention. Finally, I owe a special debt of gratitude to my parents, to whom this book is dedicated. They have been a constant source of support and encouragement, and have called me to account with consummate skill.

A. C. L. D.

March 2001

Preface

The government has used contracts since time immemorial. In recent years, however, it has done so in a variety of novel ways. The government's contracts with private firms have become increasingly central to the provision of public services. Under the Private Finance Initiative (PFI), private firms provide capital assets and associated services to the public sector through highly complex contracts. The PFI is now the main source of funding for new projects such as prisons and hospitals. The government has also restructured many of its own internal relationships using contract techniques. Under the Next Steps programme, for example, government departments were required to hive off their operational functions to arm's length agencies. Departments are expected to manage their relationships with agencies through agreements analogous to contracts, known as 'framework documents'. As a result, contract has become a core technique of modern government.

The rise of 'government by contract' has attracted some criticism, particularly from public lawyers. As Daintith (1994) points out, there is a striking disparity between the accountability mechanisms which apply to the traditional mode of governmental activity, legislation or '*imperium*', and those which apply to contract or '*dominium*'. Legislative proposals are scrutinized by Parliament and, under the doctrine of *ultra vires*, the courts are able to monitor the actions of the executive for their compliance with the legislative mandate. By contrast, the government has inherent powers to make contracts (Craig 1999; Turpin 1989) and to change (within some limits) its own internal organizational structure (see Freedland 1994). The *dominium* mode of government can therefore bypass Parliament. It also limits scrutiny by the courts. Contracts within government are not, in general, legally enforceable. And the courts have treated government contracts with private firms essentially as matters of private law: they have been reluctant to apply rigorous public law checks (Craig 1999; Turpin 1989).

Although the lack of public law scrutiny is relatively clear, there is much less agreement as to what, if anything, should be done about it. Some commentators have suggested that public law rules ought to be developed to regulate government contracts (Freedland 1994, 1998; Harden 1992): an approach employed in French law, for example (see Brown and Bell 1998). But these suggestions have not been worked out in detail:

the literature tends not to explain exactly *how* English public law might respond to contractualization. The juridification of the government's internal relations would be highly controversial. Moreover, in relation to those government contracts which are already enforceable in private law, writers in the Diceyan tradition (cf. Dicey 1885) would raise powerful objections to a public law of contract. They fear that such a law would result in privileges for the executive (Harlow 1980) and would generate litigation as contracting parties sought to map out its boundaries, given that English law does not have a clear public/private divide (see Allison 1996; Oliver 1999).

This book makes a contribution to the debate on 'government by contract' in two linked respects. First, it develops a more specific understanding of the content that might be given to a public law of contract in relation to one particular group of government contracts, those internal to the government itself. It does this by conducting an empirical case study of contracts in the National Health Service (NHS), identifying the problems faced by the contracting parties and—drawing on public law principles—suggesting normative solutions to them. Secondly, although it does not attempt to resolve the theoretical debate about the merits of greater public law intervention in government contracting, it presents doctrinal arguments and practical proposals which suggest that public law regulation is well worth exploring. Of course, the study's immediate relevance is to internal contracts—and even here, circumstances may vary from those encountered in the NHS—but it does generate a substantial research agenda (both empirical and theoretical) for other types of government contract.

An outline of the book will clarify its scope and aims. Chapter 1 locates the study in the broader 'government by contract' debate. It begins by introducing the various uses to which contracts are put by modern government. The chapter then identifies the three main controversies surrounding the growth of government by contract. These concern: the failure of 'constitutional law' controls to constrain the government's decision to use contract in a particular context; the failure of 'administrative law' controls to constrain the government's behaviour when contracting; and the absence of regulation to ensure that the government takes account of wider public interest considerations during the contracting process.

Chapter 2 introduces the 'internal' government contracts at the heart of the study. These include framework documents between government departments and their agencies, public service agreements between the Treasury and spending departments, and service agreements between local authorities and their 'direct service organizations'. Most importantly, the chapter introduces the book's case study: contracts between purchasers and providers in the NHS.

Chapter 3 examines some of the theoretical issues surrounding the development of special public law rules for internal contracts. The literature suggests that the parties will encounter two problems: purchasers will be tempted to interfere instead of giving providers a sphere of autonomy, and providers may not feel obliged to comply with contractual targets. One response to these problems would be to argue that contractualization within government is fundamentally flawed and should be abandoned (cf. Foster and Plowden 1996; Vincent-Jones 1994*a*). But since contracts are now an established feature of the administrative landscape, the book will concentrate instead on identifying ways of making them work more effectively. Two options will be explored: regulating and enforcing internal contracts through private law; and developing a framework for the regulation and enforcement of internal contracts through public law. Private law does not appear to offer acceptable doctrinal solutions to some of the problems facing the parties to internal contracts. Moreover, private law regulation is closely linked to court enforcement. Public law is attractive because it offers the flexibility to develop new norms and alternative mechanisms of dispute resolution which are tailored to the needs of internal contracts.

Chapter 4 begins the process of developing a framework of public law norms for internal contracts by setting out a policy to guide that development. The chapter argues that government contracts can be viewed as mechanisms of accountability, particularly from provider to purchaser. One task for regulation might therefore be to set out norms which would help to make that accountability process fair and effective. The promotion of accountability as a guiding policy is appealing because accountability is a core value in public law, and therefore provides a way of drawing novel contractualization reforms into the familiar discourse of public law.

Chapter 5 develops the accountability analysis more fully to reflect the richness and variety of the empirical material on NHS contracts to be presented in Chapters 6–8. Contractual relationships may take many different forms. Two extremes are identified. Hard contracts involve formal, short-term relationships in which the purchaser 'plays the market' in order to get the best deal. Soft contracts involve less formal, longer term relationships in which the purchaser uses persuasive strategies in order to get a good performance from the provider. These models will be used to categorize the behaviour of NHS purchasers when calling providers to account through their contracts. The chapter also describes the research methods used in the NHS case study.

In Chapter 6, the presentation of empirical data begins with a consideration of the accountability mechanisms which surrounded contracts between purchasers and providers. Purchasers faced rigorous accountability mechanisms to central government, but relatively weak accountability mechanisms to patients and the public. The claim that the reforms would give purchasers discretion to pursue issues of their own choosing was not, as a result, realized in practice. Two important principles about effective delegation will be suggested on the basis of these findings. The chapter also addresses the issue of defining the roles of purchaser and provider. Although purchasers did not attempt to 'micromanage' providers, there were disputes about the definition of the parties' respective roles in specific instances. Ways of minimizing such disputes are suggested. Finally, the interaction between particular NHS contracts and the other accountability mechanisms applicable to providers will be examined. In general, purchasers relied quite heavily on other mechanisms and assumed that the issues addressed by such mechanisms could therefore be omitted from their contracts. These data will be used to suggest elements to be considered in an explicit cost-benefit analysis of the interaction between one accountability mechanism and others in the same field.

Chapter 7 focuses on the relationship between the parties to the contractual accountability process, using the hard and soft models set out in Chapter 5. Fundholders tended to negotiate and draft their contracts in accordance with the hard model, but varied across the range from hard to soft when enforcing their contracts. Health Authorities usually mixed hard and soft standards and negotiating styles even within the same contract. At the enforcement stage, they used an intermediate approach somewhere between the two extremes suggested by the models. The chapter then develops a public law analysis of these relationships by considering the ways in which familiar due process norms could be applied to them. In particular, it attempts to mould due process norms so that they fit each of the different types of contractual relationship illustrated by the data.

Chapter 8 addresses the enforcement of NHS contracts. It asks whether purchasers were in a position to render the contractual accountability process effective, by setting the standards of their choice and ensuring that the provider complied with them. The data showed that purchasers struggled to enforce their requirements for a number of reasons, including the weakness of competitive market pressures in the NHS context, and the difficulty of gaining access to third party enforcement in the form of arbitration. These factors were significant regardless of whether the purchaser adopted a hard or a soft enforcement strategy. Again, various reforms will be suggested on the basis of the data. For example, it will be argued that in the absence of a competitive market, purchasers and providers should have access to a dispute resolution mechanism in order to attach a greater sense of obligation to their contracts.

Chapter 9 draws together the various norms developed over the course of the study, and explores the possibility of generalizing them to other types of internal contract. The chapter concludes by examining whether the study's findings might have wider implications for 'external' government contracts. It offers a significant agenda for further empirical and theoretical research.

Contents

Table of Directives

Table of Statutes

Table of Statutory Instruments

Table of Cases

1 Government by Contract

Government by contract is a convenient shorthand. But what does the term denote and why is the phenomenon significant? The aim of the first part of this chapter is simply to delineate the potential scope of 'government by contract'. The discussion does not suggest that all the contracts described share similar features, or that the law should regulate them in the same way. These issues would have to be addressed before any proposals about the regulation of government contracts could be made (a task beyond the scope of the present study). The second part of the chapter explores three aspects of the critique of government by contract: the absence of controls on when government can use contracts; the weakness of controls over the government's behaviour during the contracting process; and concerns about the place of 'public interest' values in government contracts. All three offer some guidance as to the issues which may need to be addressed in a study of internal government contracts. The chapter as a whole forms an important backdrop to Chapter 2, in which internal contracts, and the more specific controversies surrounding them, will be explored in detail.

The government's use of contracts

It is possible to identify at least six (albeit somewhat fluid) categories of contracting activity in which the government engages: procurement; providing public services by contracting with private bodies ('contracting out'); the private finance initiative (PFI) and other public/private partnerships; 'agreements' between the government and self-regulatory organizations; various types of agreement internal to government such as NHS contracts or Next Steps agency framework documents; and contracts of employment with staff.

Procurement contracts are probably the most straightforward and familiar type of government contract.[1] Procurement is the term generally used to describe central government's contracts for goods (computer systems, weapons and office furniture, for example), services (such as the provision of management consultancy or legal advice) and works (the construction of buildings and roads) (Turpin 1989). The procurement function has traditionally been devolved to individual departments and agencies within

---

[1] The key guidance document is HM Treasury (1998*d*). HM Treasury's Central Unit on Procurement also publishes a series of detailed guidance documents. See, generally, Arrowsmith (1992; 1996); Turpin (1989).

central government. The recent Gershon review found that there were wide variations in the deals secured by different departments, and recommended the creation of a central agency, the Office of Government Commerce, to monitor departments' performance and to conduct aggregated procurement on behalf of several departments where appropriate (HM Treasury 1999*b*; and see HM Treasury 1999*a*).

The tendering process for contracts above the relevant financial thresholds[2] must comply with the European rules on public procurement (see, generally, Arrowsmith 1996; Fernández Martín 1996).[3] These rules are designed to ensure that member states do not discriminate in favour of their own national firms. They therefore encourage governments to use transparent tendering procedures[4] and limit the grounds on which firms can be excluded from the process[5] or bids rejected.[6] Essentially, governments are obliged to accept the cheapest bid or the 'most economically advantageous' offer, selected on the basis of criteria notified to bidders in advance.[7] A full description of the details of the regime is beyond the scope of this book, though some of its significant features are discussed later in this chapter. The procurement process ultimately results in a legally enforceable contract with the chosen supplier. A procurement contract for a standard product purchased in a competitive market, such as office supplies, is likely to be relatively discrete.[8] Other contracts may be more

---

[2] For central government bodies the thresholds (from 1 January 2000 to 31 December 2001) were £93,896 for supplies and services and £3,611,395 for works contracts. The thresholds are posted on the Treasury web site at http://www.hm-treasury.gov.uk/pub/html/docs/cup/ecpro/main.html.

[3] Articles 28, 43 and 49 of the Treaty are applicable, but in practice the following directives (as amended) are usually of primary importance: Directive 93/37 for Public Works (1993 OJ L199/54), Directive 93/36 for Public Supplies (1993 OJ L199/1), Directive 92/50 for Public Services (1992 OJ L209/1), and Directive 89/665 for Public Sector Remedies (1989 OJ L395/33). The European Commission has recently proposed the consolidation of these directives into a single directive incorporating various reforms designed to simplify and streamline their requirements (European Commission 1996; 2000). The directives are implemented in UK law by the Public Works Contracts Regulations 1991 (SI 1991/2680), the Public Supply Contracts Regulations 1995 (SI 1995/201), and the Public Services Contracts Regulations 1993 (SI 1993/3228), all as amended. A separate but similar regime, beyond the scope of this work, governs the procurement practices of public utilities.

[4] See SI 1995/201, r. 9–13. (The Public Supply Contracts Regulations 1995 will be used as an example throughout this chapter.)

[5] SI 1995/201, r. 14–20.   [6] SI 1995/201, r. 21–3.   [7] SI 1995/201, r. 21.

[8] The term denotes a low-trust, short-term, arm's length relationship between the contracting parties, and contrasts with 'relational', which denotes a high-trust, long-term, close relationship between the parties. This bipolar classification of contractual relationships, with variations in the terminology, is common in the socio-legal literature: see, for example, Flynn *et al.* (1996); Fox (1974); Macneil (1974); Sako (1992). It is explored further in Ch. 5.

relational, for example, where a weapons system has to be designed and developed over a number of years. The second and third categories of government contract mentioned above, contracting out and the PFI, can be seen as more advanced and complex forms of procurement.

The 1980s saw an increasing emphasis by the government on the notion of '*contracting out*': inviting private companies to tender for the provision of a service which had hitherto been provided by the government (see generally Foster and Plowden 1996; Harlow and Rawlings 1997). This occurred at both the national and the local level. The policy reflected a distrust of public service provision, derived from public choice theory (Downs 1967; Niskanen 1971; Tullock 1965): private sector provision was seen as preferable because (due to the profit motive) it would be more efficient and more responsive to consumers (Hartley and Huby 1986). The policy has been continued since 1997, albeit with softer rhetoric, by the Labour government.

In central government, all departmental activities (including those of Next Steps agencies, discussed below) were subject to a regular review, in which one of the central questions to be addressed was whether any functions could be contracted out to the private sector (HM Treasury 1991; Office of Public Service and Science 1993). This process continues today. Every departmental activity must be examined once every five years to decide whether the activity should be abolished, privatized, internally restructured, contracted out (by inviting private bids), or market tested (allowing existing in-house staff to compete against private bidders) (Cabinet Office 1998a). The guiding principle is the achievement of 'value for money', defined as the delivery of 'better quality services at optimal cost'.[9]

Local authorities were also required to undertake market testing and contracting out.[10] Competitive tendering was made compulsory in 1980 by Part III of the Local Government Planning and Land Act 1980. Initially this applied to construction and maintenance work, but the scope of the scheme was extended by successive statutes and secondary legislation to cover a much wider range of functions, including refuse collection and legal services.[11] Local authorities were required to allow private contractors to submit bids against their in-house provider or 'direct service organization' (DSO) and increasingly detailed regulations were issued with a view to ensuring a 'level playing field' between DSOs and private

---

[9] Statement by the Chancellor of the Duchy of Lancaster, Hansard, Vol. 300, col. 94–5 (4 November 1997).

[10] Key documents include Department of the Environment (1991; 1996).

[11] See Ch. 2.

bidders.[12] The Secretary of State had power to issue directions to authorities to force them to comply with these rules.[13]

The Labour regime for contracting out at the local level[14] removes the obvious element of compulsion, although many aspects of the changes may be more presentational than real (Vincent-Jones 2000). The new regime centres around the concept of 'best value'. Under s. 3(1) of the Local Government Act 1999: 'A best value authority must make arrangements to secure continuous improvement in the way in which its functions are exercised, having regard to a combination of economy, efficiency and effectiveness.' Authorities are required to conduct regular reviews of their activities,[15] examining several questions including whether they are meeting performance targets in respect of a particular activity and how they are performing by comparison with private bodies and other authorities.[16] They must also submit an annual 'Best Value Performance Plan', which must be audited,[17] explaining how they intend to fulfil their duties under the regime.[18] Although authorities are not directly obliged to contract out, it is questionable whether they will be able to satisfy 'best value' without engaging in some market testing (DETR 1999: paras. 15–50, especially para. 36). And their 'best value' obligations may be enforced by directions issued by the Secretary of State under s. 15 of the 1999 Act.

The next stage in the Conservative government's increasingly innovative use of contract was to employ it as a means of obtaining private sector funding for capital projects: the *PFI*. Experimental schemes of this kind began in the 1980s, and became formalized as a programme in 1992 (Freedland 1998: 290).[19] The PFI enabled the government to begin new building projects without having to pay for them 'up front', thus at least appearing to reduce or contain public expenditure (Freedland 1998: 299).

[12] See, for example, the Local Government (Direct Service Organisations) (Competition) Regulations 1993 (SI 1993/848). For discussion see Harlow and Rawlings (1997).
[13] Local Government Planning and Land Act 1980, ss. 19A and 19B; Local Government Act 1988, ss. 13 and 14; as amended, Local Government Act 1992.
[14] See generally Local Government Act 1999; and DETR (1998*b*; 1999).
[15] Under s. 5 of the 1999 Act and the Local Government (Best Value) Performance Plans and Reviews Order 1999 (SI 1999/3251).
[16] The targets are set by order under s. 4 of the 1999 Act: see the Local Government (Best Value) Performance Indicators Order 2000 (SI 2000/896).
[17] 1999 Act, s. 7.
[18] Under s. 6 of the 1999 Act and the Local Government (Best Value) Performance Plans and Reviews Order 1999 (SI 1999/3251).
[19] In the Chancellor of the Exchequer's Autumn Statement (see Hansard, Vol. 208, col. 996 (12 November 1992)). Key documents under the Conservative government included HM Treasury (1993; 1995*b*).

It was claimed that the PFI would enable the public sector to harness private sector skills, and to transfer to the private sector many of the risks associated with major projects (HM Treasury 1997*b*). The PFI continues to operate under the auspices of the Labour government, now subsumed under the broader heading of 'Public/Private Partnerships' (PPPs) (DETR 1998*a*; HM Treasury 1997*b*; 1997*c*; 1999*c*; 2000).[20]

Freedland (1998) describes three different types of PFI contract. One is where the private firm provides capital assets which are rented to the public authority. Another occurs where the private firm provides capital assets which are rented out to the public: the example Freedland uses here is the provision of a bridge by a company which is then permitted to collect tolls from motorists. A third involves a combination of the first two models, with the private firm providing the capital assets and securing some revenue from both sources. The provision of capital assets distinguishes contracts in this group from standard procurement contracts, although it is important to note that the private contractor's role is usually more extensive. A contract to build a hospital might require the private contractor to maintain the building over a period of years, and to provide certain services such as cleaning or laundry, for example. Indeed, recent guidance emphasizes the importance of drafting these contracts in terms of service provision (the provision of a fully maintained building for thirty years) rather than asset provision (the construction of a building):

> The PFI transforms Government Departments and Agencies from being owners and operators of assets into purchasers of services from the private sector. Private firms become long term providers of services rather than simply upfront asset builders, combining the responsibilities of designing, building, financing and operating the assets in order to deliver the services demanded by the public sector. (HM Treasury 1997*b*: para. 3.01)

Another type of 'contract' with a private partner arises where the government strikes *a deal with a private self-regulatory organization.*[21] The government offers the organization autonomy, for example, to control who can engage in a particular activity, in return for an undertaking on the organization's part to regulate the conduct of its members. The deal is

---

[20] Other types of PPP include various forms of privatization and the commercial exploitation of government services (HM Treasury 2000). The process of negotiating a PPP may be supported by Partnerships UK, itself a PPP set up by the Treasury.

[21] On 'government by agreement' see Turpin (1999: 404–8). On self-regulation see, generally, Baldwin and Cave (1999: ch. 10); Ogus (1994: 107–11).

enforced by the implicit threat that if the organization fails to control its members, the government will regulate the area directly. These agreements—though they are highly unlikely to take effect as legally enforceable contracts—have received some legal recognition. In *R v Panel on Take-overs and Mergers, ex p. Datafin*,[22] for example, the fact that a self-regulatory organization was perceived as performing functions on behalf of the government was sufficient to make it subject to judicial review and to the rules and principles of public law.[23] But there is a sense in which these agreements are marginal instances of 'government by contract'. The 'contract' itself may be implicit, a rationalization of the situation by commentators rather than a clear transaction between the parties.

The government's relationship with the General Medical Council (GMC), the medical profession's regulatory body, illustrates the varying utility of the contractual analysis in this context. Traditionally, the GMC has been permitted to control who may join and who must leave the profession, and the standards of conduct doctors must meet (see, generally, Smith 1994; Stacey 1992). In return, the government has given both doctors and the GMC itself substantial autonomy, even within the state-funded NHS. Any agreement between the government and the profession has been, at best, vague. Recently, however, the government has introduced a greater degree of state regulation of both public[24] and private[25] health care providers, and has become increasingly clear about the standards it expects the GMC to meet (accountability, transparency and so on) if it is to retain the privilege of self-regulation (Department of Health 1999: ch. 3). The understanding between the government and the GMC is, arguably, becoming more explicitly 'contractual' as a result. Nonetheless, agreements of this type are included somewhat tentatively in the category of government contracts.

Another, rather different group of 'government contracts' (to be discussed in detail in Chapter 2) are those *agreements concluded between different branches of the government itself.* Examples include the framework documents agreed

---

[22] 1987 QB 815.

[23] This raises the intriguing question of whether the parties' 'contract' should then be classified as an internal contract—a category discussed below—because both parties are in the public sector. Importantly, however, not all self-regulatory organizations are classified as public bodies: see, for example, *R v Disciplinary Committee of the Jockey Club, ex p. Aga Khan*, 1993 1 WLR 909. For discussion, see Craig (1999: 774–8).

[24] Implemented in the Health Act 1999. See Department of Health (1997; 1998a; 2001). For discussion see Davies (2000).

[25] Implemented in the Care Standards Act 2000. See NHSE (1999a; 1999b); Department of Health (2000).

between Next Steps agencies and their parent departments,[26] service agreements between local authorities and DSOs,[27] agreements concluded between the Treasury and government departments as part of the Comprehensive Spending Review,[28] and 'internal market' contracts such as NHS contracts.[29]

These internal agreements do not in general take effect as contracts enforceable in private law because the parties to them lack separate legal personality (Freedland 1994: 89; Harden 1992: 46).[30] The implications of this are a significant concern of this book and are explored in detail in Chapter 3. Some commentators questioned whether unenforceable contractual relationships would be recognizably different from the hierarchical relationships which preceded them. The purchaser might simply continue to manage the provider, instead of giving it autonomy within the limits set by the parties' contract. The difficulty with this argument, however, is that contractual relationships may fit anywhere on a spectrum from discrete to relational,[31] and—particularly at the relational end of the spectrum—may be difficult to distinguish from managerial relationships (see Sako 1992). It is certainly wrong to assume that relationships are contractual only when they are discrete. Chapter 2 will return to this point.

A final category of government contracts consists of contracts of employment.[32] Employees of the National Health Service, public corporations and local government work under contracts of employment in the usual way. Confusingly, however, not all public sector workers have such contracts. Members of the armed forces clearly do not have contracts of employment, and considerable uncertainty surrounds the position of civil servants.[33] In practice, the precise status of government workers is often

[26] The Next Steps programme originated with the Ibbs Report (Efficiency Unit 1988). See also Cabinet Office (1998*b*); Prime Minister (1994; 1995).

[27] Initially under the Compulsory Competitive Tendering (CCT) regime, under the Local Government Planning and Land Act 1980; the Local Government Act 1988; and the Local Government Act 1992. Similar agreements are likely to arise under the 'best value' regime: Local Government Act 1999, and see DETR (1998*b*; 1999).

[28] Known as Public Service Agreements (PSAs). See HM Treasury (1998*a*; 1998*b*; 1998*c*). For discussion, see Daintith and Page (1999: 192).

[29] Under the National Health Service and Community Care Act 1990. See Department of Health (1989*b*). An internal market was also created in the BBC: see Coffey *et al.* (1997).

[30] In the NHS, Trusts did have legal personality separate from their purchasers, but legal enforceability was excluded by statute: National Health Service and Community Care Act 1990, s. 4(3).

[31] See n. 8 above.

[32] On public sector employment generally, see Deakin and Morris (1998: 182–8).

[33] Cf. *R v Civil Service Appeals Board, ex p. Bruce*, 1988 ICR 649; *R v Lord Chancellor's Department, ex p. Nangle*, 1991 IRLR 343.

insignificant: their rights will depend on the application of statutory provisions. Civil servants, for example, benefit from many of the statutory employment protection provisions,[34] and from anti-discrimination law.[35]

Powerful arguments have been made for the creation of a special regulatory regime for state employees (Fredman and Morris 1989). But there is a fundamental question as to whether that regime should be developed by analogy with that for other government contracts, or whether it should be treated as a *sui generis* issue. It has long been accepted that the contract of employment does not share the usual factual background or many of the legal incidents of the ordinary commercial contract. Considerable caution would therefore have to be exercised in generalizing norms developed in the context of—for example—procurement contracts, to the employment sphere.

'Government by contract' is thus a shorthand for a wide variety of instances in which the government acts by negotiating an agreement with another organization or person. Some have a long history (contracts of employment and traditional procurement, for example); others are more recent, such as the PFI. Some are enforceable in law (contracts with private firms under the PFI or 'best value', for example); others—internal contracts and agreements with self-regulatory organizations—are unenforceable 'contract-like' structures. These and other differences should be taken into account when making proposals to regulate 'government by contract': indeed, it may not be appropriate to treat all types of government contract in the same way. Chapter 9 will revisit this issue.

Debates and controversies

The debate about 'government by contract' forms an important part of the background to this book's study of internal government contracts, because many of the issues surrounding government by contract more generally are relevant to internal contracts. Three central debates will be explored: the failure of constitutional law to regulate the government's decision to use contract in a particular context; the failure of administrative law to control the government's behaviour when contracting; and the danger that public interest values may not be given sufficient prominence in a contractual scheme. There is, of course, a degree of overlap between these three topics: they are divided merely for ease of exposition.

---

[34] Trade Union and Labour Relations (Consolidation) Act 1992, ss. 273–6; Employment Rights Act 1996, ss. 191–3.
[35] Equal Pay Act 1970, s. 1(8); Sex Discrimination Act 1975, s. 85; Race Relations Act 1976, s. 75; Disability Discrimination Act 1995, s. 64.

Constitutional law controls

One of the most fundamental controversies about government contracts is what Freedland describes as the failure of constitutional law to control the circumstances of their use (Freedland 1994). Essentially, contractualization is a matter for the government. No parliamentary authority is required for a decision to provide a service through a contract with a private firm, or to restructure the government's internal relationships along contractual lines.

Turpin (1972: 19) explains the source of the government's contracting power succinctly:

Power to conclude particular classes of contract may be conferred upon Ministers by statute, but in addition the Crown possesses a general capacity to make contracts which rests upon no statutory authority.

The government has also asserted a broad power to determine its own internal organization in order to implement agencification and contractualization *within* government (Freedland 1994). There has been some debate in the literature as to whether the government's contracting capacity (and its power to organize its internal affairs) are more appropriately referred to as prerogatives. One definition of prerogative powers sees them as those powers which are unique to the Sovereign (Blackstone 1765–9: 232); another uses the term 'prerogative' more broadly to include all those governmental powers which are not derived from statute, whether or not they could also be exercised by the ordinary citizen (Dicey 1885: 350). The use of the term 'prerogative', while historically less accurate, serves to emphasize the scope of the power as used by modern government and the weakness of the constraints to which it is subject, drawing on the overtones of unbridled power which attach to 'prerogative' but not to 'capacity' (Daintith 1979; Freedland 1994: 91–2).[36]

There are examples of legislation on government contracts, but for the most part, they amount only to a partial constitutional law check on the government's activities.[37] This is because they tend to empower the government without imposing any significant constraints. The Deregulation and Contracting Out Act 1994 is a notable example of

[36] Though cf. Harris (1992); Wade (1985: 190–9). I am grateful to Paul Brand for helping to clarify my thinking on this point.

[37] The one exception to this generally facilitative picture has traditionally been in the area of local government. The compulsory competitive tendering policies of the 1980s and 1990s imposed a rigid statutory regime. But even this has been relaxed under the Labour government's 'best value' framework.

this.[38] The Act does not provide a compulsory statutory regime for the government to follow when contracting a service out. Instead, it simply facilitates the process by allowing the minister to delegate discretions to the contracting partner in the same way that discretions can be delegated to civil servants under the *Carltona* doctrine.[39] This may amount to a cavalier treatment of the underlying rationale of *Carltona* (Freedland 1995). Moreover, the government has combined these statutory powers with prerogative powers into a 'very extensive inherent power and authority to conduct the business of the state, and in particular to manage the finances of the state' (Freedland 1998: 292). Treasury guidance—governmental self-regulation—therefore assumes importance as the main source of regulation in this area.

If Parliament rarely has a legislative role in government contracting, it does have one residual function which might, in theory, act as a check.[40] It could refuse to provide the government with the funds to fulfil a contract or fund an agency. In practice, however, this is highly unlikely. Parliament's role in controlling public expenditure is to approve the supply estimates, and to pass the Consolidated Fund Act and the Appropriation Act based on the estimates. As McEldowney (2000: 199) explains:

Since 1982, there have been three specific days to consider the Estimates. The Commons may only reduce the estimates, but even this is unlikely if the government of the day has an overall majority . . . During this century[41] the Commons has not rejected an estimate and the scrutiny function appears a limited one.

In any event, the estimates are broadly framed, so if Parliament wished to challenge a specific contract or agency, it would probably have to do so in express words.[42] And the government would still have access to the Contingencies Fund, which can be used for payments in cases of

[38] See also the Government Trading Act 1990 and the Civil Service (Management Functions) Act 1992 (on which see Freedland (1994)).

[39] *Carltona v Commissioners of Works*, 1943 2 All ER 560; Deregulation and Contracting Out Act 1994, ss. 69 and 72.

[40] Parliament also performs an important role in scrutinizing the government's contracting activities *ex post*. The departmental Select Committees and the Public Accounts Committee conduct detailed studies of particular projects, aided by National Audit Office reports. These reports may suggest lessons for the future, but they do not amount to a 'constitutional law control' because they do not in general give Parliament the opportunity to scrutinize *proposed* projects.

[41] Presumably this denotes the twentieth century, rather than the twenty-first.

[42] This was the position in *Churchward v R.*, 1865 LR 1 QB 173. The effect of a refusal to provide funds for a contract is unclear—whether it would go to validity or enforceability (see Turpin (1972: 25–7); Craig (1999: 153–4))—but as Turpin (1972) explains, it seems highly unlikely that a contractor would ever be disadvantaged by a failure to obtain funds.

'urgency'. The only effective control over the use of this fund lies with the Treasury (McEldowney 2000).

The limited nature of the constitutional law controls on the government's contracting activities has two significant consequences. First, because the government rarely requires facilitative legislation, Parliament has few opportunities to impose constraints on the government's powers. Of course, Parliament might grant unfettered powers, but it seems more likely that the government would concede some controls on, for example, the purposes for which the powers could be used, in order to attract support for the legislation. Secondly, in the absence of parliamentary involvement, there has been little opportunity for public debate about the merits of government by contract either as a policy or in specific instances. This is particularly significant where a novel use of contract has radical implications. For example, the process of market-testing (which takes place under the government's inherent powers to organize its internal structure and to make contracts) may lead to the *privatization* of agency functions (Freedland 1994: 94–5). In short, the failure of constitutional law to control government by contract means that it lacks democratic legitimacy.

Administrative law controls

Administrative law is the second major area of controversy. Two slightly different types of problem can be identified. One is where administrative law does contain doctrines which are applied to contracts, but with arguably unpalatable results. The doctrines of contractual capacity and 'no fettering of discretion' illustrate this problem. The other is where the courts fail routinely to apply to contracts administrative law doctrines—like natural justice—which would protect contractors. The latter problem is perhaps more commonly discussed in the government by contract literature, but both problems are important. There is, of course, a third, much more general version of the administrative law problem: where government contracts, notably internal contracts, are not subject to any law at all, administrative or private. This problem will be explored in Chapter 2.

Two caveats are in order before the administrative law debate is addressed. One is that a full account of all the details of the law in this area is beyond the scope of the present study (see, generally, Craig 1999). The other is that in addition to the doctrinal issues to be examined here, there is a complex theoretical problem which would also have to be resolved before the administrative law treatment of government contracts could be strengthened. Some commentators would argue that government contracts should continue to be regulated solely or at least primarily by private law. This would avoid bringing a public/private divide into the field of contract, with all the well-known difficulties of deciding when the special public law rules would apply (cf. Allison 1996; Oliver 1999). It might also offer better protections to contractors (Harlow 1980). Others would argue that, in addition to the practical claims to be made here, there are sound theoretical reasons for applying public law norms to government contracts (Fredman and Morris 1989). This study cannot address this controversy in full, although it will be adverted to again in Chapters 3 and 9.

Contractual capacity and 'no fettering'

Litigation on government contracts is, not surprisingly, rare. Both contractors and the government generally prefer negotiation or arbitration to resolve disputes (Turpin 1989).[43] These methods are usually cheaper than litigation, and may enable the parties to rebuild their relationship once the dispute has been settled. The fact that litigation is rare means that the law in this area is rather uncertain. But there are two important public law doctrines which are superimposed on the ordinary rules of contract law. Both weaken the position of the contractor. The government may seek to escape contractual liability on the grounds that it did not have the capacity to enter the contract in the first place,[44] or that the contract constitutes a fetter on its discretion.[45]

The issue of capacity to enter into a contract generally arises in relation to statutory bodies. The statute is likely to delimit the body's powers, making it possible to argue that a particular contract is *ultra vires*.[46] In *Attorney-General v Great Eastern Railway*,[47] it was held that the actions of

---

[43] For similar findings in the private sector, see Macaulay (1963).

[44] This has a parallel in company law, though here the rigours of the common law doctrine have been modified by statute: Companies Act 1985, s. 35(1), as substituted, Companies Act 1989, s. 108.

[45] The government might also invoke the argument that the agent who concluded the contract did not have the authority to do so. Although this is not unique to public law, it adds a further element of risk for contractors who may not understand the precise powers of public officials (Craig 1999: 151–3).

[46] The *ultra vires* argument might also be applied to ministers where the Crown's inherent power to contract in a particular instance had been superseded by a specific statutory power, by analogy with *Attorney-General v De Keyser's Royal Hotel*, 1920 AC 508. See Craig (1999: 146–8) for a general discussion of the issues surrounding the Crown's capacity to contract and ministers' powers.

[47] 1880 5 App Cas 473.

a statutory corporation must be authorized expressly or implicitly by the empowering statute, though the courts would be willing to imply a power to engage in activities incidental to the corporation's main purpose. Thus, in *Attorney-General v Fulham Corporation*,[48] for example, the Corporation was empowered under the Baths and Wash-houses Acts 1846 and 1847 to set up wash-houses. The Corporation sought to provide a laundry and delivery service in addition to self-service washing troughs. It was held that this laundry business would be *ultra vires*, because the statute only envisaged making provision for people to do their own washing. The interest rate swap transactions in *Hazell v Hammersmith LBC*[49] provide a modern illustration of the same point.

The difficulty for the contractor is that if the *ultra vires* argument is successful, the contract will be held to be unenforceable: *Crédit Suisse v Allerdale BC*.[50] This outcome is undesirable in policy terms for two reasons.[51] First, it places the risk of *ultra vires* on the contractor, who is inevitably less well placed than the public body to determine whether or not a particular act is within the body's powers. Secondly, it gives the public body the unattractive option of using its own excess of power to escape a bad bargain. Moreover, the court in *Crédit Suisse* refused, albeit *obiter*, to accept the proposition that grounds of *ultra vires* other than absence of statutory authority, such as improper purposes or *Wednesbury* unreasonableness,[52] might trigger a discretion on the part of the court to decide whether or not to enforce the contract. Any form of *ultra vires* was thought to have the same extreme consequences.

Craig argues forcefully that the court should have a discretion in all cases, or at the very least, in those where a ground of *ultra vires* other than absence of statutory authority is being relied upon (Craig 1999: 150). In the case of local authorities, the rigours of the *Crédit Suisse* decision have been mitigated by the Local Government (Contracts) Act 1997. This provides, by s. 3, for local authorities to be able to certify that they have power to enter into a particular contract. The certification is conclusive for all proceedings except judicial review and audit review (s. 2(1), s. 5(1)). And even if the contract is successfully challenged in judicial review or audit review, the court is given a remedial discretion under s. 5(4) and provision is made for suitable discharge terms to apply (s. 6–7).

---

[48] 1921 1 Ch 440.   [49] 1992 2 AC 1. See Bamforth (2000).
[50] 1997 QB 306.
[51] Both are noted in the judgment of Peter Gibson LJ, 1997 QB 306 at 344.
[52] *Associated Provincial Picture Houses v Wednesbury Corporation*, 1948 1 KB 223. See, generally, Craig (1999).

Nonetheless, contractors remain unprotected in relation to other statutory authorities not within the Act.

The other risk faced by those contracting with public bodies is that the contract might be found to be *ultra vires* because it amounts to a 'fetter' on the public body's discretion. It is often said that the test for fettering is whether the contract is incompatible with the statutory purpose (Craig 1999; Wade and Forsyth 2000). This is derived from the judgment of Parke J in *R v Inhabitants of Leake*.[53] Commissioners had the power to construct drains with earth banks on either side. The issue was whether they had power to dedicate the top of the earth bank as a highway. Parke J said:

> If the land were vested by the Act of Parliament in commissioners, so that they were thereby bound to use it for some special purpose, incompatible with its public use as a highway, I should have thought that such trustees would have been incapable in point of law, to make a dedication of it; but if such use by the public be not incompatible with the objects prescribed by the Act, then I think it clear that the commissioners have that power.[54]

There was no evidence that the commissioners needed to use the bank for a statutory purpose—cleaning the drain, for example—inconsistent with the highway.

In practice, however, the courts' main focus in these cases is on the *imaginative* reconciliation of the various statutory powers involved in the case. In *British Transport Commission v Westmorland CC*,[55] the court found that the dedication of a highway over a railway bridge was not incompatible with a statutory power to demolish the bridge because, on the facts, the Commission was unlikely to need to exercise the power to demolish. Incompatibility was to be assessed by reference to probabilities, not possibilities.[56] Another strategy, illustrated by *Blake v Hendon Corporation*,[57] is to rank the powers so that one power takes precedence over an apparently inconsistent power. In *Blake*, the local authority had power to dedicate a park to the public which seemed to be inconsistent with another power to grant leases over the land. It was held that the power to grant leases was an auxiliary power which could only be exercised where it would promote the main purpose of providing a pleasure ground to the

---

[53] 1833 5 B. & Ad. 469.
[54] 1833 5 B. & Ad. 469 at 478.   [55] 1958 AC 126.
[56] 1958 AC 126 at 144, per Viscount Simonds: 'We live in a world in which our actions are constantly guided by a consideration of reasonable probabilities of risks that can reasonably be foreseen and guarded against, and by a disregard of events of which, even if we think of them as possible, we can fairly say that they are not at all likely to happen.'
[57] 1962 1 QB 283.

public. If this purpose was best served by dedication, it did not matter that dedication precluded the exercise of the (evidently superfluous) auxiliary power to grant leases.

But there are cases in which it is simply impossible to reconcile the conflicting powers. In *Dowty Boulton Paul v Wolverhampton Corporation*,[58] the corporation had granted the company a right to use the municipal airport for a term of 99 years. It then decided to refuse to renew the airport's licence because it wanted to develop the airfield for housing under other powers. Similarly, in *Cory v London Corporation*,[59] the plaintiffs entered into a refuse collection contract with the Corporation in its capacity as a sanitary authority. The Corporation then made by-laws, in its capacity as port health authority, which rendered the contract unprofitable for the plaintiffs. In both these cases, the competing powers were incompatible and, as Cane points out, 'the court is called upon to balance the public and private interests involved and to decide which deserves more weight' (Cane 1996: 149).

Unfortunately, in neither case did the court articulate a very clear set of reasons for its choice. In *Dowty*, the lease was upheld on the basis that it was a valid exercise of a statutory power. In *Cory*, the court refused to imply a term that the contract would not be made more onerous, holding that the corporation was under a duty to make the by-laws regardless of their impact on the plaintiff. But it does seem possible to rationalize the decisions. In *Dowty*, the corporation did not appear to have any particularly strong reasons for its change of plan. It was not therefore surprising that the plaintiff's private interests weighed heavily with the court. In *Cory*, by contrast, the suggested contractual term would have defeated a strong and specific public interest in raising hygiene standards, so the court preferred the public interest to the plaintiff's private rights.

Again, harsh remedies operate in this area. If a concluded contract is found to be *ultra vires*, it will be unenforceable. The contractor has no remedy in damages. Nor does the exercise of a regulatory power which renders the contract more onerous amount to a breach of contract, for which damages could be claimed. Under *Cory*, a public body cannot validly undertake not to exercise its regulatory powers in a way which would harm the contractor. It might be possible to argue that the contract is frustrated in these circumstances—a point conceded in *Cory*—but, as Craig points out, this solution may not be acceptable in every case (Craig 1999: 531–2).

---

[58] 1971 1 WLR 204.   [59] 1951 2 KB 476.

In most cases, contractual price variation clauses and other standard terms are likely to address the problem. This probably explains why there is relatively little case law on the issue. Nonetheless, as various writers have argued (Craig 1999: 532–3; Wade and Forsyth 2000: 336), it would be possible to make the law much more acceptable in this area by adopting some of the flexible French remedies (see Brown and Bell 1998: 206–10). French law permits the public authority to modify the terms of the contract (to require more water to be supplied to a growing town, for example)[60] provided that it adjusts its payment in order to preserve the financial balance of the contract. Similarly, under the doctrine of *fait du prince*, where the exercise of regulatory powers upsets the balance of the contract, the contractor is entitled to adjust its charges to the authority or the consumer unless the change in the law is of general application. These approaches seem preferable to placing all the risk on the contractor, even though in practice this might be mitigated by a sympathetic government.

Natural justice

The second type of administrative law failure in relation to government contracts occurs when the courts refuse to apply familiar administrative law doctrines—natural justice, for example—to the government because it is exercising power through a contract. This causes two significant problems. First, it limits the protection available to contractors. Secondly, it enables the government to evade public law scrutiny by replacing direct service provision with provision through contract.

Natural justice is clearly of value in ensuring that tendering procedures are properly conducted. In *R v Legal Aid Board, ex p. Donn & Co.*,[61] a tendering procedure was found to be unfair on two counts. First, the committee considered the applicants' bid on the basis of incomplete papers, due to a clerical error, and did not reconvene to reconsider when the mistake was discovered. Secondly, the committee formed a question about the applicants' fitness to conduct the litigation which was the subject of the tendering exercise but failed to offer them an opportunity to address that question. In *R v Lord Chancellor's Department, ex p. Hibbit & Saunders*,[62] the court found that a tendering process was unfair because the department engaged in financial negotiations with some, but not all, of the bidders who met the non-financial criteria.

---

[60] As in *Compagnie Générale des Eaux* (CE 12 May 1933), 1933 Recueil Hebdomadaire de Jurisprudence 368.
[61] 1996 3 All ER 1.   [62] 1993 COD 326.

But these cases illustrate an important hurdle in the way of disappointed bidders. It is that they will be denied judicial review if they cannot show a sufficient 'public element' in the case.[63] This test is inherently imprecise (Craig 1999: 773). It was found to be satisfied in *Donn* on the basis of a list of factors, including the importance to the plaintiffs, defendants, court and public at large of selecting the most appropriate solicitors to conduct the litigation. But in the *Hibbit* case, even though the procedure was clearly unfair, the court refused to find a 'public law element', and preferred to characterize the decision as a purely commercial one. It remains to be seen which approach will be preferred in future.

As Freedland points out, this issue may turn on how widely the court defines the decision it is reviewing. Judicial review tends to focus on 'the ultimate decision rather than the strategies and the whole of the process which generated that decision' (Freedland 1994: 101). This is problematic because the public body's ultimate choice of a contracting partner may appear to be a matter of commercial judgement with no public law element. A broader consideration of the tendering process might make it easier to characterize the case as raising public law issues. But *Donn* and *Hibbit* show that the ultimate choice itself can be characterized in different ways. In *Hibbit*, it was seen, narrowly, as a business decision; in *Donn*, it was seen as an important public decision about the conduct of litigation. This also affects the perception of the decision as public or private.

In practice, many tendering exercises[64] are governed by the European public procurement directives (see, generally, Arrowsmith 1996; Fernández Martín 1996).[65] In addition to controlling the criteria on which tenders can be excluded and contracts awarded, the regime imposes a number of procedural requirements on the purchaser.[66] The aim is to prevent governments from giving preference to domestic firms when awarding contracts. There is strong pressure[67] to use either an entirely open tendering procedure, in which anyone may submit a bid,[68] or the restricted procedure, under which the authority may choose a pool of at least five bidders from those who express an interest.[69] The contract must then be awarded either to the lowest-priced bid, or to the 'most economically advantageous offer', which allows the authority to take

---

[63] Natural justice in private law (discussed further below) would not avail at the pre-contractual stage because there is no concluded contract into which the courts could imply suitable terms.

[64] For the financial thresholds, see n. 2 above. For exclusions, see SI 1995/201, r. 6.

[65] See n. 3, above.   [66] See, esp., r. 9–13, SI 1995/201.

[67] SI 1995/201, r. 10.   [68] SI 1995/201, r. 11.   [69] SI 1995/201, r. 12.

account of factors like quality and after-sales service, all of which must be set out in advance of the competition.[70] Authorities are required to publish details of the award in the Official Journal[71] and to 'debrief' disappointed bidders.[72]

These rules do offer some procedural protections to bidders: everyone who responds to the advert must be considered, and the public authority is obliged to give reasons for its decision. On one view, the rigid, rule-based nature of the tendering process also promotes procedural fairness: it ensures that tenderers know how their bids are to be assessed and that all bids will be assessed in the same way. It could, however, be argued that the directives give effect only to one view of what procedural fairness might require here.[73] The directives deliberately minimize opportunities for negotiation between the contractor and the public authority. This could be seen as disregarding the usual fairness requirement of hearing the other side. It forces the public authority to rely heavily on formal tenders, even though contractors might have a better chance of conveying their ideas and capabilities during negotiations. In procedural fairness terms, therefore, the European regime is not wholly satisfactory.

Procedural fairness is not only a concern at the tendering stage. It might also be relevant during the life of the parties' contract. The purchaser may have important decisions to make affecting the contractor's rights: whether the contractor has failed to provide the service to the specified standards and should therefore have its monthly payment reduced, for example (see HM Treasury 1997*a*). The European public procurement regime does not extend beyond the contract award stage. And the applicability of public law procedural fairness is unclear: it would probably depend upon the uncertain 'public law element' test set out above. It might be possible to import natural justice into the contract through the private law technique of implied terms (discussed further in Chapter 3), but again, it is difficult to predict how the courts would respond to such an argument.

Conclusion

Administrative law is perceived as offering limited protection to contractors and thus as an inadequate regulatory framework for government

---

[70] SI 1995/201, r. 21.   [71] SI 1995/201, r. 22.   [72] SI 1995/201, r. 23.
[73] For more general critique on this issue, see Arrowsmith (1997: 400–10). The Commission's recent proposal to reform the regime would permit authorities to use the negotiated procedure for complex contracts, thus permitting a dialogue with bidders (European Commission 2000: 6–9; and Articles 29 and 30 of the draft directive).

contracts. The application of the ordinary doctrine of *ultra vires* places an enormous risk on a contractor doing business with a statutory body. The 'no fettering' doctrine fails to offer nuanced solutions to the problem of balancing contractors' private interests and the public interest in regulatory changes. And the extent to which contractors may receive basic natural justice protections, either at the tendering stage or during the life of the contract, is unclear.

Public interest values

A third area of controversy relates to the values served by government contracts. By definition, a contract involves an agreement about what is to be purchased for a particular price. One of the claimed advantages of contractualization was that it would encourage greater precision about public services and their costs, thereby improving financial accountability (Harden 1992: 71). But commentators have expressed concerns that this focus on financial accountability might exclude other 'public interest' values which ought also to be respected (see, for example, Freedland 1994). A variety of examples might be given to illustrate this argument. Two will be focused on here: the extent to which the law precludes the use of 'contract compliance' policies in government contracts, and the relationship between contractualization and public participation in government.

Contract compliance

Government contracts represent attractive business opportunities for private firms. In order to win such contracts, firms may be willing to agree to many of the government's proposed terms and conditions. Not surprisingly, therefore, governments sometimes seek to use contracts to enforce other policies: by requiring contractors to locate in a deprived region and employ long-term unemployed workers, or to recognize trade unions for collective bargaining, for example (McCrudden 1999c: 7–8).

Contract compliance policies are highly controversial. On the one hand, it is argued that such policies are inefficient: the government may fail to select the most economically advantageous bid if it focuses on non-commercial considerations. And given the weakness of the constitutional law controls on contracting, discussed above, the government's use of contracts for non-commercial ends is largely unaccountable (Daintith 1979). On the other hand, it may be argued that contract compliance is a useful way of reinforcing the government's other democratically mandated policies (Leonard 1990; McCrudden 1999*d*). Indeed, it may seem particularly inappropriate for a government committed to labour standards, for example, to be forced to contract with a notoriously bad employer. Taxpayers' money would be used to subsidize behaviour of which the government disapproved (McCrudden 1999*c*: 9). And the contractor's ability to put in a low bid might be directly related to its unfair labour practices (McCrudden 1999*c*: 10).

The European public procurement regime appears to preclude the use of contract compliance. The directives specify that a tender can only be excluded if the contractor fails checks on its economic and financial standing and its technical knowledge and ability.[74] The contract must be awarded either to the lowest priced bid, or to the bid which is most economically advantageous (taking account of factors such as the period for completion and technical merit).[75] This was the view of Advocate-General Darmon in the *Beentjes* case.[76] He argued that the criteria for excluding tenders were exhaustive, and so precluded the use of contract compliance. And at the award stage, any criteria used to determine the 'most economically advantageous' offer had to relate to the contractor's product rather than to the suitability of the contractor.

But the European Court of Justice has been rather more generous. In *Beentjes*, it accepted the Advocate-General's view that the directive's provisions on the exclusion of tenderers were exhaustive, but it did permit a social clause as an 'additional specific condition',[77] provided that two criteria were met. First, the condition had to be compatible with Community law, and in particular, with Treaty principles on the right of establishment and the freedom to provide services. In other words, the condition would not be acceptable if it discriminated against bidders from other Member States. Secondly, the condition had to be publicized in the contract notice. In the *Beentjes* case itself, this meant that a condition requiring the contractor to use long-term unemployed workers to make up 70 per cent of the workforce might be permissible. It had been included in the contract notice, and the national court was left to determine whether or not it was discriminatory.

After *Beentjes*, the Commission took the view that the 'additional specific condition' permitted by the decision could take effect as a term of the contract, but not as an award criterion (see, for example, European Commission 1996: paras. 5.42–3). In the more recent case of

---

[74] See, for example, SI 1995/201, r. 14–16.   [75] SI 1995/201, r. 21.
[76] *Gebroeders Beentjes BV v State of the Netherlands* (ECJ Case 31/87), 1988 ECR 4635.
[77] 1988 ECR 4635, at 4661.

Commission v France,[78] however, the ECJ rejected this interpretation of *Beentjes*. In this case, the French authorities had included a condition relating to a local project to tackle unemployment in contract notices for the construction and maintenance of school buildings. The Court stated that 'The condition relating to the employment of long-term unemployed persons, which was at issue in [*Beentjes*], had been used as the basis for rejecting a tender and therefore necessarily constituted a criterion for the award of the contract' (para. 52). It reiterated the requirements that the social clause must be expressly stated in the contract notice and must be non-discriminatory.[79] This significantly facilitates the use of contract compliance. Under the Commission's interpretation of *Beentjes*, public authorities had little leverage when negotiating social clauses with contractors, because they were forced to disregard the contractor's potential ability to comply with them when awarding the contract. Indeed, authorities might have been compelled to award a contract to a firm which expressed no desire to meet their social terms. The ability to take account of these issues at the award stage should enable public authorities to use social clauses more effectively.

Where a contract is not covered by the European regime, there are at least two relevant domestic legal provisions. One is statutory: local authorities are forbidden by s. 17 of the Local Government Act 1988 to take account of 'non-commercial considerations' when awarding contracts. The restrictive impact of this provision may, however, be somewhat mitigated by a new power under s. 19 of the Local Government Act 1999 for the Secretary of State to remove items from the list of non-commercial matters for the purposes of s. 17.[80] At common law, the doctrine of 'improper purposes' may also restrict the use of contracts for social ends. In *R v Lewisham LBC, ex p. Shell*,[81] the council boycotted Shell because of its involvement in South Africa. The court distinguished the council's aim of promoting good race relations in its area[82] by ceasing to trade with a company with interests in South Africa during the apartheid era, which was held to be legitimate, from its aim of pressurizing the company to withdraw from South Africa, which was held to be unlawful.

---

[78] Case C-225/1998, Sept. 2000, unreported.

[79] Although this satisfies the transparency and non-discrimination requirements of the WTO Agreement on Government Procurement (1994), it is not clear whether it is legitimate to include social criteria when assessing the 'capability' of potential bidders under Art. VIII (b). For discussion, see McCrudden (1999*c*).

[80] This power has been exercised in the Local Government Best Value (Exclusion of Non-commercial Considerations) Order 2001 (SI 2001/909).

[81] 1988 1 All ER 938.   [82] Under s. 71, Race Relations Act 1976.

The current compromise solution in both European and domestic law of permitting the use of contract compliance within limits is unlikely to appeal to the protagonists at either extreme of the debate. But what is most worrying is the absence of coherent and explicit public policy on this issue. At the European level, the commercial model of procurement, designed to prevent protectionism, sits uncomfortably with Community social policy. And at the domestic level, much of the current law is explained by attacks on left-wing councils by the Thatcher government. The policy on contract compliance at both levels would be more legitimate if it were more explicitly formulated after a full public debate.

Public participation

A second set of 'public interest' concerns arises in relation to public participation in government. Two different but linked criticisms were made. One was that contractualization in fact reduced or limited the accountability of public services to members of the public. The other was that contractualization was surrounded by a misleading rhetoric of *increasing* the responsiveness of services to their consumers.

Contractualization required public bodies to adopt more 'commercial' modes of behaviour. It was therefore argued that their governance arrangements should be reformed along commercial lines. In the NHS, for example, Health Authorities were governed prior to 1990 by large boards of appointees who were intended to represent particular interests. The boards included members of the medical professions, local authority representatives (who had at least been elected to the local authority, if not to the Health Authority) and members of local patient groups. They were replaced in 1990 by much smaller boards of appointees with 'business experience', in the style of a company's board of executive and non-executive directors (Department of Health 1989*b*; Ferlie *et al.* 1996). Proponents of the reforms argued that the new boards would be more effective:[83] the old boards had been criticized for their lack of cohesion, strategic focus, and control over service providers (Day and Klein 1987). Moreover, extensive citizen participation in the running of public services was argued to be unnecessary provided that those services were responsive to their needs (Hunt 1995; Wistow and Barnes 1993).

Commentators criticized the changes on several grounds. They challenged the way in which board appointments were made: the process was shrouded in secrecy and there was a suspicion that appointments

---

[83] Ferlie *et al.* (1996) found some empirical evidence for this.

were being used to reward the government's political supporters (Stewart 1995).[84] Moreover, they argued that business experience was not necessarily a better qualification for the task of, for example, rationing health care, than was the ability to represent some sector of the community (Longley 1990). Most significantly, they argued that the reforms reduced the accountability of public bodies to the local community. Although the old boards were not democratically elected, the reforms heralded a 'democratic deficit' because they paid even less attention to notions of representativeness[85] than the system they replaced (see, generally, Ferlie *et al.* 1996).

Commentators also claimed that the reforms reduced public accountability by blurring responsibilities for service provision (Bruce and McConnell 1995). One problem is that where services are provided by private firms, it may be claimed that the details of the contract are commercially confidential.[86] This may limit the public's access to information about the terms and conditions on which services are provided to them. Moreover, service users may be uncertain about whom they should complain to when things go wrong. An example will illustrate this difficulty.

If the consumer brings an application for judicial review, which body should be chosen as the defendant? In some cases, this issue is straightforward. In a case against a Next Steps agency, for example, the agency has no legal personality separate from its parent department (Freedland 1994: 89; Harden 1992: 46). But it is rather more complex where the department has placed a contract with a private firm. One option is to give the department continuing responsibility for contracted-out services. This appears to be the effect of s. 72 of the Deregulation and Contracting Out Act 1994.[87] Thus, where the Act is used (it will be remembered that this is not mandatory) it is possible for the aggrieved citizen

---

[84] These concerns led to the establishment in 1994 of the Committee on Standards in Public Life, and a gradual opening up of appointment procedures in accordance with the Committee's recommendations.

[85] Though the 'new right' response to this might be to argue that the old boards were more radical politically than, and therefore not genuinely representative of, local people.

[86] A considerable amount of information is available on standard contract terms: see, for example, HM Treasury (1990). And some information on specific projects emerges through sources such as National Audit Office reports and House of Commons Public Accounts Committee reports. Nonetheless, aggrieved individuals might have difficulty obtaining copies of specific contracts.

[87] S. 72(3) excludes criminal offences and the contractor's liabilities in relation to the contract with the public body.

to sue the minister, office-holder or local authority whose functions are being exercised by the contractor. The other option is to apply public law principles to the private contractor. As Craig (1999) points out, there is precedent for this in the sense that bodies performing functions on behalf of the government—such as the City Panel on Take-overs and Mergers—have been subjected to judicial review.[88] Indeed, the case for extending the application of public law seems even stronger where the body's relationship with government is more formal.

But there is a problem which affects both these solutions. Would either party be allowed to argue, in response to the claim, that the other party was to blame? The minister might claim, for example, that the contract gave him or her no power to control the contractor's activities on a particular issue. Or the contractor might allege that it had not been given sufficient funds to maintain a particular level of service. The 1994 Act does not give the minister the former option: he or she is deemed responsible regardless. But it is important that the common law should not permit these arguments either. Otherwise, the contractualization of the service could provide a way of evading liability altogether: each side could simply blame the other whenever a problem arose. Of course, it would be necessary to determine *as between the parties to the contract* who is at fault, but this determination should not be allowed to affect the rights of consumers.

Paradoxically, however, contractualization did not purport to reduce the accountability of public services to their users. It was surrounded by a rhetoric of consumer empowerment. This rhetoric is exemplified by the Citizen's Charter initiative, a relative late-comer to the 'new public management' introduced by the Conservative government in the early 1990s (HM Government 1991; Barron and Scott 1992; Willett 1996). The Citizen's Charter set out general rights and expectations for the consumers of government services. Public bodies were required to publish information about performance and to institute complaints procedures to address consumers' grievances.

Here, the complaint was that contractualization was not pushed as far as the consumerist rhetoric might have suggested (Bruce and McConnell 1995; Stewart 1995; Weir 1995). It would have been possible, theoretically at least, to use contracts to shape relationships between consumers and public services, thereby giving consumers a clear set of enforceable rights.[89]

---

[88] *R v Panel on Take-overs and Mergers, ex p. Datafin*, 1987 QB 815.

[89] For a fascinating study of the potential impact of the Unfair Terms in Consumer Contracts Directive (93/13/EEC) on this issue, see Whittaker (2000).

But the Charters were largely ineffectual: the Patients' Charter (Department of Health 1991; 1995) contained a handful of legal rights enshrined in pre-existing legislation alongside a host of unenforceable aspirations.[90] And contracts were introduced only between public service purchasers and providers (Harden 1992). Patients could not be parties to NHS contracts, for example, despite claims that the reforms would increase consumer choice (see, for example, NHSE 1994; 1995*a*). If a patient was unhappy with a service, he or she would have to persuade the purchaser (a fundholding GP or Health Authority) to contract with another provider, or move to another GP with different purchasing policies. Of course, the very notion of consumer empowerment might itself be questioned. Consumers are not the only group with a legitimate interest in the running of public services: taxpayers and staff should also have a voice (Foster and Plowden 1996). Nonetheless, it is important to recognize that the reforms did not offer the empowerment they proclaimed.

Conclusion

The advocates of government by contract focused on its potential to encourage the precise specification of service standards, a more explicit focus on costs, and improvements in performance as a result of market pressures. These issues are obviously important: both taxpayers and users benefit from the efficient provision of public services. But contractualization was controversial because its proponents failed to engage with the way in which the policy might affect other significant public interests. Should contracts be used to enforce social goals? How could contracts be introduced whilst empowering, or at least not disempowering, members of the public? These are difficult questions, but a well-designed contractualization policy would address them in an explicit and honest way.

Conclusion

Government by contract is an important modern phenomenon. Although contracts themselves are nothing new, they are being put to a variety of novel uses as techniques for organizing the internal relationships of government agencies, and for harnessing the efforts of private firms to provide complex combinations of assets and services to the

[90] For example, the Charter contained a number of unenforceable standards about the time patients would have to wait for treatment in various circumstances, alongside a statement of patients' right of access to medical records, enshrined in the Access to Health Records Act 1990.

public sector. This chapter has explored some of the controversies surrounding government by contract: the concern that Parliament is unable to control the executive's decision to use a contract in a particular context; the concern that the law does not provide an adequate regulatory framework to protect contractors; and the concern that the contractualization of government has ignored important public interest values.

These controversies are in various ways applicable to the internal government contracts at the heart of this study. The government's power to reorganize its internal management structure along contractual lines appears to be an inherent capacity requiring no parliamentary scrutiny. Internal contracts are even less well regulated than procurement or PFI transactions, for example, because they are not legally enforceable. And the concern that contractualization may sideline public participation is particularly significant: much of this critique has developed in 'internal markets' within public services, such as the NHS. Chapter 2 will introduce internal government contracts in more detail, and explore some of the controversies which particularly affect contracts in that category.

2 Government by Internal Contract

For the purposes of this study, the concept of an 'internal government contract' encompasses any agreement between two bodies, both of which are in the public sector.[1] This chapter will examine some of the main examples of this phenomenon: in central government, framework agreements between government departments and their agencies, and Public Service Agreements (PSAs) between the Treasury and government departments; in the public sector more generally, contracts between purchasers and providers in the NHS, and service agreements between local authorities and their direct service organizations (DSOs) (and, to some extent, their in-house social care providers). There are other examples—internal contracts in the BBC, for instance (see Coffey *et al.* 1997)—but this chapter will focus on these four significant cases.

Two themes of particular importance to this study will run through the discussion. First, to the extent permitted by the available evidence, the similarities and differences between the various types of internal contract will be examined. This information will help to determine whether or not internal contracts are a coherent category for the purposes of study and reform. More specifically, it will help to determine the extent to which reform proposals based on research about one type of internal contract—such as the NHS case study to be used in this book—might be generalizable to other types of internal contract. Secondly, the legal status of each of the internal contracts described in the chapter will be explored. Perhaps the most significant common feature of internal contracts is the fact that they are highly unlikely to be enforceable in law. The implications of this will be taken up in Chapter 3, which addresses some of the critiques of internal contracts and potential avenues for reform.

Contracts in public services

One important aspect of the 'new public management'[2] was the attempt to 'marketize' the delivery of public services. This involved the creation

---

[1] This chapter will focus on contracts which form part of a specific contractualization programme. It would, of course, be possible for branches of government to conclude *ad hoc* agreements to which this study's proposals might also apply.

[2] For enthusiastic advocacy, see Osborne and Gaebler (1992). For an introduction to the large critical literature, see Ferlie *et al.* (1996); Foster and Plowden (1996); Hood (1991; 2000); Power (1997); Rhodes (1997).

of separate purchaser and provider roles in place of hierarchical management structures. Relationships between public sector purchasers and public sector providers were governed by internal contracts. This section will examine internal contracts in both the NHS and local government, describing the former—the book's case study—in some detail.

Purchasing and provision in the NHS

Prior to the National Health Service and Community Care Act 1990[3] ('the 1990 Act'), the provision of care in the NHS was hierarchically managed.[4] Funds were distributed from the centre to Regional Health Authorities (RHAs).[5] RHAs gave budgets to District Health Authorities (DHAs) which managed the provider units in their area. The reforms sought to dismantle the hierarchical relationship between DHAs and providers, by giving providers organizational independence from DHAs, and by creating a new role for DHAs as the purchasers of care from these providers.[6] This structural change is commonly referred to as the 'purchaser/provider split' or the creation of an 'internal market'.[7]

The reforms reflected two key 'new public management' principles: that the task of providing services should be separated from the task of deciding what should be provided, and that competition could be used as an effective stimulus to greater efficiency and higher quality (see, generally, Foster and Plowden 1996). The first principle is derived from public choice arguments that service providers have an interest in maximizing their own budget, and to some extent their own convenience, and will not necessarily do what is in the best interests of the public or consumers (Downs 1967; Niskanen 1971; Tullock 1965). It was claimed that the reforms would make providers of care more accountable

---

[3] See Department of Health (1989*b*). There is a large introductory literature: see, for example, Spurgeon (1993); Levitt *et al.* (1995); West (1997). For an introduction to the comparative analysis of the reforms, see Ranade (1998). On 'new public management' in the NHS more generally, see Ferlie *et al.* (1996); Longley (1993); Walsh *et al.* (1997).

[4] For the reforms in their historical context, see Webster (1998) and Klein (1995). For a full history of the NHS, see Webster (1988; 1996).

[5] Abolished from April 1996 by the Health Authorities Act 1995. Their functions were taken over by the regional offices of the NHS Executive. For history of the regional tier of NHS management, see Webster (1998).

[6] The arrangements described are those of 1996–7, when the empirical study (described in Ch. 5) was conducted. See also Montgomery (1997*a*).

[7] Both terms are problematic. The first does not convey the novelty of the purchasing role (see Lapsley and Llewellyn (1997)); the second tends to imply a degree of competition which may not in fact be present (Montgomery 1997*a*). Competition is discussed further in later chapters.

because they would be answerable to independent purchasers for the quantity, quality and cost of the treatment given (Department of Health 1989; cf. Harden 1992). The second principle, that of competition, reflects the preference of these theorists for private sector ways of operating (Osborne and Gaebler 1992; Enthoven 1985). Under the old arrangements, providers had no incentive to treat more patients: to do so would make it harder to stay within budget, and any extra financial allocation in respect of extra patients would not filter through the system until the next financial year (Department of Health 1989). The White Paper emphasized the principle that 'money would follow the patient' under the new funding arrangements (Department of Health 1989). Purchasers could buy from whichever provider offered the best deal, and could pay the provider immediately for the work done. This plays on the same notion of bureaucratic self-interest which is challenged by the first principle: providers would seek to please their purchasers in order to attract more patients, and thereby maintain their market share or increase their income. Thus, the enhanced accountability under the first principle would be reinforced by competitive pressures.[8]

Providers were permitted under s. 5 of the 1990 Act to apply for 'NHS Trust'[9] status, which gave them their own board of directors and legal and organizational identity separate from their parent DHA. Each Trust was created by a Statutory Instrument which included a statement of its functions, but in practice this was usually very brief, referring simply to the provision of (for example) 'hospital' services from the Trust's address. Trusts usually specialized in a particular kind of service: acute, community, ambulance, and so on. Schedule 2 of the 1990 Act lists general powers and duties of Trusts. As explained above, instead of receiving a portion of the DHA's annual budget under the old hierarchical management system, Trusts were to attract income by selling their services to purchasers. They were placed under a statutory duty to ensure that they brought in enough income each year to cover their expenditure,[10] but were not allowed

---

[8] The White Paper itself played down the terminology of markets and competition (Department of Health 1989*b*), perhaps because of its negative connotations (for example, the possibility that unsuccessful hospitals would be forced to close), but this terminology formed a key part of the literature on which the reforms appeared to be based (Enthoven 1985, and see Webster 1998).

[9] Another example of misleading terminology: although provision is made for money to be held on trust for the purposes of a particular Trust (s. 11 of the 1990 Act), they are themselves statutory corporations (s. 5(5) of the 1990 Act), not trusts in the private law sense. See Hughes (1991).

[10] 1990 Act, s. 10(1).

to make a profit or cross-subsidize different services: the price of each service was to reflect the cost of providing it (NHSME 1990). Moreover, they were confronted with stringent financial targets.[11] For example, Trusts were obliged to achieve a return on their assets, with the express aim of encouraging the efficient use of estate and putting them on an equal footing with private sector providers (Department of Health 1989). By the time of this study in 1996–7, it was the norm for providers to have Trust status.

Health Authorities'[12] historical role was to exercise on behalf of the Secretary of State his statutory duties to provide health services. This continued after the reforms. Under the National Health Service Act 1977, s. 1(1):

It is the Secretary of State's duty to continue the promotion in England and Wales of a comprehensive health service designed to secure improvement:
(*a*) in the physical and mental health of the people of those countries, and
(*b*) in the prevention, diagnosis and treatment of illness,
and for that purpose to provide or secure the effective provision of services in accordance with this Act.

More specific duties to provide services such as hospital accommodation, ambulance services and maternity services are given in s. 3 of the 1977 Act. The National Health Service (Functions of Health Authorities and Administration Arrangements) Regulations 1996[13] permit the Secretary of State's more specific duties to be performed on his behalf by Health Authorities.[14] They may provide services directly, or arrange for them to be supplied through NHS or other contracts. Thus, as the reforms were implemented and providers became Trusts, Health Authorities delivered services increasingly through placing contracts rather than through direct management. They received a budget from the regional tier with which to do so, and were expected to remain within that budget each year. They were subject to other financial targets too, such as the requirement to achieve an annual efficiency gain (for example, 2 per cent more work for the same level of funding) in their contracts with providers (NHSME 1990).

Health Authorities were, however, not the only type of purchaser under these reforms. Larger[15] GP practices were given the option of joining the fundholding scheme, a voluntary arrangement under which they were

---

[11] 1990 Act, s. 10(2).

[12] The Health Authorities Act 1995 replaced DHAs and Family Health Services Authorities with unitary Health Authorities. The latter terminology is used hereafter.

[13] SI 1996/708.   [14] SI 1996/708, r. 3.

[15] Initially with a minimum list size of 9000, reduced to 7000 in 1992 and 5000 in 1996 (Audit Commission 1995).

given a budget and took responsibility for purchasing most types of non-emergency care for their patients (see, generally, Glennerster *et al.* 1994; Audit Commission 1996).[16] (Health Authorities took responsibility for purchasing emergency care for all the patients in their area, and purchasing non-emergency care for GP practices which did not take up the fundholding option.) Fundholding practices were obliged to apply their budgets to purchase such goods or services listed for purchase by fundholding practices[17] 'as are necessary for the proper treatment of individuals on the lists of patients of the members of the practice and are appropriate in all the circumstances having regard, in particular, to the needs of all those individuals'.[18] They were expected to keep within their budgets each year.[19] Fundholding represented a radical departure from previous arrangements: prior to the reforms, GPs had no real influence over the management of provider units. They simply referred patients to consultants for treatment as required. It was claimed that by making providers answerable to GPs, these new administrative arrangements would introduce a new mechanism of accountability (Department of Health 1989). This mechanism was remarkable in professional terms because it gave one group of doctors, GPs, the opportunity to challenge the practices of another group, consultants, thereby having the potential to alter the balance of power within the medical profession quite significantly. Fundholding was also claimed as an advance in consumer accountability, because GPs were perceived to be more closely affected by the views of patients: much was made of the point that fundholding allowed decisions to be taken 'close to the patient' (NHSE 1994; 1995*a*: 5–6). Importantly, however, patients were not themselves able to place contracts with providers (Harden 1992).

Purchasers (of either type) and providers needed some means of relating to one another: making clear what was to be provided and for how much money. Agreements between purchasers and providers within the NHS took the form of 'NHS contracts', defined in s. 4(1) of the 1990 Act as arrangements 'under which one health service body ("the acquirer")[20] arranges for the provision to it by another health service body ("the provider")

---

[16] From 1994 onwards, there were a number of 'total purchasing pilots' in which fundholding practices also purchased emergency care. From 1996, 'community fundholding' was introduced in which smaller practices (3000 patients and above) could hold a budget for community nursing, drugs and practice staff only (see Audit Commission 1995).

[17] National Health Service (Fund-holding Practices) Regulations 1996 (SI 1996/706), r. 20(2).

[18] SI 1996/706, r. 20(1).   [19] SI 1996/706, Schedule 2, para. 3.

[20] The term 'acquirer' has been replaced by the term 'purchaser' in both official documents and academic commentary.

of goods or services which it reasonably requires for the purposes of its functions'.[21] Although the term 'contract' is used throughout, s. 4(3) provides that 'whether or not an arrangement which constitutes an NHS contract would, apart from this subsection, be a contract in law, it shall not be regarded for any purpose as giving rise to contractual rights or liabilities.'[22] Instead, provision is made in the remainder of s. 4 for a special system of arbitration to determine disputes,[23] coupled with powers given to the Secretary of State to issue binding directions to health service bodies in order to enforce arbitration decisions.[24] (Purchasers of both types were also permitted to buy care from the private sector through ordinary private law contracts.)[25]

The NHS arbitration system was unusual in that it applied to problems arising during contract negotiation (s. 4(4)) as well as to disputes arising during the life of the contract (s. 4(3)). It was as much a mechanism of market regulation as one of dispute resolution, reflecting an acknowledgement on the part of the centre that the market would not be fully competitive and that contracting parties might be tempted to abuse monopoly positions. Moreover, the decision-making model used by the regional offices appeared to be more managerial than adjudicative (McHale *et al.* 1997: 199). This was illustrated by the way in which one regional office in the case study had interpreted the requirement to conduct pendulum arbitration (NHSME 1989)[26] so as to allow it to find for one party or the other on each separate element of the claim, rather than on the claim as a whole. The aim was to impose the regional office's preferred solution—a compromise—rather than to adjudicate on the parties' competing claims, as a court would do.

But the most striking feature of NHS arbitration was the extent to which the parties were deterred from using the procedure. Formal statutory arbitration was very rarely used.[27] Regional offices of the NHS Executive

---

[21] Core texts include Flynn *et al.* (1996); Flynn and Williams (1997); Walsh *et al.* (1997). There are also a number of 'practitioner' works, including Øvretveit (1995); Hodgson (1996).

[22] Some of the reasons for this are discussed in McHale *et al.* (1997). For discussion of the legal effects of this attempt to 'oust' the courts, see Jacob (1991); Miller (1992); Barker (1993).

[23] Detailed provisions are made in the National Health Service Contracts (Dispute Resolution) Regulations 1996 (SI 1996/623).

[24] 1990 Act, s. 4(6), s. 4(7).

[25] This study found that use of the private sector was not widespread. This contrasted with the position in social care: local authorities were obliged to spend 85 per cent of their budgets in the independent (private and voluntary) sector (see Walsh *et al.* 1997).

[26] This was intended to discourage arbitration by raising the stakes.

[27] Hughes *et al.* (1997) have discovered only one example.

operated an informal conciliation and arbitration system which avoided the statutory procedure (with its obligation to publish the results) (Hughes *et al.* 1997). Moreover, contracting parties were firmly discouraged even from using this informal system. Health Authorities and providers were told that invoking it would be seen as a sign of management failure.[28] Thus, conciliation was used only *in extremis*, usually by Health Authorities with their main local provider. There was no evidence of its use by fundholders. Lack of recourse to dispute resolution procedures was not in itself a major difference between NHS and private law contracts: the reluctance of businesses to litigate is well-documented (Macaulay 1963; Beale and Dugdale 1975). But contracting parties in the NHS were as much concerned about incurring criticism from the centre as they were about causing damage to their own relationship.

The content of NHS contracts was similar to that of commercial contracts. They contained terms specifying their duration, the price to be paid, the amount of activity to be provided, quality standards and so on (Allen 1995). Their drafting was, however, often informal in style (Allen 1995). This probably reflected the fact that lawyers were rarely involved in the process. The only exception to this in the present study was for contracts with private sector providers: advice from solicitors might be sought because these contracts were legally enforceable. The fact that NHS contracts were not subject to private law doctrine was apparent from some of their terms: for example, many contracts made explicit use of penalty clauses, drafted in such a way as to make it unlikely that they would be enforceable under English law (Treitel 1999).

Not surprisingly, the 1990 reforms were highly controversial in the NHS, as 'new public management' reforms were in other sectors. Three main sets of criticisms were made. First, it was argued that the reforms were highly bureaucratic, leading to increased paperwork and management costs.[29] Proponents of the reforms claimed that these costs could be justified by the system's benefits: better quality through competition, for example (Department of Health 1989). Secondly, it was argued that the reforms violated the fundamental principle of equity: that patients with the same clinical needs should receive equivalent NHS services (House of Commons Social Services Select Committee 1988). In particular, it was claimed that the patients of fundholding practices received preferential treatment from

---

[28] Interview data. See also McHale *et al.* (1997).

[29] For discussion see Glennerster *et al.* (1994); Audit Commission (1996); Flynn and Williams (1997); Walsh *et al.* (1997); Webster (1998). The argument has also influenced recent reform proposals (Department of Health 1997).

providers when compared with the patients of non-fundholding practices.[30] Thirdly, commentators questioned the feasibility of implementing competition in health care: some empirical evidence about the role of competition is explored in later chapters.

In response to some of these concerns, the Labour government introduced a further round of reforms in the Health Act 1999. The accompanying rhetoric claimed that the Act would abolish the internal market, but in practice, many elements of the 1990 system have been retained (Department of Health 1997: paras. 2.1–2.2). The most significant change is on the purchasing side: fundholding has been replaced with a system of Primary Care Groups (PCGs), each covering a population of around 100,000 (Department of Health 1997: ch. 5; House of Commons Select Committee on Health 1999). All GPs are obliged to join a group. At the first stage of development, PCGs simply advise the Health Authority on its purchasing strategy. At later stages of development, PCGs may take on a budget and become purchasers themselves (Department of Health 1997: para. 5.11). The Health Authority is left with the limited role of supervising the activities of PCGs and Trusts in the light of the locally agreed Health Improvement Plan. It seems likely that smaller Authorities will be merged with their neighbours at this stage (Department of Health 1997: para. 3.17; ch. 4). Eventually, PCGs may become Primary Care Trusts (PCTs).[31] This will cause a partial blurring of the purchaser/ provider divide because PCTs will take over the role of providing community services (district nursing and so on) currently performed by community Trusts under contracts (Department of Health 1997: para. 5.13).

Purchasers under the new regime continue to relate to providers through unenforceable NHS contracts. Again, the rhetoric surrounding the contracts is softer, but the fundamentals remain unchanged. There is a greater emphasis on longer-term contracts: for at least three years rather than for a single year as was common under the 1990 regime (Department of Health 1997: para. 9.11). Moving a contract to another provider is still permitted, but as a last resort (Department of Health 1997: paras. 9.11–9.14). Purchasers are required to give the 'losing' provider ample opportunity to improve its performance and to ensure that moving the

---

[30] For discussion of the complexities of this argument, and empirical evidence, see Glennerster *et al.* (1994). The empirical study conducted for this book found greater evidence for the claim that some fundholding practices were able to purchase shorter waiting times than the local Health Authority (on behalf of non-fundholders). See also Goodwin (1998).

[31] Health Act 1999, ss. 2–7.

contract does not have any significant destabilizing effects. Nevertheless, there is a continuing emphasis on the negotiation and monitoring of contracts as a means of making providers accountable to their purchasers. In particular, the government expects purchasers to implement a range of new national standards (which focus much more heavily on clinical care than did national standards under the 1990 regime (Davies 2000)) through their contracts (Department of Health 1997: paras. 5.28– 5.30). It is too early to comment on the impact of these various changes: NHS contracts under the 1990 regime will be the primary focus of this book.

Compulsory competitive tendering and best value

The 'marketization' of local government services began in the early 1980s, with the introduction of the compulsory competitive tendering regime (CCT). The significance of this regime for present purposes is that it resulted in the creation of internal contracts where in-house teams managed to bid successfully against private firms. The 1997 Labour government has replaced CCT with a similar but less strict scheme called 'Best Value'.

CCT was introduced by Part III of the Local Government Planning and Land Act 1980.[32] Authorities could not simply provide services directly. In-house teams had to compete with external bidders, and were only allowed to provide services where they submitted the best (essentially the cheapest) bid. DSOs were relatively successful: Walsh and Davis (1993) found that in the authorities they studied, private firms won on average only 22 per cent of contracts between 1989 and 1992.[33] The 1980 Act applied to construction and maintenance work (ss. 5–9). The Local Government Act 1988 added services such as vehicle maintenance, refuse collection, catering and cleaning (s. 2(2)). Under s. 2(3), the Secretary of State was empowered to extend CCT to other services. This power was exercised quite extensively. For example, it was used in 1989 for leisure management[34] and in 1994 for legal services.[35]

---

[32] In addition to the 1980 Act, the final legislative scheme for CCT consisted of Part I, s. 32 and Schedule 6 of the Local Government Act 1988, and ss. 8–11 and Schedule 1 of the Local Government Act 1992.

[33] There were, however, considerable variations between authorities and between different services, and signs of growing interest among private firms.

[34] Local Government Act 1988 (Competition in Sports and Leisure Facilities) Order 1989 (SI 1989/2488).

[35] Local Government Act 1988 (Competition) (Defined Activities) Order 1994 (SI 1994/2884).

Because many local authorities were opposed in principle to the legislation, it was not merely facilitative but also contained very significant elements of constraint and compulsion. A full account of the complex legislative scheme is beyond the scope of this work (see, generally, Arrowsmith 1996), but an illustration of the point is provided by the Local Government (Direct Service Organisations) (Competition) Regulations 1993.[36] These regulations specified various types of conduct which had 'the effect of restricting, preventing or distorting competition' for the purposes of s. 9(2)(b) and (d) of the Local Government Act 1992. Such conduct included permitting people other than the head of the DSO or the authority's legal or financial advisers to work on the DSO's bid (r. 4(3)(a)); giving the DSO information additional to that given to other bidders (r. 4(3)(b) and (c)); and taking account of costs the authority would incur in disbanding the DSO other than those defined in the regulations (r. 5(a)(iv)). Authorities' compliance with these and other requirements was monitored by central government (through the Department of the Environment) and the Audit Commission. The Secretary of State had extensive powers of intervention where it appeared that an authority had not conducted a CCT exercise in accordance with the rules (Vincent-Jones 1997).

Despite the rigidity of the tendering procedures, authorities retained some discretion as to how far they separated the roles of purchaser and provider once the contract had been awarded to the DSO. Vincent-Jones (1997: 154) found three broad types of organizational structure: continued departmental organization with no clear purchaser/provider split; 'soft client-contractor structures' involving a close working relationship and limited organizational separation; and 'hard' splits in which purchaser and provider functions were clearly separated. His research suggests important, though different, roles for internal contracts in the second and third types of structure. In the second situation, the contract helped to 'increase accountability for performance' (Vincent-Jones 1997: 158) but was not adhered to rigidly. In particular, the parties resolved disputes informally rather than using the contract's default provisions. In the third situation, the contract was treated as defining the parties' relationship. It was interpreted in a strict and adversarial way, even though it was not legally enforceable because of the DSO's lack of separate legal personality.

The change of government in 1997 has brought about a shift of emphasis away from compulsion (see, generally, Vincent-Jones 2000). The key

---

[36] SI 1993/848.

concept under the new regime is 'best value', which is 'a duty to deliver services to clear standards—covering both cost and quality—by the most effective, efficient and economic means available' (DETR 1998*b*: para. 7.2).[37] The achievement of best value hinges on 'fundamental performance reviews' of local authority services (DETR 1998*b*: ch. 7). Each service should be reviewed once every five years,[38] drawing on both national and local performance indicators.[39] These reviews should involve four elements: questioning the need for the service and its current mode of provision; comparing the service against performance indicators; consulting widely with interested parties; and competition (DETR 1998*b*: para. 7.18).[40] This seems to suggest that competition takes its place as just one of the techniques for securing best value.

Nonetheless, competition and contracting-out have key roles under the best value regime (DETR 1999: paras. 36–48). Paragraph 7.28 of the White Paper stresses the need for competition: 'Retaining work in-house without subjecting it to real competitive pressure can rarely be justified' (DETR 1998*b*). The government does, however, contemplate a wider range of options than simply putting the service out to tender: joint ventures with the private sector or restructuring the in-house team to meet external performance indicators are also acceptable (DETR 1998*b*: para. 7.29; DETR 1999: para. 44). The continuing role of contracting out is made plain in paragraph 7.27: 'Services should not be delivered directly if other more efficient and effective means are available' (DETR 1998*b*). The element of compulsion, though perhaps rather less overt, remains under the new regime. If an authority cannot tackle its own failure to achieve best value,[41] the Secretary of State has wide-ranging powers under s. 15 of the Local Government Act 1999 and may, for example, require the authority to accept external management assistance, to cease to provide services directly, and to put services out to competition (DETR 1998*b*: para. 7.47).

The move away from compulsion and formality means that the role of internal contracts under best value is rather less clear than it was under

[37] See also the statutory definition of a 'best value authority': s. 3 Local Government Act 1999.

[38] 1999 Act, s. 5; Local Government (Best Value) Performance Plans and Reviews Order 1999 (SI 1999/3251), Article 5.

[39] 1999 Act, s. 4; Local Government (Best Value) Performance Indicators Order 2000.

[40] See also 1999 Act, s. 5(4).

[41] An authority's achievement of best value will be monitored by its auditor, who will audit its best value performance plan (1999 Act ss. 6–7), and by the Audit Commission, which is given a power of inspection (1999 Act s. 10).

CCT. Nevertheless, it is difficult to imagine how a local authority could satisfy the requirements of best value without specifying performance targets for in-house services through some kind of internal contract, and maintaining separate accounting arrangements in order to give the in-house service a distinct budget. Again, however, such contracts would not be legally enforceable because the in-house service provider would not have legal personality separate from that of the authority itself.

Contracts for social care

Social care services are those provided for groups such as the elderly, the mentally ill, those with physical disabilities, and those with learning disabilities, either in the user's own home or in an institution. Under the National Health Service and Community Care Act 1990,[42] local authorities were given the lead role in the delivery of social care.[43] Various measures were taken to ensure that they delivered care through purchasing rather than direct provision. Nonetheless, internal contracts are a relatively recent development in this field.

Like the reforms in other sectors, those in social care reflected 'new public management' and public choice ideas. It was claimed that the introduction of a purchaser/provider split would help to make providers more responsive to user needs (see Wistow *et al.* 1996: 3–16). This reflected a more specific concern in the social care sector to provide services in the community rather than in residential institutions, in part because this would enable service users to retain a greater degree of independence, and in part because community provision is usually cheaper than residential provision (see Walsh *et al.* 1997: 18).

The reforms involved a significant transfer of resources from the social security budget to local authorities. The Department of Health required 85 per cent of this money to be spent in the independent sector, by placing contracts either with voluntary associations or with private firms (Wistow *et al.* 1996: 14–15). This meant that authorities could not significantly expand their own direct provision of care in order to meet their new responsibilities. Their role was to purchase care in a mixed market. Some authorities 'externalized' a part of their in-house provision, for example, by creating not-for-profit trusts to run residential homes (Walsh *et al.* 1997: 81–96). This enabled them to continue supporting these providers

---

[42] The Act was preceded by Griffiths (1988) and a White Paper, Department of Health (1989*a*). For an account of the development of the policy, see Wistow *et al.* (1996: 3–16).

[43] Full implementation of the Act was delayed until April 1993.

despite the restrictions on how their budgets could be spent. Where services remained in-house, however, authorities were reluctant to introduce contractualization. Most continued to manage their providers through hierarchical structures rather than internal contracts (Walsh *et al.* 1997: 139). Market techniques were not popular and were not introduced where it was not mandatory to do so (Walsh *et al.* 1997: 81–96).

Social care services are now covered by the 'best value' scheme, described above. A recent report by the Social Services Inspectorate (SSI) suggests that this will bring about two major changes in authorities' relationships with their in-house providers (SSI 1999).[44] First, authorities will no longer be able to protect in-house providers from competition with private firms and voluntary organizations for the award of contracts (SSI: 1999: para. 5.4). This is a necessary implication of the obligation to demonstrate that any chosen mode of provision offers 'best value'. Secondly, authorities will need to formalize their relationships with internal providers in order to obtain the information about cost and quality which will form the basis for comparisons between competing providers (SSI 1999: para. 5.38). The SSI report advocates the structuring of relationships with in-house providers as internal contracts (SSI 1999: para. 5.13). It is claimed that such contracts would put in-house provision on the same footing as private provision, as a prelude to competition, and would encourage authorities to monitor in-house provision more rigorously. It remains to be seen how this emerging area of internal contracting will develop.

Central government

Internal contracts were introduced into central government under the Conservative government's Next Steps programme in the late 1980s. More recently, they have been used by the Labour government to structure the relationship between the Treasury and spending departments under the Comprehensive Spending Review. Each will be examined in turn.

Next steps agency framework agreements

The Next Steps programme involved the division of government departments into a civil service core with a policy-making role, and semi-autonomous agencies with responsibility for implementing policy in a

---

[44] See also Department of Health (1998*b*), especially paras. 2.60–2.61; ch. 7.

particular setting.[45] Agencies were to relate to their parent departments through internal contracts called 'framework agreements', which would set out agencies' budgets and the performance targets they had to meet.

The Next Steps programme grew out of the financial management initiatives in the civil service in the early 1980s.[46] The Ibbs Report (Efficiency Unit 1988) suggested that structural change was necessary in order to make financial management more effective.[47] The framework agreements themselves would improve cost control, by setting clear budgets, and service delivery, by setting clear targets. And both the budgets and the performance targets would be challenging because they had been set by the central department, not by self-interested service providers. Agencies would be motivated to comply by both individual and corporate incentives. The role of agency chief executive was given a high profile, in contrast to the role of service delivery manager in the pre-Next Steps civil service. In particular, the chief executive's remuneration package was linked to the agency's compliance with its targets (Greer 1994: 60). This meant that the personal status and the pay of the agency head were at stake if the agency performed badly. Moreover, agencies themselves were encouraged to develop a corporate identity and to explore new ways of working. These changes were both reflected in, and reinforced by, the greater flexibility given to agencies, for example, in personnel management (Greer 1994: 98–100).

To some extent, these pressures were reinforced through competition. The government's market testing programme required departments to consider whether any of their functions—which included parts of agencies' functions, or even entire agencies—could be contracted out to the private sector (HM Treasury 1991). Thus, an agency might be required to bid against private firms for some or all of its functions. As Foster and Plowden (1996) point out, however, agencies were rarely designed with privatization or market testing in mind. They might consist of odd agglomerations of activities which would not be attractive to a private provider. It therefore seems unlikely that competition has had more than a marginal effect on agencies.

The framework agreements between agencies and departments are not enforceable in law. As Harden explains:

---

[45] Key documents include Efficiency Unit (1988); Cabinet Office (1998*b*); Prime Minister (1994; 1995). For critique see, generally, Foster and Plowden (1996); Freedland (1994); Greer (1992; 1994); O'Toole and Jordan (1995).

[46] For the history of the reforms see, generally, Greer (1994); Zifcak (1994).

[47] The idea of creating accountable units within departments is not novel: see the Fulton Report (Committee on the Civil Service 1968: 61–2).

Relationships between Next Steps agencies and departments . . . cannot take the form of private law contracts, because the parties have no separate legal identity. Legal identity precedes and cannot be derived from a contractual relationship. Thus if an organisational separation of interests in the public sector is to have any legal dimension, it must come from public law. Next Steps agencies . . . have no corporate personality deriving from public law; otherwise they would be able to make contracts. (Harden 1992: 46)

Freedland (1994) notes the incongruity of this position. Agencies are held at arm's length from government and encouraged to develop a corporate identity separate from that of their parent departments. But this is not reflected in their legal status: agencies are fictional organizations, so their framework documents are fictional contracts.

Public service agreements

Public Service Agreements are a more modern version of the internal contract within central government. Like framework documents, they set performance targets for a particular part of the government machine. But Public Service Agreements are, in effect, 'contracts' between the Treasury and spending departments (HM Treasury 1998*a*: para. 1.15).

Public Service Agreements (PSAs) grew out of the Comprehensive Spending Review. This review examined all aspects of the government's expenditure, and sought to focus it more effectively on the government's policy priorities. One of the themes running through the review is the introduction of an element of reciprocity between spending departments and the Treasury: 'The Government is determined to improve public services by securing a commitment from all departments to modernise and reform in return for the money allocated to them' (HM Treasury 1998*a*: para. 1.9). Public Service Agreements make this reciprocity explicit. They 'will include [departments'] new objectives and measurable efficiency and effectiveness targets' (HM Treasury 1998*a*: para. 1.15). The targets include percentage efficiency gains to promote value for money; departmental contributions to the achievement of government policies such as the reduction of fraud and the greater use of information technology; and service standards specific to the department itself (HM Treasury 1998*c*: ch. 2).

The Chancellor of the Exchequer chairs a Cabinet Committee (known as 'PSX') which oversees a 'continuous process of scrutiny and audit' (HM Treasury 1998*a*: para. 1.15) to monitor departments' performance against their PSAs. A Public Services Productivity Panel, with members drawn

from the private sector, has also been created to advise the government
on improving the efficiency of departments and services (HM Treasury
1998*b*: para. 3.114). Both the government's annual report, and departmental annual reports, will describe performance against the targets (HM
Treasury: 1998*c*: 2). The sanctions for failing to meet the targets are, however, rather less clear. The Cabinet Committee's role is described as advisory (HM Treasury 1998*c*: 2). In particular, it has been stated very clearly
that: 'Should a target not be met, there is no question of money being
deducted from the budget for that department' (HM Treasury 1998*c*: 2).

The question of legal enforceability is unlikely to arise in relation to
these agreements. It is impossible to envisage the Treasury attempting
to take another department to court for failing to meet its performance
targets. In theory, departments can enter into contracts in their own name
and not that of the Crown (Daintith and Page 1999: 32) but a court faced
with a dispute between departments might decide to treat the executive
as a unity.[48] The doctrines of justiciability and absence of an intention
to create legal relations might also be used to dismiss a case between the
Treasury and a government department. Like framework agreements,
PSAs have a strong element of fiction. Nonetheless, they do indicate a
desire at the centre of government to control departments (which have
a surprising degree of functional autonomy) using the specification of performance targets through 'contracts' as a technique (Daintith and Page
1999: 192).

Internal contracts as category

In order to justify the study of internal contracts as a group, it is necessary to demonstrate that they have a basic core of common features. It
is also important to highlight differences, in order to ensure that generalizations of research findings from one type of contract to another are
not made inappropriately. The first part of this section examines three
crucial issues: the legal status of internal contracts; the degree of organizational separation between purchasers and providers; and the extent
to which the parties have a meaningful choice about contracting with
one another. The discussion may also be of more general assistance when
considering whether or not experiences with internal contracts can be
applied to external government contracts (an issue to be discussed in

---

[48] This was done using the concept of the Crown in *Town Investments v Department of the Environment*, 1978 AC 359.

Chapter 9). In the light of this discussion of core features, the second part of this section explains and justifies the choice of NHS contracts as a case-study of internal contracts. It identifies both theoretical and practical reasons for that choice.

Internal contracts: similarities and differences

All the contracts considered in the first part of this chapter meet the definition of an 'internal contract': they are agreements between two public bodies in which one undertakes to perform specified activities in return for a budget supplied by the other. But what else do they have in common?

First, and most significantly, none of the contracts explored in this chapter are legally enforceable. Usually, this is because the parties to them lack separate legal personality; in the NHS, a specific statutory provision seeks to exclude the courts.[49] On the theoretical level, this has led some writers to deny the validity of the contractual metaphor and to employ a term such as 'pseudo-contract' instead (Foster and Plowden 1996: 171; Harlow and Rawlings 1996: 210). Terms of this kind play an important role in emphasizing the limited nature of contractualization reforms: not all the usual connotations of the word 'contract' apply to internal contracts. But they should not be allowed to close off the possibility of reforms which would implement contractualization more fully and effectively: which would make internal contracts more 'contractual'. Chapter 3 will return to this point.

On a practical level, the fact that internal contracts are not legally enforceable means that it is not clear what consequences will follow from a breach or a dispute about performance. Of course, in competitive markets, contracts are generally self-enforcing: the provider complies for fear of losing business to its competitors. The parties use litigation only as a last resort when their relationship has broken down (Macaulay 1963; Beale and Dugdale 1975). Nonetheless, litigation may serve as an important underlying threat (Deakin *et al.* 1997). One common issue in internal contracts might therefore be the need to find effective methods of enforcement in the absence of the possibility of litigation. Various types of sanction are suggested in the literature. In relation to PSAs, it was noted above that the overseeing Cabinet Committee would simply proffer advice to a department which was failing to meet its targets (HM Treasury 1998c:

---

[49] National Health Service and Community Care Act 1990, s. 4(3).

2). Under the Next Steps programme, the agency head's performance related pay might be tied to targets in the framework agreement. And in both local government and the NHS, the parties themselves provided for sanctions, such as penalty clauses, in their contracts.

A second significant issue is the extent to which the two parties to the contract, the purchaser and the provider, are in fact separate organizations. For many commentators, this is an important indicator of the extent to which hierarchical managerial relationships really have been replaced by contractual ones. The purchaser/provider split was most complete in the NHS. It was expressed both in legal form and organizational structure. Trusts were created as statutory corporations with their own board of directors,[50] answerable directly to the NHS Executive. And with the introduction of GP fundholding, Trusts were answerable not only to Health Authorities (their former managers) but to a range of new purchasers with whom they had not previously had a managerial relationship.

In other contexts, the split is less clear. Separate legal personality was not used in local government or in the Next Steps programme. But as the example of PSAs shows, organizations may have a surprising degree of institutional separation even if the legal position is uncertain. Empirical research on both CCT contracts and Next Steps agency framework documents has shown that organizational relationships may vary considerably in practice. Some may be arm's length and formal, placing heavy reliance on the precise terms of the contract. Others are close and informal, using the contract selectively or not at all.

As later chapters will explain, it is inappropriate to place too much reliance on the presence of 'arm's length' relationships as indicators of successful contractualization. Research on commercial contracts has shown that they may fit anywhere on a spectrum from discrete to relational (Fox 1974; Macneil 1974; Sako 1992). At the relational end, the respective roles of the contracting parties are blurred. To suggest that only discrete relationships are contractual is to ignore a substantial body of evidence about other types of contractual relationship. In fact, it is the variety of relationships engendered by internal contracts that is one of their most significant common features.

A third issue is the extent to which the parties have a choice about whether or not to contract with one another. At one level, this is simply a practical question about the competitiveness of the markets in which

---

[50] National Health Service and Community Care Act 1990, s. 5.

internal contracts take place. It relates to whether or not the contracts can be enforced effectively, and is closely linked to the discussion about legal enforceability, above. Local government services seem most clearly competitive, since authorities were obliged to seek tenders under CCT and are now encouraged to engage in market 'creation' under best value. In the NHS, as later chapters will demonstrate, some purchasers had a good choice of providers within reasonable travelling distance, whereas others (those in rural areas, for example) were forced to contract with one provider for most services. In the Next Steps context, although some aspects of an agency's work might be market-tested, this policy has had less impact on each agency as a whole. Thus, although there might be competition to provide a particular prison, it seems unlikely that there would be meaningful competition for the entire work of the Prisons Agency. PSAs are ambiguous in terms of competition. Although departments compete against one another for their share of government funds, they do not compete for functions.[51] There is no option, either for the Treasury or a spending department, of refusing to agree a PSA. But spending departments do have a strong incentive to co-operate in order to maximize their budgets.

The weakness of competition in some internal contracting contexts has provided commentators with another reason for criticizing the use of the term 'contract' (Vincent-Jones 1994*a*). The traditional conception of a contract is that it results from the mutual promises of free individuals, who can choose whether or not to enter into the contract and on what terms. The principle of freedom to enter into a contract remains a key part of the modern law of contract.[52] But in the NHS, for example, little respect was accorded to this principle (Allen 1995). The parties were (*de facto* at least) obliged to enter into NHS contracts. Purchasers had to perform their statutory function of ensuring that care was provided,[53] and in the absence of any directly managed units this could only be done by contracting with providers. Providers had to secure income to cover their outgoings:[54] this could only be done by contracting with purchasers. If the parties were unable to reach an agreement, the Secretary of State had the power to impose particular terms, and potentially an entire

---

[51] There are, of course, boundary disputes between departments and occasional boundary changes, but these take place outside the PSA process.

[52] Though even this is not unconstrained (Collins 1997).

[53] SI 1996/708 (Health Authorities); SI 1996/706 (fundholding practices).

[54] 1990 Act, s. 10(1).

contract, on the parties.[55] And where competition was weak, purchasers might be forced to contract with a particular Trust which had a local monopoly over provision.[56] The extent to which any particular internal contract diverged from traditional expectations about freedom of contract is, of course, a question of degree requiring empirical investigation. But it seems likely that at least some internal contracts would take place in highly constrained circumstances.

Internal contracts have three common (and unusual) features: they are not legally enforceable; they take place between organizations which need not be formally separate; and they do not necessarily result from freely given promises in competitive markets. These common features make it appropriate to consider internal contracts together for the purposes of research and reform. Chapter 3 will address some of the issues raised here in more detail as part of a discussion of the controversies affecting internal contracts and the possibilities for reform.

The choice of case study

The remainder of this book, in particular Chapters 6–8, explores the possibility of reforming the regulatory framework for internal contracts by drawing on an empirically researched case study of NHS contracts. It was necessary to focus on one example for the study because of constraints on research time. NHS contracts were chosen on both theoretical and practical grounds.

On the theoretical level, a good case study should produce results which are likely to be 'generalizable' to other contexts. In terms of competition and choice, NHS contracts appeared to be somewhere in the middle of the spectrum: purchasers had some choice at the margins.[57] It was hoped that the study would offer insights into both the position of a purchaser in a competitive internal market, and the position of a purchaser which had no choice but to contract with a particular provider. Thus, lessons from a study in the NHS might be applicable to internal contracts at either extreme of the competitiveness spectrum.

The NHS market did involve a more formal organizational split than any of the other types of internal contract. But it seemed likely that this would be an advantage. In particular, it would enable the research to test the assumption, commonly made by commentators, that a more formal separation between purchaser and provider is essential to the success of

---

[55] See s. 4 (6) and (7) of the 1990 Act.   [56] See Ch. 8.   [57] See Ch. 8.

contractualization. And in any event, early empirical evidence suggested that NHS contracts in fact resulted in a variety of relationships, across the discrete-relational spectrum, like CCT and possibly even Next Steps. The other major difference between NHS contracts and other internal contracts was the arbitration system. Two factors suggested that the NHS would be a good case study despite this difference. First, there was evidence that arbitration was rarely used, making NHS contracts more like other internal contracts with no dispute resolution mechanism. Secondly, occasional uses of NHS conciliation were worthy of further investigation in case the process provided a model for generalization to other areas.

Moreover, NHS contracts had considerable advantages in terms of the practicalities of empirical research. The contracts themselves were public documents, and could be accessed with relative ease. The NHS offered a considerable choice of research sites: when some purchasers and providers refused to participate in the research, it was possible to find replacements. The sheer number of NHS contracts also made it possible to study and compare several different relationships over a relatively short period of time. Moreover, at the time of the study, NHS contracts were highly topical and the subject of debate both within and outside the NHS. The study took place in 1996–7, some four or five years after the introduction of the internal market. The initial shock of the reforms had subsided, and a process of mature assessment was taking place. Within the NHS, staff were actively considering how best to develop and use contractual relationships. The interviewees were therefore able to share the results of their own reflections on their work. Outside the research sites, there was a growing body of literature and empirical evidence on the reforms from a variety of disciplinary perspectives, notably economics and sociology. This work was an invaluable source of analysis and supplementary data to complement the empirical work conducted specifically for this study.

NHS contracts seemed to be a good choice of case study on both theoretical and practical grounds. Nonetheless, any claims as to the wider applicability of the NHS case study will be made tentatively and cautiously throughout this book. The case study should be viewed as a starting-point for further research, rather than as a resolution of the relevant issues in other contexts.

3 Controversies and Reform

Internal contracts, like government by contract more generally, have attracted much critical comment in the literature. Two important critiques will be examined in the first section of this chapter. One, derived primarily from the Next Steps literature, questions whether contractualization does in fact lead to arm's length relationships between purchasers and providers. Commentators have noted the difficulty of drawing a satisfactory distinction between the role of the department and the role of the agency, and have suggested that the minister may continue to interfere in the agency's activities (for example, Foster and Plowden 1996). A second critique, more closely linked to internal market reforms, asks whether there are sufficient sanctions to render contracts effective. In the commercial context, perhaps the most significant sanction is provided by market pressure (Macaulay 1963). As Chapter 2 noted, however, most internal contracts, with the exception of some local government and NHS contracts, were not awarded in particularly competitive conditions.

It will be argued in the first section of this chapter that both these objections reflect, at least in part, a more fundamental problem, namely the fact that internal contracts are not regulated or enforced by the law. The problem of role definition arises in part because the parties do not take the terms of the contract seriously and do not seek formal contract variations when their circumstances change. The problem of enforceability is not caused solely by the fact that litigation is not available—the weakness of competitive pressure is also to blame—but its absence is a contributory factor. Research by Deakin *et al.* (1997) has shown that a high degree of juridification in contractual relationships may help to prevent disputes, even when recourse to the courts themselves is rare.

Of course, empirical research is required to assess the extent of the problems suggested by the literature. But there is little point in engaging in such research if there are no realistic options for reform. The second part of this chapter therefore examines possible ways of developing a suitable normative framework and dispute resolution mechanism for internal contracts. Further exploration of the potential of public law—rather than private law—will be advocated. In terms of regulation, established private law doctrines do not appear to offer nuanced solutions to some of the problems which are likely to arise in internal contracts. It may be preferable to develop new norms through public law. And public law would facilitate (to a greater extent than would private law) the use of a mechanism of alternative dispute resolution in place of the unattractive prospect of enforcement through the courts.

Controversies surrounding internal contracts

Some of the controversies about government by contract in general, discussed in Chapter 1, were also applicable to internal contracts. Constitutional law failed to impose any controls on the government's decision to reorganize its internal affairs along contractual lines. Moreover, the reforms of which internal contracts were a part did not appear to take sufficient account of other public interest values, notably public participation. But the debate about administrative law controls which takes place in relation to those government contracts which are legally enforceable is eclipsed for internal contracts by a much broader debate stemming—arguably— from the fact that they are not regulated or enforced by law at all. Two main issues have been raised in the literature. One is the problem of the division of roles between purchaser and provider. The other is the problem of ensuring that the parties comply with their contractual commitments.

The division of roles

As Chapter 2 explained, contractualization within government generally involved replacing hierarchical management relationships in single organizations with contractual ones between separate purchaser and provider organizations. It was argued that this would enhance the accountability of providers. But commentators felt that it would be difficult to achieve a clear separation of roles between purchasers and providers, and that the attempt to do so might blur, rather than clarify, responsibilities.

It was claimed that the reforms would improve accountability in three major respects. First, the move from line management to 'contract' would make it possible to formalize standards of performance, monitoring mechanisms and so on.[1] The accountability process would be more explicit and transparent.[2] Secondly, it was believed that separating policy-making or purchasing from provision would make it less likely that those responsible

---

[1] Some of the difficulties of devising clear performance measures are discussed in Greer (1994: 68–75) and Zifcak (1994: 43).

[2] See the Next Steps Review 1993, quoted in Freedland (1994). For a strikingly similar account of the advantages of contract in a very different context, see Nelken (1987).

for calling to account would identify with those responsible for provision. The 'new public management' was in part driven by ideas from public choice theory that bureaucrats are inherently self-interested, working to enhance the budget and status of their organization, rather than working in the interests of those they are meant to serve (Downs 1967; Niskanen 1971; Tullock 1965). They cannot be trusted to run an effective and efficient service of their own accord. Independent scrutiny, for example from a purchaser, is needed to ensure genuine accountability (HM Treasury 1991; Ferlie *et al.* 1996). Thirdly, competition (in services like the NHS) could support or even supplant entirely the formal processes of contractual accountability: service providers would meet the required standards because they would be afraid of losing out to their competitors if they did not.[3]

But commentators were not convinced that a clear dividing line could be drawn between purchaser and provider roles. Some official documents appeared to suggest that there is an inherent distinction between the two roles: purchasers would decide on policy; providers would implement that policy (for example, Efficiency Unit 1988: 10; NHSME 1989: para. 2.11). It is, however, notoriously difficult to draw a dividing line between policy and operations (Simpson 1996; Woodhouse 1994). For example, ministers were supposed to maintain 'arm's length' relationships with the nationalized industries, but in practice, they were often tempted to interfere behind the scenes with operational details (Foster 1992: ch. 3; Prosser 1986). In relation to Next Steps agencies, it was therefore suggested that the more politically sensitive an agency's work, the less likely it would be to receive genuine independence (Greer 1992; 1994; Zifcak 1994). Similar difficulties would also exist in reverse: supposedly operational agencies would acquire a key role in giving policy advice, because of the considerable expertise they would develop in their area.[4]

The absence of an inherent distinction between purchaser and provider roles was exacerbated by two weaknesses in the institutional structure used to implement contractualization. First, it was noted in Chapter 2 that, with the exception of the NHS, purchaser/provider splits have not in general been given legal recognition in the form of separate legal personality for the two new organizations. In practice, of course, a corporate identity might be developed in other ways: most Next Steps

---

[3] See, for example, Department of Health (1989*b*) which makes the same point in a positive way: successful providers would attract more resources.

[4] Greer (1994: 68) points out that all the Department of Social Security's agencies' framework documents contained an objective relating to the giving of good quality policy advice.

agencies have their own logos, for example. Nonetheless, informal purchaser/provider splits rely heavily on the parties to exercise restraint. Secondly, because internal contracts are not legally enforceable, there is nothing to hold the parties to their terms. This means that providers in particular cannot protect themselves from purchaser interference by pointing to the terms of the contract between them. For example, if political priorities changed, a minister might insist that a Next Steps agency behaved in a different way without negotiating a formal variation to the terms of the framework agreement (Zifcak 1994: 87).

Obviously, if these fears were realized in practice, the reforms would fail to secure any of the advantages, discussed above, of separating provision from purchasing. Moreover, Parliament and the public might be confused by the existence of the two ill-defined roles. In particular, each side might be tempted to evade being called to account by blaming the other if a problem arose (Bruce and McConnell 1995). Early empirical evidence suggested that much of this criticism was warranted. The fact that there is no inherent distinction between purchasing and provision was evidenced by the wide variety of different relationships which could result from the introduction of a purchaser/provider split (Greer 1994; Vincent-Jones 1997). And the notorious problems of the Prison Service Agency illustrated the inevitability of ministerial interference in the work of a politically sensitive agency, and the problem of mutual blame for the agency's failings (Foster and Plowden 1996; House of Commons Public Service Committee 1996).

But the picture is complicated by another key piece of evidence from the local government context. Vincent-Jones (1997) found that local authorities which had maintained close links with their DSOs (such as retaining purchaser and provider functions within the same department) seemed to have more constructive working relationships than those which had set up DSOs as separate organizations. An attempt to divide up the roles too sharply might therefore create its own set of problems. Empirical evidence on this issue in the NHS will be discussed in Chapter 6.[5]

Compliance

A second debate in the literature concerns the enforceability of internal contracts: would providers comply with them? This links to the first

---

[5] The chapter will also discuss the issue of central government's purported delegation of power to purchasers. Although the relationship between the centre and purchasers was not clearly structured as a contract, it raises similar issues of autonomy and control.

concern: if purchasers were unlikely to respect the terms they had set for providers, it is difficult to see why providers would respect those terms either. This debate was perhaps most clearly articulated in relation to 'market' situations such as the NHS, social care and local government, but it is applicable across the range of internal contracts (see, generally, Collins 1999: 303–20).

In the commercial context, the normal expectation is that contracts will be self-enforcing (Macaulay 1963). This is because they take place in competitive markets. The provider competes against others to win the contract, to retain the purchaser's custom, and to obtain future orders. It maintains high standards of performance because it is afraid of losing out to its competitors. Some instances of contractualization were introduced with this in mind. In the NHS and in social care, for example, it was claimed that competition between service providers would maintain and even raise standards of performance and cost-effectiveness (Department of Health 1989*a*; 1989*b*).

As Chapter 2 explained, commentators questioned the extent to which market pressures would operate in these various contexts. In the NHS, for example, the competitiveness of the market was affected by a number of factors.[6] One was geographical. In most areas, there was a natural flow of emergency cases to particular hospitals. Purchasers could not alter this flow and had to maintain contracts with those hospitals in order to pay for the care they provided. Even in relation to elective treatments, over which purchasers had some control, there was a limit to how far patients were prepared to travel for treatment (Barker *et al.* 1997). Studies have used, for example, a travelling time of 30 minutes as an estimate of patients' average mobility (Propper and Bartlett 1997). Another problem was capacity: particularly during the winter, most hospitals are short of space and do not have the spare capacity to 'poach' patients from other providers. In other contexts, different constraints applied. In CCT, for example, it was often claimed that the packaging of particular services by authorities did not necessarily make them attractive to private firms,[7] and more fundamentally, that the market in private service provision was not sufficiently well developed to take on all the new opportunities created by the policy (for example, Walsh *et al.* 1997: 103–13).

[6] There is a large literature on this point. See, for example, Klein (1995); Propper and Bartlett (1997); Barker *et al.* (1997); Spurgeon *et al.* (1997).

[7] See, for example, Department of the Environment Circular 10/93 (paras. 7.9–7.10) quoted in Harlow and Rawlings (1997: 256–7).

Of course, competition is not the only possible means of making contracts enforceable. The parties might try various self-help strategies, such as making deductions from contract payments if the terms are not met. These strategies were used in local government (see, for example, Vincent-Jones 1997; Walsh *et al.* 1997: 128–39) and NHS internal contracts. Their impact in the latter context will be discussed in Chapter 8. But even sanctions of this type were not apparent in some contexts. In PSAs, for example, the overseeing Cabinet Committee is confined to an advisory role if a department is not meeting its targets (HM Treasury 1998*c*: 2).

More fundamentally, as Chapter 2 made clear, internal contracts are not generally enforceable in law. It is well known that businesses rarely litigate even when it would be possible to do so. They prefer to preserve relationships and reputations for fair dealing by negotiating solutions to their disputes (Macaulay 1963). But the underlying threat of litigation may, nevertheless, serve an important role. Collins (1999: 317) identifies two linked functions performed by the prospect of enforcement in private law. Private law sanctions force people to make credible commitments, and hold them responsible for deviating from those commitments. He argues that in the absence of private law sanctions, internal contracts will be ineffective. The parties will not strive to meet the standards contained in the contracts, and as a result, will pay little attention to the way in which the contracts are drafted in the first place. In short, unenforceable contracts will not be taken seriously. And the problem is exacerbated by the absence of other modes of enforcement, particularly competitive pressure.

If commentators were right to predict that the parties to internal contracts would not take them seriously, the problems which would result are readily apparent. One of the major claims made for contractualization was that it would make service providers accountable to purchasers for their performance. But if purchasers were unable to enforce their contracts, providers would have no incentive to comply. Purchasers would become superfluous and, in effect, providers would determine standards of performance for themselves.

Conclusion

Both the controversies identified in this section—about role definition and effectiveness—seem to be linked to the fact that internal contracts are not regulated or enforced by law. Purchasers may be tempted to interfere in providers' activities without contractual authorization because there is no legal regulation of the circumstances in which contracts can be concluded or varied. And providers may be tempted to breach the targets set for them because the law does not provide a means of enforcing the contracts.

Although some of the arguments made in this section do have empirical support, further research is needed in the various internal contracting contexts in order to test their validity more thoroughly. But if the problems exist in practice, finding an appropriate solution is by no means a simple task. The discussion so far seems to point in the direction of using the law to regulate and enforce internal contracts, but this would be immensely controversial. Some discussion of the theoretical possibilities for reform therefore seems appropriate before any empirical study is undertaken. The next section tackles this thorny issue.

The options for reform

A simple solution to the problems of internal contracts would be to advocate their abolition. Some governments have pursued contractualization as an ideology, and may therefore have introduced contracts into some sectors in which economic theory would not normally advocate that mode of governance (Vincent-Jones 1994*a*). The conditions necessary for effective contracting—experienced purchasers, mutual trust between the parties and so on—may not obtain in all contexts (Vincent-Jones 1994*a*). Moreover, the emphasis on entrepreneurial behaviour and risk-taking may undermine key public service values of probity and caution (Foster and Plowden 1996). The literature contains many useful critiques of this kind, but this book does not seek to add to their number. Internal contracts have been used and developed by governments of both main political parties, and therefore seem to be a relatively durable feature of the public sector landscape. There is therefore an urgent need for scholars to consider ways of making these contracts work more effectively, without prejudice to the wider discussion of their desirability.

There are two possible avenues for reform of the legal structures surrounding internal contracts: to give effect to them as ordinary private law contracts, or to develop a public law regime of regulation and enforcement.[8] At first glance, the public law solution might seem to be the most

---

[8] It would also be possible to use a combination of public and private law norms. For the sake of clarity this chapter does not consider this more complex option.

natural: internal contracts take place between public bodies, and public law is the usual mode of regulation within the public sector. But the position is complicated by the fact that government contracts have traditionally been treated largely as matters of private law. It is therefore necessary to ask whether the private law solution should be adopted, or whether the possibility of developing a new public law framework for internal contracts should be explored instead. This issue will be examined below. But first, it must be established that regulation and enforcement are relevant to internal contracts.

Contract as symbol

It might be claimed that internal contracts were meant to have symbolic value only. They were intended to set out the parties' aspirations: the targets they hoped to achieve if all went well. The decision not to make them legally enforceable might reflect a deliberate desire merely to invoke the *rhetoric* of contract.[9] This would suggest that the notion of securing providers' compliance with the contracts is misplaced, or at least overstated. All that is required is that providers should work towards the targets. Similarly, it would be wrong to argue that purchaser behaviour under the contract ought to be regulated. Because the provider is not obliged to comply with the contract, it does not matter if the purchaser wishes to change or redefine the objectives to be achieved. The purchaser need not follow a procedure for negotiating contract variations with the provider. In effect, the contractual relationship is simply a hierarchical management relationship with a greater degree of formality about the aims to be pursued.

Some aspects of the 'new public management' did involve aspirational statements of objectives. The Citizen's Charter, for example, set out various rights and expectations for the consumer of public services, few of which could be 'enforced' in any sense (HM Government 1991; Barron and Scott 1992; Willett 1996). It might be argued that public services would be improved simply by achieving a new clarity about their aims (Harden 1992: 71). But this claim sits uncomfortably with the public choice premises on which much of the 'new public management' was based. One of these premises was that bureaucrats are inherently self-interested

---

[9] Many commentators were keen to emphasize the fact that internal contracts were not 'real' contracts (for example, Harlow and Rawlings 1997; Hughes 1991), but little attention has been paid to the possibility of a symbolic interpretation (though cf. Vincent-Jones 1994*a*).

and cannot be trusted to serve the public unless they are subject to stringent mechanisms of accountability (Downs 1967; Niskanen 1971; Tullock 1965). Unenforceable commitments are only likely to succeed in a context in which there *is* a public service ethos, making staff willing to work towards compliance even without the threat of sanctions. Moreover, the proponents of 'new public management' did not envisage internal contracts as unenforceable. Their main focus was on disciplining providers through competitive pressure: where a DSO was subject to regular competition with private firms, its contract could hardly be said to be unenforceable in practice. The weak nature of internal contracts themselves only becomes apparent in situations—somewhat neglected by 'new public management' theory—in which there is no effective market for the service. 'Contract as symbol' does not seem plausible as a statement of the reformers' intentions.

Even if contractualization was not meant to have merely symbolic effect, it might be felt that (given the problems of competition, for example) this was the most appropriate *ex post* interpretation to give to the reforms. But two arguments cast doubt on this more limited claim. First, the introduction of contractualization seems likely to have been a highly expensive business (for example, Webster 1998: 203–4; though cf. Walsh and Davis 1993). It is, of course, difficult to measure the cost of setting up the reforms in the first place, or to compare the transaction costs of contracts with those of the hierarchical management relationships which preceded them. But it seems likely that substantial expenditure is involved in activities such as restructuring services along purchaser and provider lines; conducting tendering exercises (where applicable); negotiating contractual targets; drafting contract documentation and so on. It is not clear how these costs could be justified if the resulting contracts are purely symbolic.

A second argument against the symbolic interpretation is that its main advantage—flexibility—would not necessarily be destroyed by a greater emphasis on the regulation and enforcement of internal contracts. Such contracts often govern complex public services (cf. Day and Klein 1987), and as a result, many of the commitments they contain need to be provisional and contingent. For example, a hospital's undertaking to meet a particular waiting time target for elective surgery is based on the assumption that there will not be a sudden rush of emergency cases necessitating the cancellation of elective operations. The hospital, as the provider of a public service, could not simply turn away the emergency cases in order to meet its contractual commitment. Any attempt to enforce that commitment strictly would produce undesirable results. But this claim rests on a misunderstanding of the possibilities of contract drafting and enforcement. The agreement between the parties might be written (admittedly at some extra cost) in such a way as to admit of legitimate excuses for non-performance. Even if the agreement was not so drafted, it might be possible to imply a suitable term. Thus, a policy of giving more than merely symbolic effect to internal contracts could be adopted without losing vital flexibility.

Private law or public law?

If internal contracts should not be seen merely as symbols, but should be regulated and enforced in some way, it is necessary to decide how to regulate and enforce them. A comparison of the respective merits of public and private law for these purposes is far from straightforward.

The first methodological problem in conducting such a comparison lies in defining what is meant by public law and contract law. There are fundamental debates about each subject's underlying policies and principles. It might be possible to say, for example, that public law is about constraining the activities of government,[10] and that contract law is about enforcing the promises made by the parties (Fried 1981).[11] But both these propositions can be contradicted. Public law also involves giving the government a substantial degree of discretion,[12] through doctrines such as *Wednesbury* unreasonableness[13] and justiciability. This seems analogous to contract law's respect for the autonomy of the parties. And contract law commonly protects weaker contracting parties from abuses of power—this is true of employees and consumers, for example—a characteristic which it shares with public law (see, generally, Collins 1997). Indeed, much of the most interesting recent scholarship on the public/private divide is concerned to highlight the extent to which bodies of doctrine on both sides of the divide share similar values (Oliver 1999).

A second methodological problem is that it is difficult to compare the public and private law treatments of contracts because they are at radically different stages of development. The private law of contract is a long-established, sophisticated body of doctrine. If internal contracts were made enforceable in private law, the implications of this reform could

---

[10] Famously labelled 'red light theory' by Harlow and Rawlings (1997: ch. 2).

[11] There are, of course, numerous theories of contract law: on the protection of reliance, see Atiyah (1986); on the promotion of exchange, see Kronman and Posner (1979).

[12] The 'green light theories' described by Harlow and Rawlings (1997: ch. 3).

[13] *Associated Provincial Picture Houses v Wednesbury Corporation*, 1948 1 KB 223.

be predicted relatively easily. It would be known what norms would apply to contract formation, breach and so on. Public law, by contrast, does not contain a similar body of doctrine for contracts. Where the government makes a contract with a private firm, that contract is enforceable in *private* law, and there are only a few embryonic rules of public law which apply in addition, as Chapter 1 explained (see, generally, Craig 1999: 121–62). This means that the application of public law rules to internal contracts is much more speculative. What is being considered is the possibility of extending existing doctrines—natural justice, for example—which are already applied to other governmental functions, to government contracts.

These methodological difficulties have significant implications for the nature of the argument to be made in this chapter. It will be suggested that there are two problems with the use of the ordinary law of contract to regulate internal government contracts. In terms of regulation, it will be argued that contract law does not offer the kinds of norms which might be desirable for internal contracts. In a study of this kind it is not possible to examine exhaustively all the norms of the law of contract which might be relevant. Instead, some examples will be given in the hope of persuading the reader that creative possibilities outside the constraints of the law of contract are at least worth exploring. In relation to enforcement, several arguments point to the desirability of using an alternative dispute resolution mechanism for internal contracts, rather than allowing recourse to the courts. It will be suggested that this poses more problems for a private law solution than it does for a public law solution. It will therefore be argued that the development of public law norms for internal contracts warrants further investigation.

Regulation

This discussion of the regulatory potential of private law will focus on two key examples: natural justice and penalty clauses. An application of the principles of natural justice to internal contracts could serve a number of purposes. During contract negotiations, the purchaser could be obliged to give the provider an opportunity to comment on all aspects of the proposed contract documentation, for example. This would be particularly desirable in non-competitive internal contract situations in which the provider did not have the option of refusing to contract with the purchaser. During the life of the contract, natural justice might require the purchaser to give the provider an opportunity to explain its conduct before levying penalties for default. This would help the purchaser to make a fair and accurate decision as to whether or not the penalty was appropriate.

As Chapter 1 noted, natural justice in the law of contract is a doctrine of relatively limited application. At the contract negotiation stage, the common law imposes few obligations[14] and the courts have refused to acknowledge any general doctrine such as a duty to bargain in good faith.[15] There are exceptions, the most notable being the doctrine of misrepresentation, which enables a person to obtain damages or rescind a contract or both where he or she has been induced to enter into it by a misleading statement or, under more limited circumstances, by the non-disclosure of material facts (see, generally, Treitel 1999: ch. 9). But natural justice does not apply at this stage. Because there is no contract, the courts cannot use the technique of an implied term to require its observance.

The implied term technique is, however, of some assistance once the contract has been concluded. The cases in which natural justice requirements have been implied fall into three broad groups: expulsion from an association or a club, expulsion from a trade union, and removal from office (see, further, Beatson 1995; Oliver 1999). Although the courts have held that expulsion from an association or club should require observance of natural justice, they have not applied the rule consistently: compare *Weinberger v Inglis*[16] and *Lapointe v L'Association de Bienfaisance et de Retraite de la Police de Montreal.*[17] In the trade union cases, review tends to be intensive: see, for example, *Stevenson v United Road Transport Union.*[18] This is also true of the cases concerning removal from office (e.g. *Ridge v Baldwin*),[19] although here the courts have an element of discretion in deciding whether or not to characterize a person's employment as having the status of an 'office'. Although some relatively broad constructions have been given, for example in *Malloch v Aberdeen Corporation*,[20] the courts have not gone so far as to make natural justice a more general requirement of the employment relationship (Deakin and Morris 1998).

---

[14] The government is, however, required to use fair and transparent tendering procedures under the European public procurement regulations, described in Ch. 1.

[15] See, for example, *Interfoto Picture Library v Stiletto Visual Programmes*, 1989 QB 433. For a persuasive argument in favour of adopting a general duty to negotiate with care, see Collins (1997: ch. 10).

[16] 1919 AC 606.

[17] 1906 AC 535. See also *Wood v Woad*, 1874 9 LR Exch. 190; *Shearson Lehman Hutton v Maclaine Watson*, 1989 2 Lloyd's LR 570.

[18] 1977 ICR 893. See also *Lee v The Showmen's Guild of Great Britain*, 1952 2 QB 329.

[19] 1964 AC 40.   [20] 1971 1 WLR 1578.

These cases seem to have two main strands of reasoning. First, emphasis is placed on the need for the club, union or employer to satisfy itself of particular issues before the individual can be expelled or dismissed. In *Stevenson*,[21] for example, the union official was entitled to continue in office while he 'gave satisfaction' to the executive committee of the union. Natural justice, in the form of a hearing, was necessary in order to decide whether there was evidence that the official had failed to perform his duties. This reasoning might well be applicable to internal government contracts. A court could imply a requirement to hold a hearing before permitting the purchaser to decide that the provider had failed to deliver services to the required standard and to deduct money from its monthly contract payment. The second strand of reasoning reflects the impact of the relevant decision on the individual. In *Lee*,[22] for example, the plaintiff's expulsion from the union in a closed shop situation would have deprived him of his livelihood. The applicability of natural justice to internal contracts might therefore turn on how important this point is to the reasoning of the courts in these cases. A public body might attract some sympathy where its survival depended upon its contract with the purchaser, but the imbalance of power between two public bodies might be less obvious to a court (and therefore less likely to attract sympathy) than the imbalance between an individual and a powerful collective or employer.

Private law does not therefore seem to offer the natural justice protections which would be desirable for internal contracts. Natural justice does not apply during contract negotiations and its application during the life of the contract, through implied terms, is uncertain. Of course, private law could be developed: as suggested above, implied terms could be extended to cover internal contracts. But there are two important points to note about such a proposal. If the suggestion is to extend private law doctrine solely in relation to internal contracts, this development might not count as 'private law'. Although implied terms are a private law technique, the development might be more appropriately classified as public law if it could only be invoked as between two public bodies. But if the suggestion is to extend private law doctrine to encompass natural justice protections more generally, much broader issues of the reform of contract law are raised. The situations in which natural justice can currently be implied in private law are notable for the fact that they bear a strong resemblance to administrative decisions. In the trade union cases, for example, a powerful organization is making a judgement about how

---

[21] N. 18, above.   [22] Ibid.

to respond to the behaviour of an individual. It is not at all clear that it is desirable to extend this type of protection to, for example, ordinary commercial settings.

The alternative is to develop natural justice norms for internal contracts through public law. Natural justice is, of course, a well-established doctrine in public law: it is one of the three grounds for judicial review set out in Lord Diplock's speech in the GCHQ case.[23] But its application to government contracts is uncertain because they are normally treated as matters of private law. As Chapter 1 demonstrated, the application of natural justice at the tendering stage depends on whether the court is willing to discover a sufficient 'public element' in the case.[24] The application of the 'public element' test is inherently imprecise (Craig 1999: 773). But this does at least suggest that if the public/private problem did not arise—because of a clear decision that internal contracts were to be governed by public law, for example—natural justice would be readily applicable during contract negotiations. There is no public law precedent on the application of natural justice during the life of the contract, but again, if decisions about whether or not to deduct money from the contractor's monthly payment were accepted as being of a public character, there would be no difficulty in applying natural justice to them. In particular, there would be no need to construct an argument for doing so around any of the justifications for implying terms into contracts: natural justice would simply be imposed by the law. Chapter 7 will explore in greater detail how this might be done.

The second example to be examined here of the problems inherent in any attempt to regulate internal contracts through private law is that of the rules on penalty clauses. It is arguable that the government as purchaser should have access to a wide range of self-help remedies in order to ensure compliance with its contracts and thus to secure the delivery of effective and efficient public services. But the common law restricts the use of clauses which do not amount to a reasonable pre-estimate of the purchaser's likely loss.

Why might the government as purchaser need to include sanctions in its contracts? A purchaser might be at a disadvantage in relation to a provider in one of several ways. In many internal contract settings, as Chapter 2 noted, the purchaser may have no alternative sources of supply: it may have no choice but to contract with the provider regardless

---

[23] *Council of Civil Service Unions v Minister for the Civil Service*, 1985 AC 374.

[24] The leading cases are *R v Legal Aid Board, ex p. Donn & Co.*, 1996 3 All ER 1, and *R v Lord Chancellor's Department, ex p. Hibbit & Saunders*, 1993 COD 326.

of its performance. The purchaser might become dependent on the provider over the course of a long-term relationship, or the provider might have greater expertise in the subject-matter of the contract than has the purchaser. In any of these situations, the provider might be tempted to offer a service which is too highly priced or of low quality. Public choice theory (a key part of the background to contractualization reforms) rejects the notion that public bodies can be trusted to act in the public interest (Downs 1967; Niskanen 1971; Tullock 1965). But even if one does not accept this as a reliable prediction of behaviour, it is surely the case that public bodies might default inadvertently, for example, by failing to notice ways in which they might improve their performance.[25]

If the provider does default, members of the public might receive inadequate or expensive services as a result of the contract. Instances of inefficient or ineffective public expenditure are not usually tolerated: various mechanisms of accountability (audit or parliamentary questions, for example) are triggered when problems arise. There seems to be no reason why such failings should be tolerated when the expenditure takes the form of an internal contract. If government purchasers are not to make bad bargains, they must be given special powers. These powers might include the right to use contractual sanctions to punish recalcitrant providers.

At common law, however, such sanctions may not be enforceable. Where a contractual term provides for the payment of a sum of money in the event of a breach, the courts decide whether the term should be construed as a liquidated damages clause, which is enforceable, or a penalty clause, which is not (Treitel 1999: 929–37). A penalty clause is for 'a payment of money stipulated as *in terrorem* of the offending party'[26] to compel performance of the contract, whereas a liquidated damages clause is an attempt genuinely to estimate the loss likely to be occasioned by the breach.

This would create two problems in internal contract settings. One is that the purchaser might not have suffered any loss as a result of the breach. Many internal contracts govern the provision of services to members of the public rather than to the purchaser. If an operation is cancelled at the last minute, it is the patient who suffers a loss (by taking time off work unnecessarily, for example) and not the purchaser.[27] In order to recover,

---

[25] Empirical evidence on this issue is presented in Ch. 8.

[26] *Dunlop Pneumatic Tyre v New Garage and Motor Co.*, 1915 AC 79 at 86.

[27] It is possible that the patient might be able to claim under the Contracts (Rights of Third Parties) Act 1998. But, as Treitel (1999: 601) points out, it is not sufficient to satisfy s. 1(1)(b) for the third party to show 'that he would happen to benefit' from the contract. And the parties themselves might argue under s. 1(2) that they had not intended that the third party should be able to enforce the relevant term.

the purchaser would have to bring itself within one of the recognized exceptions to the general rule that damages cannot be awarded in respect of a third party's loss. Various analogies are possible—with the local authority exception[28] or perhaps even the family holiday exception[29]—but the law in this area is far from clear. And the purchaser would probably have to account to the third party for the money received,[30] so that recovery would effectively be limited to situations in which the purchaser wanted to pay compensation to service users. This might not be appropriate in all public service contexts.

The second problem is quantification. The present law upholds genuine attempts to estimate loss (even if they turn out to be rather too low or rather too high) but characterizes all other sums of money as punitive. This may be unduly harsh. There is little to be gained by permitting purchasers to use penalties which are so high that the provider could not conceivably pay them and continue to perform the contract. This would lead to considerable disruption in the provision of public services. But not all 'penalties'—sums in excess of the anticipated loss—are punitive to that extent. Some may be designed to act as a *deterrent* to poor performance. An example will illustrate the point.

An NHS Trust might be required to pay £500 to the purchaser for each patient who waited longer than a year for an operation. Let us assume that this clause is enforceable because the purchaser uses the £500 to buy an operation for the patient at another hospital: it is a reasonable pre-estimate of the cost to the purchaser of making alternative arrangements. The Trust does suffer a loss, although not of £500. Even though it has not incurred the cost of performing the operation, a part of the price would have covered its fixed costs (buildings maintenance, staff salaries, and so on) which do not diminish even though the operation is not performed. But the provider might feel that this small loss is not enough to prompt a drive to reduce its waiting lists. This is problematic for the purchaser: it wants the provider to improve its performance rather than to treat the sanction as a form of 'taxation'. A small increase in the size of the penalty, over and above the purchaser's loss—say to £600—might

---

[28]   *St Albans City and District Council v International Computers*, 1996 4 All ER 481. But this analogy might not work where the public body purchaser was not in direct receipt of funds from service users.

[29]   *Jackson v Horizon Holidays*, 1975 3 All ER 92. The public authority would be seen as arranging something on behalf of the service users but without the creation of a relationship of agency.

[30]   By analogy with *The Albazero (Albacruz v Albazero)*, 1974 2 All ER 906; *Alfred McAlpine Construction v Panatown*, 2000 4 All ER 97.

be enough to deter the provider from breaching the standard. Thus, while there is no reason to permit extortionate penalties, there may be good reasons for allowing penalties somewhat in excess of the purchaser's actual loss. This would be particularly important in internal contract settings in which competition is weak.

There are, of course, ways of drafting contracts so as to include sanctions without violating the law. For example, the courts have been less inclined to treat provisions allowing the victim of a breach to withhold payment as punitive.[31] Nonetheless, there may be a case for offering a greater degree of choice and flexibility: some contracts may not lend themselves to a regime of potential deductions from monthly payments or the end payment. The rules could, of course, be changed simply for internal contracts, but for the approach to be classified as 'private law'—as argued above—the new rules would have to apply to all contracts. The law on penalties has been subject to much criticism in the literature on the ground that there is no reason to disallow clauses to which the parties have given their consent, given that the danger of exploitation could be dealt with through doctrines such as duress and undue influence (see, for example, Downes 1996; Goetz and Scott 1977; Kaplan 1977). A proposal for wholesale reform would therefore attract considerable support.

Nevertheless, it is arguable that this would not work well for internal contracts and that a more tailored solution (not therefore classifiable as 'private law') might be appropriate. First, the doctrine of duress applies primarily to illegal acts, and it is not clear how far it (or the doctrine of undue influence in equity) would extend to abuse of a monopoly position (Collins 1997: ch. 8). The latter seems far more likely than the former to occur in the public sector context. A power to review the amount of the penalty to ensure that (although not confined to a pre-estimate of damages) it is not excessive would seem more appropriate.[32] Admittedly, this would create considerable uncertainty as to where the line of enforceability would be drawn. Such uncertainty would probably not be tolerable in commercial contracts, but in the more regulated world of internal contracting, central guidance could be used to give the parties examples of penalties which were likely to be enforceable. Secondly, it might be desirable to couple special penalty powers with some procedural safeguards. The importance of this point will become clear in

---

[31] See, for example, *Eshelby v Federated European Bank*, 1932 1 KB 423, though cf. *Gilbert-Ash v Modern Engineering*, 1974 AC 689.

[32] The amount would, of course, be a relevant factor in an assessment of whether or not the contract had been agreed under conditions of duress.

Chapters 7 and 8. For example, the purchaser might be required to give the provider a hearing in order to investigate the circumstances of the breach properly before invoking the penalty. This might make the regime seem unduly bureaucratic and burdensome in commercial settings, although it is a familiar requirement in public law.

Again, then, public law seems to offer advantages as a source of regulation for internal contracts. Admittedly, public law does lack an obvious doctrinal peg on which to hang special penalty powers. But in terms of the general aims of public law, penalty powers may not be as difficult to justify as they seem to be at first sight. Public law is not merely concerned with controlling and constraining the government. It has a second key strand: that of facilitating governmental activity in the public interest (Ogus 1994: v). Penalties clearly fit this aspect of public law thinking. Moreover, it would at least be easier to couple public law penalty powers with constraining safeguards, such as natural justice requirements. These issues are discussed further in Chapter 8.

Enforcement

The discussion so far has suggested that there may be a case for breaking away from familiar private law doctrines and developing tailored public law norms to *regulate* internal contracts. There is also a case for *enforcing* internal contracts in a public law forum. Given the special circumstances of internal contracts, enforcement through the courts does not seem an attractive option: an alternative dispute resolution (ADR) mechanism would be preferable. But the very essence of a contract in private law is that it is an agreement between the parties which would be recognized and enforced as a contract by the ordinary courts. Even under a private law ADR scheme, ultimate recourse to the courts might sometimes be necessary. It will be suggested here that access to the courts might be less troublesome under a public law regime.

The enforcement of internal contracts by the ordinary courts is unattractive for three reasons, one theoretical and two practical. On the theoretical level, internal contract disputes might raise issues of justiciability for the courts (see, generally, Allison 1996: 185–7; Cane 1996: 34–9; Craig 1999: 860–4). There does not appear to be any difficulty of principle in requiring the courts to decide a case involving two public bodies. There is precedent for litigation between two local government bodies,[33]

---

[33] For example, *Bromley LBC v Greater London Council*, 1983 1 AC 768.

between local and central government,[34] and even between a statutory body and central government.[35] And some cases might raise quite 'ordinary' issues of contract interpretation which the courts could readily resolve. But others might raise complex polycentric and politically sensitive issues, for example, about the appropriate levels of funding for particular public services.[36] The courts might not be—and might not feel themselves to be—an appropriate forum in which to resolve problems of this nature.

But the most fundamental objections to court enforcement of internal contracts are practical ones. Collins—who favours, in principle, the enforcement of internal contracts through the courts—ultimately rejects this option on the grounds that it would be too costly (Collins 1999: 318). The government would not wish to spend scarce public funds on lawyers' fees. Indeed, the government would doubtless be criticized for allowing litigation between public bodies, and as a result would seek to ensure that public bodies did not turn to the courts to resolve their disputes. Although the minimization of litigation is a worthy aim, this might mean that the parties to a genuinely difficult dispute which did need authoritative resolution would not have access to a suitable forum in which their problems would be addressed.[37]

Another practical problem with enforcement through the courts is the likely impact of litigation on contractual relationships. It is well known that in commercial contexts, businesses litigate only when relationships have broken down irretrievably (Beale and Dugdale 1975; Macaulay 1963). The formal, adversarial character of court proceedings makes it virtually impossible to resume trusting relations once the case has been concluded (see, for example, Shapiro 1981: ch. 1). In a competitive market, this is not a significant problem: both parties can seek other contracting partners. But it is a worry in internal contracts. Because many internal contracts are not concluded in competitive markets, the parties may be trapped into a long-term relationship. If a dispute arises, the parties need a mechanism which helps them to resolve the dispute and *rebuild* trust. A court battle seems unlikely to fulfil this goal.

These problems point towards the use of some form of ADR[38] for internal contracts. Various types of ADR might be explored: one possibility

[34] For example, *Nottinghamshire CC v Secretary of State for the Environment*, 1986 AC 240.
[35] For example, *R v Secretary of State for Employment, ex p. Equal Opportunities Commission*, 1995 1 AC 1.
[36] The term originates in the writings of Fuller (see, especially, Fuller 1978). For a helpful commentary see Allison (1996: ch. 9).
[37] Unless the government provided an accessible ADR scheme, discussed below.
[38] For an introduction to the large literature on this topic, see Freeman (1995); Smith (1996).

would be to model a scheme on that designed for the NHS.[39] It will be recalled that this involved arbitration as a last resort, preceded by informal conciliation to resolve or at least narrow down the dispute (Hughes *et al.* 1997; McHale *et al.* 1997). An internal dispute resolution process would be less afflicted by problems of justiciability. It could be staffed by experts—lawyers and civil servants, for example—and chaired by a minister, so that it would have both the expertise and the political authority to deal with polycentric issues. Allison (1996: 138–52) attributes the success of the French Conseil d'État in part to its close links with the administration. This gives it an in-depth knowledge of the conditions faced by the government, and ensures that its decisions command respect.

Recourse to an internal dispute resolution procedure might also be less likely to attract adverse comment. The costs of the procedure could be kept to a minimum through, for example, the use of conciliation at an early stage of the dispute, and the employment of departmental legal advisers rather than counsel. If recourse to the mechanism nevertheless attracted public and parliamentary criticism, it would be possible to insist that the proceedings were kept confidential.[40] While it ill behoves a public lawyer to advocate any form of secrecy in government, the accessibility of the dispute resolution mechanism must be the paramount consideration.

Finally, an ADR mechanism could be designed so as to offer the parties the best chance of maintaining their relationship despite the dispute, or at least of rebuilding it once the dispute has been resolved. The two-stage NHS procedure offers the possibility of seeking a friendly settlement through conciliation before the adversarial arbitration stage is reached. Moreover, even if the dispute cannot be settled, conciliation should help to narrow down the subject-matter at issue and to prevent the parties from becoming overly aggressive at arbitration. Of course, no dispute resolution mechanism can preserve all relationships: the fact that there is a dispute at all is a sign of low trust between the parties. But certain types of ADR might perform better than the courts in this regard.

In private law settings, ADR may fulfil one of two possible roles. One is simply to reduce the likelihood of, rather than to prevent, litigation.

[39] National Health Service and Community Care Act 1990, s. 4; National Health Service Contracts (Dispute Resolution) Regulations 1996 (SI 1996/623).
[40] Most forms of ADR take place in private. This may be particularly attractive to the parties in certain types of case (see, for example, Hunter and Leonard (1997) on sex discrimination). But this aspect of ADR has been criticized even outside the governmental context (Fiss 1984; Hunter and Leonard 1997).

Thus, an ADR clause might be designed to commit the parties to use ADR *before* going to court, leaving open the possibility of litigation if ADR is unsuccessful. The other role is to provide a genuine alternative to the courts by seeking to exclude their involvement as far as possible. At common law, clauses which purport to remove a party's right to bring a case to court are not valid.[41] But one way to achieve this result is to conclude an arbitration agreement within the meaning of the Arbitration Act 1996. Under the Act, the parties to an arbitration may agree to exclude the power of the courts to determine preliminary points of law (under s. 45) or appeals on points of law from the arbitration award itself (under s. 69), provided that (in the case of a domestic arbitration as defined in s. 85) they agree to do so *after* the arbitration proceedings have begun (s. 87). Even if the parties do not so agree, the jurisdiction of the courts is limited in various ways. For example, a party seeking to appeal from the arbitral award under s. 69 can only do so with the agreement of the other parties to the proceedings or by obtaining leave of court, which can only be granted under certain circumstances set out in s. 69(3). In short, the 1996 Act sacrifices the legal accuracy of decision-making in order to promote arbitration as a quick and conclusive alternative to litigation.

It seems rather strange to argue that internal contracts should be made enforceable in private law, but that the courts should be almost entirely excluded from the enforcement process. The sacrifice in accuracy might turn out to be quite significant. As noted above, existing private law doctrines might not fit the circumstances of internal contracts very comfortably. Arbitrators might be able to deal with this by a flexible and discretionary application of the law. But this would produce a body of special law for internal contracts which would not have the authority of the courts, and which would in fact make a mockery of the idea that internal contracts were enforceable in private law (cf. Fiss 1984).

The problem of sacrificed accuracy does not arise so strongly in relation to an ADR mechanism applying public law norms to internal contracts, because the courts' involvement in this area has been so limited. The ADR mechanism would be charged not with the task of applying an existing body of doctrine, but with developing a body of doctrine from more general public law principles. Although the courts would determine those general principles, they would not have any ownership of the more precise rules. There would be a partial overlap, but not full competition, between the two jurisdictions.

---

[41] *Czarnikow v Roth Schmidt*, 1922 2 KB 478.

The public law solution does, however, have one disadvantage. It is that the courts are highly wary of attempts to exclude their jurisdiction (Craig 1999: ch. 24). It would be extremely difficult to insulate the ADR mechanism itself—the arbitral tribunal, for example—from the reach of judicial review. This again presents all the disadvantages of litigation (adversarialism, cost and adverse publicity). But there are two factors which might reduce the courts' involvement. One is that, as noted above, at least some internal contract disputes might not be justiciable. The other is that the courts do sometimes limit their scrutiny where the body under review is applying a different legal regime. The Parliamentary Commissioner for Administration (PCA) is concerned with decisions taken with 'maladministration',[42] which overlaps with the grounds of judicial review but is much broader, covering failings such as delay and rudeness (see, generally, Craig 1999: 233; Harlow and Rawlings 1997: 424–5). The courts have acknowledged the PCA's wide discretion and have limited their scrutiny to the conduct of the investigation and the adequacy of the reasoning given to support the findings.[43] Thus, even if the courts did attempt to review the ADR mechanism, they might confine themselves to procedural matters rather than to the substance of the specialist doctrine it was developing.

In conclusion, it is clear that ADR has many advantages over court enforcement for internal contracts. It would avoid expense and adverse publicity; it would offer expert solutions to disputes; and it could be designed to maximize the chances of maintaining cordial long-term relationships. This also points—though perhaps less clearly than the doctrinal arguments advanced above—to the development of a public law regime for internal contracts. Such a regime would be able to exclude the courts without sacrificing legal accuracy because it would not be purporting to apply an existing body of law.

Conclusion

This chapter has sought to problematize the notion of unenforceable internal contracts. It has been suggested on the basis of the critical literature, with some empirical support, that it may be difficult for the parties to

---

[42] Parliamentary Commissioner Act 1967, s. 5(1).

[43] The leading cases are *R v Parliamentary Commissioner for Administration, ex p. Dyer*, 1994 1 WLR 621; *R v Parliamentary Commissioner for Administration, ex p. Balchin*, 1997 COD 146; *R v Parliamentary Commissioner for Administration, ex p. Balchin (No. 2)*, 2000 2 LGLR 87. For critique, see Giddings (2000).

an internal contract to take their contract seriously when there are no real consequences if it is ignored. The purchaser may be tempted to interfere in the provider's work and vary the terms of the contract without the provider's consent. The provider may simply refuse to comply with controversial or challenging targets.

It has further been suggested that treating internal contracts as mere symbols would not be consistent with the underlying premises of the reforms, or with the amount of effort which has been expended on the creation of contractual structures in public services. But this does not mean that the obstacles which currently prevent internal contracts taking effect as ordinary private law contracts should simply be removed. The law of contract would doubtless provide many rules which would be suitable for internal contracts, but even a cursory glance at its doctrines identifies some areas which would have to be reformed or adapted. And it is by no means clear that these changes ought to be extended to *all* contracts. Moreover, the suggestion that two public bodies should resolve their disputes in court is problematic on both practical and theoretical grounds. The use of an ADR mechanism may sit more comfortably with public law regulation of internal contracting than with private law regulation.

But the reader might be forgiven for thinking that this chapter has waged something of a 'phoney war'. It has been suggested that public law might provide better rules (and better enforcement mechanisms) without specifying exactly what those rules (or mechanisms) might be. The battle must, of course, be fought and won on the issue of whether or not it is possible to give specific content to the norms and procedures of a public law of contract in a way which would convince the reader of their practical utility and desirability. The remainder of this book is devoted to this task.

4 Accountability Mechanisms

How should the daunting task of developing public law norms for internal contracts be approached? As in any creative enterprise, several different strategies might be adopted. One option would be to conduct comparative studies of other jurisdictions in which there is a well-developed public law approach to government contracts. Such studies might identify norms which were suitable for 'transplantation' into English law to regulate internal contracts.[1] Another option would be to conduct empirical studies of internal contracts in order to identify the practical problems faced by the parties. Some of these problems might admit of solution through public law rules. The present study adopts this empirical approach: Chapters 6–8 will develop norms for internal contracts using the NHS as a case study. But whichever option is chosen, the creative process must be guided by some notion of what a public law of internal contracts should be trying to achieve.

A good guiding policy should meet three relatively uncontroversial criteria. The first is political acceptability. The policy must be based on values which the law ought to promote: fairness, the efficient use of public funds, and so on. The second might be termed 'productivity': the policy should be a fruitful source of inspiration for legal development. And the third is 'fit'. The policy should be appropriate to the area being regulated and, if possible, it should provide a way of linking new developments to the existing law. Although it is not desirable to tie legislators and policy-makers to the existing law for all their ideas, the law should be developed coherently wherever possible.[2]

This chapter does not attempt to provide a complete set of policies and principles for a public law of internal contracts. Their development and elaboration would be beyond the scope of a single volume. The more modest aim here is to focus on one policy which would support a significant part of that law: the policy of promoting the use of internal contracts as

---

[1] For a discussion of the dangers of transplantation, particularly in the context of public law, see Allison (1996). Transplantation from external contracts to internal contracts might be particularly problematic.

[2] Dworkin distinguishes principles, which are derived from the existing law and may be applied by judges, from policies, which are matters for the legislature and need not fit existing law (Dworkin 1986). The point being made here is that a policy which fits the existing law has the added advantage that it will promote coherent development. But fit is not an essential requirement for a policy: as Pitt (1993) points out, to insist that future development always fits the current law is to inhibit the legislator unnecessarily.

fair and effective mechanisms of accountability. It will be argued that this policy meets the three criteria listed above: accountability is a fundamental value in a democracy, and therefore politically acceptable; internal contracts can be interpreted as mechanisms of accountability; and the idea of a fair and effective mechanism of accountability is a fruitful source of norms. The discussion provides the theoretical framework for the NHS case study to be presented in the next four chapters.

Accountability as a guiding policy

One obvious way to identify a suitable policy for internal contracts would be to adopt a policy which was already a part of public law. An established policy would probably (though not inevitably) satisfy the criterion of political acceptability. It would be productive because its use in other contexts would produce detailed norms which might be applicable to contracts. And it would help to draw internal contracts into a familiar public law discourse.

The absence, demonstrated in Chapters 1 and 2, of any clear public law response to government by contract did not bode well for this approach. Perhaps surprisingly, however, the government itself drew on a public law concept—accountability—when explaining its increasing use of contractual modes of organization. The government argued that changes such as the separation of agencies from their parent departments, and the creation of 'internal markets' in public services such as the NHS, would improve the accountability of service deliverers (agencies or providers) to those who decided what services should be delivered (central departments or purchasers).[3] The claim was that contracts would improve accountability by setting out the targets to be achieved and the sanctions to be employed (reduced contract payments or the loss of performance-related pay, for example) if the targets were not met. Moreover, providers in a market setting would be motivated to perform to high standards in order to attract new contracts or to ensure that existing contracts were renewed.

The accountability justification for contractualization was highly controversial. The government focused on what might be labelled 'internal accountability', discussed further below, in which lower tiers of

---

[3] See, for example, the Next Steps Review 1993, quoted in Freedland (1994) (on Next Steps Agencies); Department of Health (1989*b*), NHSME (1989; 1990) (on NHS contracts). For a strikingly similar account of the advantages of contract in a very different context, see Nelken (1987).

government are made accountable to their superiors for the achievement of financial targets and the delivery of the government's programme. Some commentators accepted that contractualization would bring accountability benefits in this sense (for example, Harden 1992: 71). But most focused instead on 'external accountability': the government's accountability to members of the public and their representatives for its performance. They argued that contractualization did not improve external accountability because members of the public had very little input into the award of contracts and might be disadvantaged by the renewed emphasis on the economy and efficiency of service delivery (for example, Freedland 1994: 102–3). Moreover, as Chapter 1 explained, the move to contractualiza-tion was part of a package of reforms which reduced public participa-tion in other ways, for example, by emphasizing business experience rather than community work as a criterion for appointment to the boards of public bodies, such as NHS Trusts.

This debate will be examined further below. For the moment, it is suf-ficient to observe the widespread use of accountability—a familiar concept in public law—by both government and commentators, as a way of evalu-ating the contractualization reforms. This may provide a crucial clue in the search for a guiding policy for a public law of internal contracts. The remainder of this chapter assesses accountability's candidature for the position of guiding policy using the criteria of political acceptability, fit and productivity. But first, the concept must be defined.

Defining accountability

A relationship of accountability has two elements. The first element is responsibility: 'One cannot be accountable *to* anyone, unless one also has responsibility *for* doing something' (Day and Klein 1987: 5). But this does not necessarily mean that a person can only be accountable for those acts he or she has performed him- or herself: the constitutional conven-tion of ministerial responsibility is in part premised on a notion of account-ability for the acts of others, even if this ideal is not always fulfilled in practice (Woodhouse 1994). The responsibility may therefore be either for the performance of a particular task, or for the supervision of peo-ple and systems through which the task is performed. In Hart's terms, the responsibility may be a role-responsibility coupled with a liability-responsibility, or simply a liability-responsibility on its own (Hart 1968).

The second element is that others have a legitimate interest in how the responsibility is discharged: the person to be called to account must not simply be acting on his or her own behalf. This may occur, for example, when others have delegated responsibility for performing the task, or supplied the money for it. This gives them the right to ask for an explanation: they are the people *to whom* the person discharging the responsibility is to be answerable. Their relationship with the person to be called to account need not be direct. They may be members of an interested group, such as taxpayers or voters, whose 'delegation' of responsibility is, at best, indirect.

But this relationship of accountability does not necessarily result in the giving and receiving of accounts. Instituting an accountability *process* or *mechanism* is,[4] in principle,[5] optional.[6] The person with the right to call to account may choose not to exercise his or her right (though the liability to be called to account subsists even where the right is not exercised). At one level, the decision to institute an accountability process may be seen in terms of fundamental pairs of values: as a choice of control over delegation, of checking over trust. But as Power (1997) points out, one cannot eliminate trust by choosing checking, or autonomy by choosing control. Accountability does involve checking, but it cannot function without trust: trust in those calling to account, and some degree of trust in the information being supplied by those being called to account. Accountability simply involves striking a different balance between the two values.

Political acceptability

The first of the three criteria for a good guiding policy is political acceptability. The debate about internal and external accountability, described above, seems to cast some doubt on the likelihood that accountability will satisfy this requirement. If the meaning of the concept is so contested, how can it command widespread support?

Accountability is, in fact, a core value in a democracy.[7] A democratic government exercises power on behalf of its citizens, who have a legitimate interest in what is done in their name. They can express their approval

---

[4] These terms are used interchangeably.

[5] In practice, this choice may be frustrated where those who are entitled to call to account are dependent upon the co-operation of others in setting up an accountability process: members of the public may be dependent upon government in this regard.

[6] It may be mandatory in some contexts, notably where the caller to account does not act on his or her own behalf and is accountable for calling another body to account.

[7] Accountability is also relevant in a variety of private law contexts which are beyond the scope of the present discussion. See, for example, McCahery *et al.* (1993) on companies; Fridman (1996) on agency; and Martin (1997) on trusts.

or disapproval through the ballot box: elections are one key mechanism of accountability. Moreover, while a government is in office, a healthy democracy will provide a variety of ways—further mechanisms of accountability—in which its policies can be examined, checked and challenged (Weir 1995).[8] As Hirst comments: 'Assessments of how democratic a country is concentrate on the degree to which government is accountable to the people and the effectiveness of the means of ensuring accountability' (1995: 341).[9]

Democratic government involves two types of delegated power.[10] First, power is 'delegated' by the electorate to their representatives, whom they elect to govern on their behalf. Secondly, governing itself is a complex activity, particularly in the modern state, which requires power to be delegated to a variety of individuals and agencies to perform different government functions. These two types of delegated power are linked to two types of accountability process.[11] 'External' accountability processes are required, in order to allow members of the public, or their elected representatives, to call those who govern to account. 'Internal' accountability processes are required in order to ensure that the lower tiers of government are accountable to ministers.[12] The reason for choosing to use an accountability mechanism, rather than simply trusting the delegates, is different in each case.

The periodic election is obviously the most fundamental mechanism of external accountability in a democracy. It allows voters to judge the performance of their representatives, particularly those forming the government, and to decide whether or not to re-elect them on the basis of their past performance and stated future intentions. But this does not offer the electorate an adequate degree of control: in the words of one of the founding fathers of the US constitution, 'A dependence on the people is, no doubt, the primary control on the government; but

[8] The exact nature of these mechanisms depends on whether the conception of democracy being espoused is pluralist or unitary (see below).

[9] For examples of such assessments see Harden and Lewis (1986); Longley (1993); Oliver (1991). The legitimacy of government is measured in other ways, too. Baldwin and McCrudden's (1987) discussion of the legitimacy of regulatory agency action is instructive in this regard.

[10] For historical analysis, see Day and Klein (1987).

[11] It should be noted that the use of the terms 'external' and 'internal' to describe accountability processes does not correspond to the use of 'external' and 'internal' in relation to contracts. Both types of contract are 'internal' mechanisms of accountability.

[12] This distinction is similar to that drawn by Loughlin (1992) between political and administrative accountability, and by Day and Klein (1987) between political and managerial accountability.

experience has taught mankind the necessity of auxiliary precautions' (Madison *et al.* 1788).

These auxiliary precautions take the form of more regular and routine accountability mechanisms: to Parliament, the public and the courts. As Day and Klein comment, 'it is precisely day-by-day accountability, in which the rulers explain and justify their actions directly to the ruled, which distinguishes a democratic society from an elective tyranny' (1987: 7). The doctrine of the separation of powers, albeit imperfectly realized in the British constitution (Vile 1967), gives Parliament a role in calling the executive to account between elections. The deficiencies of political accountability mechanisms, despite attempts to strengthen them, for example through the Select Committee system, have been well documented (see, for example, Woodhouse 1994; Oliver 1991). Some writers have advocated a more pluralist conception of democracy, in which opportunities are provided for citizens to participate more directly in government, to relieve the heavy burden of scrutiny currently placed on Parliament. Such mechanisms are not, however, particularly well-developed in the British constitution. Finally, the courts have an important role to play in upholding the Rule of Law (Fuller 1969; Raz 1977): ensuring that public bodies comply with their legal mandate and act in accordance with a set of common law requirements of good government (procedural fairness, proportionality and so on) (Turpin 1999).

Internal mechanisms of accountability include, among others, the government's own financial controls, for example through the Treasury and the departmental Accounting Officers;[13] the work of the public auditing bodies, the Comptroller and Auditor General[14] and the Audit Commission[15] (though these bodies have important external accountability functions too); and managerial accountability through various types of internal contract. Day and Klein (1987) argue that the justification for this category of accountability is very different from that for political accountability. Government is seen here as the management of an estate: both ministers and their subordinates must be made accountable for their stewardship of public funds and their delivery of services. But internal accountability feeds into external accountability. It should

---

[13] HM Treasury (1995*a*) (as amended); Harden (1993); McEldowney (2000).

[14] The Comptroller and Auditor General is an independent officer of the House of Commons, responsible to the Public Accounts Committee, and assisted by the National Audit Office: National Audit Act 1983. See generally Harden (1993); McEldowney (1991; 2000).

[15] See the consolidating Audit Commission Act 1998; Radford (1991); Loughlin (1992), McEldowney (2000).

ensure that ministers have some control over the actions of their departments: political and public accountability are ineffective if the government cannot influence the behaviour of those implementing its policies. It also provides information to members of the public and politicians to assist them in calling the government to account. The debate surrounding contractualization has tended to ignore this link between the two types of accountability, and the importance of having effective mechanisms to implement *both*.

Two main functions are usually claimed for accountability processes, whether 'external' or 'internal'. The first is to guard against the abuse of delegated power. The existence of checks might either deter potential abuses, or detect those which have taken place. The concept of abuse may be narrowly defined, covering for example the deliberate pursuit of personal gain, or broadly defined, to include wasteful or inefficient behaviour. There are, however, two dangers identified in the literature. One is that of placing undue faith in the mechanisms of checking: Power (1997) explains that no checks can guarantee that standards are being met. The second danger relates to the balance between autonomy and control, noted above. One of the central dilemmas of the modern state has been to find ways of controlling and structuring discretion without instituting so many checks as to impede the efficient conduct of public business (Smith and Hague 1971; Galligan 1986; Thynne and Goldring 1987; Hawkins 1992). Some have seen the notion of accountability as the solution to this dilemma: an official may be given discretion provided that he or she is accountable for its exercise (Normanton 1971). But a process of accountability in fact involves the same dilemma, since it may subject the official to more or less detailed scrutiny of his or her performance. The more detailed the scrutiny, the more the official's autonomy is threatened.

More recently, theorists have begun to point to a second, constructive role for accountability processes (see, for example, Harden and Lewis 1986; Oliver 1991). An accountability process can promote efficient and effective performance of the required task because it encourages the primary actor to gather information and to exchange ideas with those calling to account, thus helping to overcome problems of 'bounded rationality' (Simon 1947). As Normanton explains: '[P]ublic accountability should not only provide administrative safeguards but should, by improving the flow and the quality of information, make an important contribution to the efficient conduct of government. Accountability can and should be *useful*' (1971: 338; emphasis in original). In part, this may be seen as the discovery or rediscovery of the second key strand to public law: facilitating the pursuit of public interest goals by government.[16] Ogus comments that 'public law is not only about preventing the abuse of power; it is also about selecting legal forms which can best achieve the instrumental goals of collective choice' (Ogus 1994: v).[17]

Thus, although the government's claims about the accountability implications of internal contracts were controversial, this was because the government and commentators were focusing on different aspects of accountability. In fact, both internal and external accountability are fundamental elements of democratic government. The controversy does not undermine the view that the promotion of accountability is a politically acceptable policy which would command widespread assent.

Fit

Accountability may be an acceptable value, but does it help to make sense of internal contracts? To answer this question, it is necessary to spend some time thinking about accountability in *analytical* terms. It will be argued that contractual relationships can be understood as relationships of accountability, and that contracts themselves can be used in order to perform or support the practical tasks associated with accountability. The discussion will also illustrate the subsidiary dimension of 'fit'—fit with public law more generally—by highlighting parallels between contracts and other mechanisms of accountability.

The first requirement for a relationship of accountability—that the body to be called to account must be responsible for the performance of a particular task—is likely to be met in all internal contracts.[18] The second requirement, that the caller to account must have a legitimate interest in the performance of the task, is satisfied in at least two respects where one public body places a contract with another. One is that the purchaser is commonly delegating some part of its responsibilities to the provider, rather than divesting itself of those responsibilities entirely. If the provider defaults, the purchaser may be in breach of its own obligations. It therefore has a legitimate interest in the performance of the delegated

---

[16] For useful typologies of understandings of administrative law, see Harlow and Rawlings (1997); McCrudden (1999*b*).

[17] Ironically, he blames the neglect of the latter on a preoccupation with accountability, taken in the sense of controlling power and preventing abuses.

[18] Contracts involve mutual obligations: the purchaser is obliged to pay the provider for its work, for example. But the purchaser's obligations are usually much more straightforward and therefore less interesting for a study of accountability.

task. Another is that the public body is in many instances paying for the performance of the task. This is obviously true of an NHS contract, for example, but it is to some extent true of a framework agreement under which an agency agrees to perform a particular task within a defined share of the department's overall budget. The purchaser has a legitimate interest in the use made of its money.

As noted above, the caller to account may decide not to 'activate' the relationship of accountability. But this seems unlikely in relation to internal contracts. First, the government's purpose in introducing the contracts was to improve internal accountability. And secondly, government purchasers may come under pressure to call their providers to account from the external accountability mechanisms to which they themselves are subject. MPs may be critical of a department if its agencies perform poorly. The Audit Commission may be critical of the performance of NHS purchasers if providers do not meet their targets. It might therefore be expected that the more effective the accountability mechanisms to which the public body is subject, the more likely it is to call its contracting partners to account. Whether this occurs in practice is, of course, a matter for empirical research.

In order to understand the notion of 'activating' the relationship of accountability more fully, it is necessary to think about the ways in which contracts might be used in practice to support the giving and receiving of accounts. What tasks are involved in accountability, and what role might contracts play in their performance? Oliver describes the components of an accountability mechanism in the following way: '[Accountability] is about requiring a person to explain and justify—against criteria of some kind—their decisions or acts, and then to make amends for any fault or error, whether by reversing the decision, or paying compensation or in some other way—even resigning from office' (Oliver 1994: 246, based on Marshall 1986). On the basis of this description, it can be seen that an accountability mechanism consists of four key features: setting standards against which to judge the account; obtaining the account; judging the account; and deciding what consequences, if any, should follow from it. These are common to all mechanisms of accountability, although they can be manifested in a variety of ways. Each element of the model is examined in turn here, but it should be remembered that the elements are often closely linked in practice, and that some variations in their chronological order are possible.

The first component of accountability involves *setting standards against which the account can be judged*: '[A]ccountability . . . presupposes agreement both about what constitutes an acceptable performance and about the language of justification to be used by actors in defending their conduct' (Day and Klein 1987: 5). The standards have an important role to play in determining the scope of the accountability process: they define which aspects of the relevant body's responsibilities are covered by the process, and implicitly, which are not. Internal contracts are potentially broad in scope: there were no formal restrictions on the terms which could be included in NHS contracts, for example. By contrast, the National Audit Office is required to call departments to account for the economy, efficiency and effectiveness of their work but not for the substance of the policies they adopt.[19]

The standards set are likely to include some which apply to the account itself, for example that it should be honest and accurate (Thynne and Goldring 1987), as well as substantive standards relating to the quality of the activity being accounted for. The nature of the substantive standards will vary according to the purpose of the accountability process. In general terms, as Oliver explains, 'it is for their stewardship of the public interest that state institutions are in practice most commonly accountable, and by this criterion that they are judged' (Oliver 1991: 23). But in many situations, more precise criteria are evolved. If the accountability process is designed to act as a safeguard against poor performance, the standards set may be minimum requirements below which performance should not fall. If it is designed to improve performance, the standards may be devised as more challenging targets. NHS contracts commonly contained standards of both types.

The identity of the standard-setter depends on the particular accountability process in question. In some cases, the person calling to account sets the standards: individual voters set their own criteria for judging the government's performance. Where a contract is used, the person being called to account is likely to have some input into the standards, because they are set out in contract terms to which both parties must agree. The extent of that input will, however, depend on the parties' relative bargaining power. In the case of professional regulation, the notion of having an outsider to set standards is abandoned altogether: the members of the profession determine what counts as acceptable behaviour (Allsop and Mulcahy 1996).

Likewise, the formality of the standard-setting process depends on the context. At one end of the spectrum, a minister's accountability to

---

[19] National Audit Act 1983, s. 6.

Parliament or the electorate proceeds on the basis of vague standards: the standards themselves may be contested on political grounds, and the minister may have to justify not only his or her performance but also the criteria against which he or she has measured it. The process involves a greater focus on debate as a result (Stewart 1984). At the other end of the spectrum, contracts can be used to set formal written standards of performance. Governments and commentators have seen this as one of the major advantages of contract over direct managerial relationships. For example, the guidance to NHS purchasers stated: 'The move to a contract system . . . [is] above all aimed at improvement in the quality and responsiveness of patient care. The separation of purchasing from provision will require contracts to state in increasingly explicit terms the quality and standard of service which is to be provided' (NHSME 1990: 6; see also Harden 1992: 71). Even here, however, there is room for informality. The purchaser may approach contract negotiations with some implicit ideas about what makes a good contracting partner, and may continue to have implicit expectations about the partner's behaviour during the life of the contract, without setting these expectations out in tender specifications or the contract itself. Moreover, even when standards are explicit, they must still be interpreted: applying the standards to the facts involves a continuous process of standard-setting (Hawkins 1984).

The second component in the accountability process occurs where *the person calling to account requires the primary actor to explain and justify his or her actions.* This component lies at the very heart of accountability: without information and explanation, the process cannot take place at all. Once again, a variety of forms and procedures may be used for obtaining accounts. The person calling to account may simply ask for oral or written information: for example, MPs use parliamentary questions or Select Committee hearings to obtain explanations from ministers. In other mechanisms, such as inspection or audit, the caller to account takes a more direct role in seeking the information. Contracts may involve either of these methods. In short-term, simple contracts, the purchaser is likely to inspect the product before paying the invoice, so that the product can be sent back if it is unsatisfactory. In longer-term relationships, the contract itself may be used to provide for monitoring procedures (Stinchcombe 1985): regular meetings or reports, rights of inspection and approval, and so on. Moreover, calling to account may either take place regularly or be triggered by signs of a possible problem. A contract might provide for monthly monitoring meetings, and for extra meetings in the event of a breach.

Day and Klein (1987) point out that the accountability process should be compulsory: it should be possible for the person calling to account to take action if the required information is not supplied.[20] This may appear to be an evaluative point: the accountability process is more likely to be effective if it is compulsory. But it is important to include this in the definition itself, whilst recognizing its close links with effectiveness. The distinction made by Day and Klein (1987) is between accountability and giving accounts.[21] When a public body voluntarily issues an annual report, for example, it gives an account but is not called to account. It has control over what goes into the report, and could gloss over areas of poor performance or exclude them from the report altogether (Normanton 1971). The element of obligation required by genuine accountability may be achieved in different ways. NHS contracts commonly included terms requiring the provision of reports on specified dates, with financial penalties if they did not appear. Other mechanisms, such as parliamentary accountability, rest on convention, public and parliamentary opinion, and media pressure. This demonstrates the close link between the definition and the question of effectiveness: where these 'sanctions' are weak, it is questionable whether parliamentary accountability processes retain a sufficient element of obligation to distinguish them from processes in which accounts are volunteered.

The third component of accountability is *judging the account rendered against the standards set.* In some accountability processes, this component is clearly separated from obtaining the accounts and deciding on the consequences to follow from them: in court proceedings, for example, the elements of hearing, giving judgment and making any resulting orders are easy to identify. In other processes, however, the components may be harder to distinguish. There is strong empirical evidence from the regulatory context for the proposition that the decision to characterize performance as inadequate is linked to the consequences that are likely to ensue (Hawkins 1984). Judgements about performance may also be closely connected to the task of obtaining information. A contract manager might monitor a provider more intensively—by requesting further reports and meetings—if the provider appeared to be in difficulties.

---

[20] See also Morgan (1993); Oliver (1991); Woodhouse (1994).

[21] Similarly, Stewart (1984) distinguishes between a 'bond' of accountability, in which the person calling to account has the power to demand accounts, and 'links' of account, in which the person being called to account volunteers information as a matter of custom or good practice to interested parties, even though they do not have the right to call him or her to account.

The fourth component of the accountability process is *applying any resulting consequences, or 'enforcement'*. The consequences may have one of at least three possible goals: to punish poor performance, to reward good performance, and to secure improvements for the future. A single accountability process may, of course, pursue more than one of these goals. A DSO's contract might provide for deductions from the monthly contract price if it fails to meet particular standards. These deductions would act as a punishment for poor performance and as a spur to renewed efforts in the future. Moreover, if the DSO performs its contract in a cost-effective way it might be rewarded by having the contract renewed for a further term.

Enforcement may be direct or indirect, and may be carried out by the caller to account, or by a third party. Contracts illustrate these various possibilities. Indirect enforcement is demonstrated by the way in which market pressures may make contracts 'self-enforcing'.[22] During contract negotiations, suppliers may accede to purchasers' demands in order to win their custom, and during the life of the contract, they may comply in order to retain purchasers' goodwill. Direct enforcement is illustrated by the inclusion of incentives or sanctions in the contract itself. NHS contracts often included penalty clauses if waiting time targets were breached. Finally, as a last resort, the 'legal system' governing the contract may offer a method of third party enforcement. As Chapter 2 explained, internal contracts are not legally enforceable, but in the NHS at least, there was a possibility (albeit remote) of recourse to arbitration in the event of a dispute.

The effectiveness of enforcement was touched on above in relation to the supply of information. If the enforcement measures for an accountability process are wholly ineffective, this might cast some doubt on whether it is right to apply the label 'accountability process' at all. For example, if ministers engage in voluntary consultation and do not commit themselves to considering the views expressed, it would not be appropriate to describe those participating in the consultation as callers to account. In less extreme cases, the effectiveness of enforcement is simply a question of the quality of the accountability process, and does not raise definitional issues. It is important to draw on empirical evidence—rather than assumptions—when assessing effectiveness. In contractual settings, the purchaser's bargaining power may vary according to factors such as the degree of competition in the market and the relative value of its contract.

---

[22] For an introduction to the analysis of self-enforcing contracts through game theory, see Hviid (1996).

The concept of an accountability mechanism is thus a powerful tool of analysis. It identifies very clearly the elements which are necessary in order to realize the value of accountability in practice. In so doing, it provides a framework for thinking about the various elements of internal contracts, and a means of linking contracts with other mechanisms of accountability. It fits contracts, and draws them into the discourse of public law.

Productivity

The third, crucial element of a good guiding policy is that it should inspire the development of norms and principles for internal contracts. Accountability is likely to do this for two linked reasons. First, the process of accountability involves a series of tasks which can be performed more or less fairly and more or less effectively. It should be possible to devise norms and principles to promote fairness and effectiveness in the performance of these tasks. Secondly, since accountability is a familiar principle in contexts other than contracting, as demonstrated above, it should be possible to develop some norms for contracting by transplantation. In a sense, the rest of this book is devoted to a demonstration of the power of 'promoting good accountability' as a guiding policy. But a brief example can be given here in anticipation of this more detailed discussion.

It was explained above that deciding whether or not standards have been met is one key component of accountability. It is a basic principle of our legal system that judgments of liability should be made only after a full investigation of the relevant evidence, during which the 'accused' should be given an opportunity to refute allegations being made against him or her. It therefore appears that one requirement of a good accountability process is that it should involve observance of the principles of natural justice at this stage.

The application of these principles can be worked out in more detail by examining specific accountability processes and making comparisons between them. Where the accountability process is a complaints procedure or a court hearing, for example, natural justice might be observed through the use of an adversarial procedure, in which the body being called to account is given the opportunity to present its case and to challenge the case being put against it. But when the accountability process is a public inquiry or an investigation by the ombudsman, natural justice might take a rather different form. The investigator would be responsible for ensuring that all relevant information was collected from the various interested parties, including the body being called to account.

In a contract, the purchaser might decide to investigate the matter itself, or the parties might opt to present their cases to an arbitrator. By selecting the most appropriate analogy from the two given above, it would be possible to suggest suitable norms of procedural fairness to ensure that the provider was given an adequate opportunity to refute or explain the purchaser's claims that it was in breach. It would also be possible to reason from basic principles: whatever the procedure adopted, it would invariably be necessary to give the provider notice of the purchaser's allegations, for example. The policy of using internal contracts as fair and effective mechanisms of accountability is helpful because it renders contracts more accessible to public lawyers and draws attention to ways in which public law might be used to regulate and enforce them. As Chapters 6–8 will show, it is indeed a productive policy.

Conclusion

Accountability provides a useful starting-point for public law thinking about internal contracts. As a well-established value in public law, it is likely to achieve widespread recognition and acceptance. The more specific notion of an accountability mechanism is a helpful tool for the analysis of contractual relationships. And it has an evaluative dimension: it should be possible to comment on ways of making the various components of an accountability process fairer and more effective, both on principle and by comparison with other similar processes. Accountability therefore meets the criteria for a guiding policy for the public law of contracts.

It would, of course, be possible to continue the discussion purely at the theoretical level. But if the aim is to make a practical contribution to the debate on internal contracts, it is necessary to demonstrate that the theory can usefully be applied to real-life problems. Chapters 6–8 present the results of a case study of NHS contracts in which the accountability mechanism is used as an analytical and evaluative tool. The next chapter introduces this case study.

5 Accountability Analysis in Practice: NHS Contracts

The next few chapters give a strongly practical focus to the analysis by presenting empirical evidence from a case study of NHS contracts as mechanisms of accountability. This chapter prepares the ground for the case study in two respects. First, it develops a more sophisticated method of classifying and analysing accountability relationships for use in the empirical study. Early pilot studies showed that while the basic concept of the accountability mechanism could provide an initial categorization of the data, it could not address the data's richness and complexity. Two models or 'ideal-types' of the contractual accountability relationship are therefore developed in the first section of this chapter, drawing on the socio-legal literature on contractual relationships. Secondly, the chapter gives a brief account of the methodology used in the empirical study. In particular, it explains the way in which NHS bodies were selected for participation in the research, and the techniques used to collect data.

The 'hard' and 'soft' models of contractual accountability relationship

The basic analysis of the contractual relationship as a mechanism of accountability provides a useful method of classifying empirical data into the core activities of standard-setting, monitoring, and enforcement. But it does not help to identify the variety of different ways in which these activities might be approached. Two possible sources of more refined analytical models suggested themselves: the literature on trust in contractual relationships, and principal-agent theory.

Principal-agent theory is concerned with the way in which a principal can control its agent's actions in the absence of competition (Ross 1973; Bamberg and Spremann 1989). It assumes that the agent will pursue self-interest at the principal's expense unless their interests can be aligned: financial penalties could be used to give the agent an interest in performing the principal's requirements, for example. This theory is obviously concerned with the agent's accountability and might have provided the more detailed insights into the parties' behaviour required for this study. But the model was rejected, for two main reasons. First, the model assumes that the agent is not subject to competitive pressures. In the NHS, by contrast, the reforms were intended to create a market (Department of Health 1989*b*).[1] Even though, as discussed below, that market was not fully competitive, it was important to employ a model which acknowledged the possibility of competition and allowed its role to be investigated. Secondly, early empirical work showed that this model did not fit the NHS parties' behaviour as closely as did the alternative model.[2] It did not account for the role of trust or for actions which did not involve the pursuit of self-interest. Moreover, the model's rationality assumption was not likely to explain all the findings of an empirical study.

The other option was to derive models from the literature on contractual relationships in socio-legal studies and transaction cost economics. This literature uses the level of trust between the parties in order to categorize contractual relationships, usually employing pairs[3] of concepts such as 'transactional' and 'relational' (Macneil 1974), 'arm's length' and 'obligational' (Sako 1992), 'low-trust' and 'high-trust' (Fox 1974), and 'adversarial' or 'collaborative' (Flynn *et al.* 1996). The models link the level of trust to particular patterns of behaviour, using, for example, broad contractual standards as an indicator of high trust, and specific standards as an indicator of low trust. This literature had two major advantages as a source of models for the present study. First, the models were developed for competitive markets.[4] Although it could not be assumed that the NHS market would be entirely competitive, the models made it possible to test the issue. This is explained below. Secondly, early empirical work showed that they accorded well with the NHS parties' behaviour, and even with the parties' perceptions of their behaviour. For example, fundholding practices often had an explicit policy of dealing with providers in a collaborative or adversarial way.

The models to be used in the present study, which will be labelled 'hard' and 'soft', distil the essence of this literature. They are not tied to any particular writer's version and are therefore given their own labels[5] to avoid confusion: the literature itself can be difficult to use because apparently similar accounts of the models may vary in subtle ways. Moreover, they are adapted to fit the study's needs, by focusing in

---

[1] The White Paper avoids explicit market terminology, probably for political reasons.

[2] Walsh *et al.* (1997) rejected the model for similar reasons, noting also its inability to explain the range of interests at work in the NHS.

[3] Some writers use a tripartite classification: for example, 'classical', 'neoclassical', and 'relational' (Macneil 1978; Williamson 1979).

[4] This is particularly apparent in the empirical studies by Macaulay (1963) and Sako (1992).

[5] The labels are not entirely novel: Lapsley and Llewellyn (1997) use 'formal' and 'soft'.

particular on the key tasks of accountability: standard-setting, monitoring and enforcement.

Before describing the models, it may be helpful to offer a brief examination of the central concept of trust.[6] Part of the dictionary definition of trust is 'reliance on some quality or attribute of a person or thing, or on the truth of a statement' (Simpson and Weiner 1989). Trust lies somewhere between faith, which presupposes no evidence for a particular belief, and confidence, which suggests good grounds for that belief (Hart 1988). Trust itself denotes the absence of evidence to contradict a belief (Gambetta 1988*b*). Importantly, although 'trust' may be used to describe situations in which one person has no alternative but to rely on another person, these are not genuine instances of trusting behaviour (Lorenz 1988: 197).

Trust provides a way of coping with situations in which we are uncertain about the way in which others will behave, and where their actions might harm us (Gambetta 1988*b*). Its relevance to contractual relationships is obvious: it provides a way of dealing with the risk that the other party might behave opportunistically (Lorenz 1988). Sako (1992) distinguishes three types of trust in contractual relationships: 'contractual trust' (that the other party will comply with its obligations); 'competence trust' (that it will perform to acceptable standards); and 'goodwill trust' (that it will exercise its discretion in a way which furthers its partner's interests). The soft model relies on a high degree of trust to deal with opportunism; the hard model involves a lesser degree of trust (all contracts require some trust) and suggests alternative strategies for tackling such behaviour.

The relationship between trust and accountability is similarly complex. Like a contractual relationship, accountability inevitably requires some trust (cf. Power 1997). At first sight, accountability implies checking, which may suggest that the hard model should be used and trust should be kept to a minimum. On closer inspection, however, effective accountability, like effective regulation (Hawkins 1984) and effective contracting (Sako 1992) may require high levels of co-operation. This may be more easily fostered through trust (using the soft model) than through the coercive strategies of the hard model. Thus, both the hard and the soft models suggest different versions of an accountability process, and—surprisingly—the soft model may be more effective than the hard model. The latter point will be explored during the empirical study.

---

[6] The discussion follows the approach of Deakin *et al.* (1997: 107–8) in distinguishing relevant 'dimensions' of trust.

Perhaps the greatest difficulty in using the concept of trust lies in the uncertainty in the literature as to how trust is created and sustained. A number of factors may be at work. Personal or cultural factors are one important group (Sako 1992; Fukuyama 1995). But empirical work has shown that such values are not a sufficient explanation: the parties themselves can strive to build trust through particular kinds of behaviour designed to demonstrate commitment and trustworthiness (Lorenz 1988). Indeed, trust can be seen as an activity requiring sustained effort (Flynn *et al.* 1997). Moreover, recent empirical work by Deakin *et al.* (1997) has demonstrated the potential for the institutional framework surrounding a particular contract to affect the degree of trust in the parties' relationship. Later chapters will explore the relevance of these various factors.

The hard and soft models

The models' main features can briefly be summarized:

Hard model:
- low-trust relationship between the parties
- standard-setting through adversarial negotiations
- comprehensive and precisely drafted standards
- monitoring through 'policing'
- enforcement through sanctions, particularly exit

Soft model:
- high-trust relationship between the parties
- standard-setting through collaborative negotiations
- broadly drafted, general standards and unwritten assumptions
- monitoring through shared information or trusting the provider to comply
- enforcement through persuasion

This section gives an introductory description of the models, acknowledging their derivation from the literature.[7] For present purposes, it is assumed that the purchaser has greater bargaining power than the provider, in the sense that the provider is anxious to win and retain the purchaser's custom (usually because the transaction takes place in a competitive market).

---

[7] The discussion here will focus on the contracts literature, but there are also important parallels, particularly at the enforcement stage, with the choice of persuasion or prosecution faced by regulatory agencies: see generally Ogus (1994), and Ch. 8.

The *hard model* describes a purchaser whose actions respond to (and reinforce) a low-trust relationship with the provider. This is immediately apparent from the way in which the purchaser negotiates the contract and sets standards for the provider's performance.[8] The hard purchaser sets out the standards it requires and demands that the provider sign up to them. A bargaining process may take place if the provider resists some of the demands. But the parties do not share information or negotiate collaboratively. The provider agrees to the contract by signing it: the purchaser is not interested in any stronger form of consent.

The hard model also has implications for the way in which the contract's terms are written. Despite the difficulty of drafting a comprehensive contract, sometimes referred to as the problem of incompleteness,[9] the parties strive to set detailed standards on as many aspects of their relationship as possible (Macneil 1974; Sako 1992). The purchaser's aim is to achieve maximum control over the provider (Fox 1974). Comprehensiveness helps to limit the number of situations in which the purchaser cannot call the provider to account because no standards have been set to govern a particular issue. The clarity and precision of the standards helps to prevent, as far as possible, disputes about their meaning.

At the monitoring stage, the hard model emphasizes the need to check up on the provider's performance. Formal monitoring procedures are included in the contract document, and reinforced by the threat of sanctions (Fox 1974). Information supplied by the provider is rigorously checked against independent information, wherever possible.[10] The purchaser behaves as if it suspects the provider of cheating or concealment, and places explicit disincentives in the way of this form of opportunistic behaviour.[11]

At the enforcement stage, the hard purchaser values compliance with its requirements above the maintenance of the relationship with its contracting partner (Sako 1992). If the provider does not comply, the purchaser simply 'exits' (Hirschman 1970) to another provider. Of course, the mere threat of exit may act as a good deterrent to poor performance. The hard purchaser might also employ what might be termed

---

[8] This is an extension of some of the ideas found in the literature, which focuses more closely on the life of the contract.

[9] Or 'presentiation': Macneil (1978).

[10] See discussion of 'competence' trust and monitoring costs in Sako (1992).

[11] The hard purchaser is also likely to check any information supplied by the provider during negotiations.

'intermediate' sanctions falling short of exit, such as penalty clauses, to respond to instances of poor performance which do not merit the ultimate sanction of taking the contract elsewhere.[12]

The *soft model* describes a very different pattern of behaviour, which reflects and reinforces a high-trust relationship between the parties. When setting standards during contract negotiations, the soft purchaser works jointly with the provider, on the basis of shared information, in order to negotiate a deal which is fair to both parties. It seeks the provider's full consent to the standards set, not just a signature to the contract. This emphasis on collaboration is reinforced by the way in which the standards are drafted. They are broad and general, and anticipate further negotiation between the parties to work out their details, or even to vary them in response to changing circumstances (Macneil 1974; Sako 1992). The soft purchaser is less concerned than the hard purchaser with the problem of incompleteness: it can rely on future negotiations to fill the gaps in the contract. The parties trust each other not to behave opportunistically during the negotiations and do not feel the need for the protection of a detailed contract document (Dore 1983).

Where the soft model is fully implemented, formal monitoring procedures are not required because the purchaser trusts the provider to comply and to perform to acceptable standards (Sako 1992). At the beginning of the parties' relationship, some checking may be necessary in order to reassure the purchaser that the provider is trustworthy (Sako 1992: 39). In any event, a trusting relationship implies a free flow of information between the parties (Dore 1983) which minimizes the problem of information asymmetry: the provider is unlikely to be able to conceal a breach from the purchaser.

At the enforcement stage, the trusting relationship of the parties to a soft contract affects their behaviour in several ways. It deters the provider from breaching, because it is afraid of losing the purchaser's goodwill (Macaulay 1963). Where a breach does occur, the purchaser eschews sanctions in favour of persuasion and works with the provider to solve the problem which has led to the breach (Dore 1983). Finally, the parties do not plan for default under this model. Any reference to the possibility of breaches might endanger their relationship by implying that the purchaser does not trust the provider to comply (Macaulay 1963).

---

[12] See Macneil (1978) and Williamson (1979) on 'neoclassical' contracts with their own dispute resolution arrangements.

A caveat: the models' hidden assumption

The studies from which these models are derived are usually based on research in competitive markets. Often, they focus on a number of small suppliers competing with one another for the trade of a large purchaser.[13] The purchaser has considerable power over the suppliers because they are afraid of losing its custom. The purchaser's superior position explains why both the hard and the soft models can claim to be effective. The purchaser's threat of exit under the hard model is effective because it is realistic—there are alternative suppliers—and potentially damaging—the provider fears the loss of income. The purchaser's use of persuasion under the soft model is effective because of an indirect reliance on exit. The provider fears the purchaser's loss of goodwill, in part because the parties value their trusting relationship and in part because a loss of goodwill might ultimately lead to the loss of the contract. Soft persuasion is backed by relatively harsh implied threats (Dore 1983).

In the NHS, as Chapter 2 indicated, purchasers were not always so privileged. Although a Health Authority might be a provider's main customer, the budgets of fundholding practices were trivial by comparison with most providers' annual incomes.[14] And purchasers did not necessarily have a large choice of alternative providers.[15] There is usually a limit to the distance most patients will travel for treatment (Barker *et al.* 1997).[16] In urban areas, the purchaser might have several providers within travelling distance. In rural areas, patients who lived on a county boundary might be within reach of more than one provider. This created limited contestability rather than competition (Walsh *et al.* 1997). But some purchasers' geographical location might mean that there was only one realistic provider for most services. This would inevitably enhance the provider's bargaining power at the purchaser's expense.[17]

Those NHS purchasers who were fortunate enough to be in strong bargaining positions would be able to implement their chosen model to

[13] See, for example, Macaulay (1963); Dore (1983); Sako (1992). Similar assumptions probably apply in Fox (1974).

[14] Audit Commission (1996) found that Trusts were dependent on fundholders for up to 20 per cent of their income. But this could consist of some 50 contracts with individual practices.

[15] See, for example, Klein (1995); Propper and Bartlett (1997); Barker *et al.* (1997); Spurgeon *et al.* (1997).

[16] Thirty minutes' travelling time is usually taken as a convenient indicator (Propper and Bartlett 1997).

[17] These and some of the other factors affecting bargaining power are explored in Ch. 8.

the full. The model's underlying assumptions would hold and purchasers would be highly likely to achieve their accountability goals. Purchasers in weaker positions might use the techniques suggested by one or other model, but might not be so successful. For example, a purchaser might have no choice but to contract with a particular provider. That purchaser might adopt a soft approach by persuading the provider to comply, or a weaker version of the hard approach by attaching sanctions other than exit to breaches of its contract. But in either case, the provider might pay less attention to the purchaser's requirements because it knows that the purchaser cannot take its contract elsewhere. The empirical study will not only seek out cases in which the models were implemented, but also cases in which the models could not be implemented to the full, in order to investigate the role of competition in the contractual accountability process.

Which model best describes NHS contracts?

Before embarking on the case study, it is worth speculating briefly as to which model might be most common in the NHS. The model for any given contract is, to some extent, a matter of choice for the parties. But the literature identifies a number of factors which are likely to influence that choice (often using the economist's assumption that the parties are acting rationally) (for example, Williamson 1979).

The *first factor*, and probably the most fundamental, is the *duration* of the relationship between the parties (Macneil 1974; Williamson 1979). The hard model is linked to short-term, discrete exchanges; the soft model to longer-term relationships. A brief encounter is unlikely to involve the close bonds inherent in the soft model. The shortest contracts in the NHS were waiting-list initiatives or one-off specialist treatments for a few patients, lasting only for the time it took to treat those patients. The shortest routine contracts were for a single financial year (Montgomery 1997*b*). A contract which was agreed for a year and not renewed could therefore count as hard, or at least towards the hard end of the spectrum. In most cases, however, purchasers renewed their one-year contracts over a longer period, or (less commonly) agreed longer contracts with annual re-negotiation of the contract price. The latter clearly counted as soft; the former were towards the soft end of the spectrum, particularly if there was a presumption that the contract would be renewed. There was also evidence that purchasers preferred on principle to build long-term relationships with providers (Flynn *et al.* 1996). Duration was therefore a strong indicator that the soft model would prevail in the NHS. Some caution was, however, required. Given the lack of choice of providers in the NHS 'market', some purchasers might be forced to renew contracts even if they were unhappy with a particular provider. A long-term relationship in the NHS might not therefore be a clear indication of a high level of trust between the parties. Chapter 7 demonstrates the importance of this caveat.

A *second factor* much discussed in the economics literature is *asset specificity* (Sako 1992; Williamson 1979). If, in order to meet the contract, the parties have to invest in specific assets which will be of much less value when put to alternative uses, a long-term relationship is required in order to obtain the maximum return on these investments. The parties are therefore likely to opt for the soft model. The importance of this factor in the NHS was primarily geographical. If a provider was proposing to build a community hospital to serve a particular area, it might want undertakings from purchasers in that area that they would use the new hospital, because there would be a limit to the extent to which it could replace their custom by attracting patients from outside. In other circumstances, for example in an urban area with a number of well-funded purchasers and an under-supply of services, a provider which found that it had spare capacity because one purchaser had taken its contract elsewhere could sell that capacity to other purchasers. Asset specificity might therefore be a problem in the NHS, but much depended on the parties' circumstances.

A *third factor* is *personal relationships*. Hard contracts do not involve wider personal relationships outside the scope of the transaction itself; soft contracts involve interactions at a number of levels (Macneil 1974). This was important in the NHS because the contracting system was introduced into a context in which many of the key actors were in relationships in other capacities and had known each other for some time. This suggested that NHS contracts would fit the soft model. In the social care context, for example, Lapsley and Llewellyn (1997) found that social workers knew each other and had shared values which rendered formal contracts entirely unnecessary.[18]

A *fourth factor* is the extent to which it is possible to *specify the exchange* between the parties. Following Macneil (1974), it is possible to distinguish hard contracts in which the parties measure their exchanges and expect precise reciprocation, from soft contracts in which they expect reciprocity

---

[18] See also Flynn *et al.* (1996).

over time but do not measure it exactly. The indications for the NHS were ambiguous. The purchaser's need to obtain as much treatment as possible within a limited budget was likely to lead to an attempt to specify the price and quantity of treatment covered by the contract relatively precisely (NHSME 1990). But there were difficulties with this. Specifying the quantity of treatment was technically difficult in some areas, notably community services (Flynn *et al.* 1996). Specifying the type and quality of the treatment to be provided was even more challenging (Allen 1995; Flynn *et al.* 1996; Walsh *et al.* 1997). The NHS is shown by Day and Klein (1987) to be heterogeneous (providing a variety of services), complex (using a variety of skills), and uncertain (in the relationship between the services provided and their outcomes or objectives). This might require a soft approach, in which the parties agreed general standards in the contract and worked out their detailed application during subsequent negotiations.

A *fifth set of factors* relates to the *institutional framework* surrounding the contracts (Sako 1992; Deakin *et al.* 1997). In the NHS, central government policy and the arbitration system were probably the most important influences. Did they encourage or facilitate the development of long-term relationships? In the NHS, the policy element was ambiguous (Hughes *et al.* 1996). On the one hand, the government acknowledged that for many services, purchasers would have only one realistic provider and would therefore be in a long-term relationship (NHSME 1989; 1990). On the other hand, the reforms were in part intended to introduce competition, so there was pressure for short-term relationships and changes of provider where possible.[19] The effect of arbitration for NHS contracts was also difficult to predict. Its applicability to the negotiation stage acknowledged that some relationships were inevitably long-term, and might require outside assistance to ensure their effective functioning (Hughes 1991). But its weakness more generally might make disputes more prevalent and long-term relationships more difficult to sustain (cf. Deakin *et al.* 1997).

Finally, the parties' *strategy* is relevant. Although the circumstantial factors discussed above are important, the parties' preference for one or other model is also likely to be influential. Because of the weakness of competition in some parts of the NHS, the parties might have no choice about the duration of their relationship: contracting with one another might be inevitable. Here, the parties' willingness to work at developing a relationship of trust was vital (Lapsley and Llewellyn 1997). But it might

---

[19] The 'money follows the patient' principle of Department of Health (1989*b*).

prove difficult to sustain that trust in a 'compulsory' relationship: a point explored fully in the empirical study. Moreover, a purchaser's ability to spend time building relationships might also be relevant: large Health Authorities had more staff and more time to devote to meetings with providers than did fundholders, for example.

To sum up, it was difficult to predict which model would best describe NHS contracts. Several factors pointed towards the soft model. But there were some ambiguities: the fact that long-term relationships might not be a matter of choice, for example. Empirical evidence will help to determine the significance of the various indicators.

Methodology

For the purposes of this study, empirical research was conducted to examine NHS contracts as mechanisms of accountability. A brief account is given here of the research methods employed.[20] Some empirical material from other studies of NHS contracts was available when this study was conducted in 1996–7,[21] but it was not focused on accountability and did not provide enough relevant, detailed information on which to base conclusions.

The sample

To gain a rounded view of the contracting process it was essential to study a sample of all three types of organization involved: Health Authorities, GP fundholders and Trusts. Wherever possible, the research included the Trusts with which the Health Authorities and fundholders in the sample had placed contracts, in order to obtain purchaser and provider perspectives on the same contract. The choice of research subjects was governed by practical and theoretical considerations. On a theoretical level, although it was not possible to take a statistically significant sample, the reliability of the results was enhanced by choosing bodies facing different circumstances and seeking common patterns amongst them (see Hutter 1988). On a practical level, factors such as the travelling time to, and any personal knowledge of, the area were relevant. The total sample size was dictated by the amount of time available for empirical work.

---

[20] Further details may be found in Davies (1999*a*).
[21] More precisely, the research began in the summer of 1996 and ended at Easter 1997, giving a convenient 'time-slice' of data.

Three Health Authorities were included in the study. In order to select Authorities facing different conditions, the criteria of access to providers and the nature of the Authority's population were used. It seemed likely that an Authority's choice of providers would affect its behaviour in the market: a greater choice of providers might lead to more frequent changes of contracting partner.[22] And the nature of an Authority's population might influence the issues it sought to address through contracts. For example, an Authority with a multicultural population might have focused more strongly on the accessibility of services to patients from different ethnic groups. In practice, the first criterion was more significant than the second, as later chapters will demonstrate.

Authority A was in a relatively densely populated area with a large teaching hospital as its monopoly provider. The county was relatively wealthy, as were parts of the main city, but there were pockets of deprivation within the city and outside. Authority B was in a rural area with a very small District General Hospital and a variety of other hospitals some distance away. There were variations in wealth, although they were not stark, and an above average proportion of elderly people in the population. Authority C was in a densely populated urban area, with a choice of potential providers. The area was very deprived, with high rates of associated conditions such as lung cancer and coronary heart disease. The population was ethnically diverse, in contrast to that in Areas A and B.

In each area, a sample of three or four fundholding practices was chosen. In order to examine market behaviour, practices with different degrees of choice among providers were selected. For example, in Area B, one of the practices chosen was in the same city as the main local provider, whereas the other two were half-an-hour's drive away on the county boundary. These two practices also had the option of using a neighbouring provider, some 40 minutes' drive away in the next county. Another important criterion was the date at which the practice had joined the fundholding scheme. The sample therefore included a spread across the first (1991–2) to fifth (1995–6) waves. This ensured that the study included practices with different levels of experience in dealing with the contracting process. It also included practices with varying degrees of enthusiasm for the scheme: early wave practices usually displayed a greater ideological commitment to fundholding than did more recent recruits.

---

[22] Studies generally take a thirty-minute drive as a guide to the distance patients are willing to travel (cf. Propper and Bartlett 1997).

Finally, a sample of Trusts was chosen, three in each area. One of these Trusts was based outside the district being studied (two were out-of-county in Area C), whereas the others were within the district. This affected the nature of Health Authorities' relationships with them quite considerably, as Chapter 6 will explain. It also provided an insight into competitive behaviour: the efforts of the out-of-county provider in Area B to win the custom of fundholders on the county border were of considerable interest. The study concentrated on acute and community providers in each area (usually the in-county community provider, the main in-county acute provider and an out-of-county acute provider). Studying both acute and community provision made it possible to compare the two types of service. But broadening out the sample to include other types of provider (mental health, learning disabilities and so on)[23] would have made it difficult to build up an understanding of specialist terminology.

Common patterns did emerge across all three areas. This suggested that the research results were reliable and generalizable. Where there were differences in the results for each area, these could often be explained by reference to an area's specific features. For example, Authority C's greater interest in moving patients to other providers was a reflection of its urban location and wider choice of providers. Moreover, there was no reason to think that the areas chosen were not typical of the NHS as a whole. Interviewees occasionally made reference to bodies not in the sample—a Trust manager might refer to other Health Authorities, for example—and these references often helped to confirm the reliability of the findings.

Within each practice, provider or Authority, a sample of staff was chosen for interview. The aim was to identify those most closely involved with contracting, although some more 'marginal' staff were also interviewed to obtain broader perspectives and to check that their involvement in contracting was indeed limited. In the three Health Authorities, the interviewees were selected in order to give a picture of the various specialisms within contracting (quality, finance, information and so on) and to include both junior and senior staff. More interviews were carried out in Authorities A and B than in Authority C, because better access was obtained to those Authorities. Each fundholding practice usually had a fund manager, responsible for day-to-day administration, and a GP designated as the 'lead' partner for fundholding purposes. These two people were most heavily involved in the contracting process, and interviews

---

[23] An ambulance provider was studied in Area B, by way of further comparison.

with both were sought wherever possible. One or two interviews and some informal conversations were held with non-lead GPs as more 'marginal' research subjects. NHS Trusts usually had a small team of contracting staff. Once again, interviews were conducted with staff involved in different aspects of contracting, including finance and quality, and at different levels of seniority. Some 'marginal' interviews were also conducted with managers of particular services within the provider, and with a small sample of clinicians.[24]

Methods of data collection

Three main research methods were employed: document analysis, participant observation, and interviewing. The use of multiple methods, or 'triangulation' (Campbell and Fiske 1959), is commonly seen as a valuable technique on theoretical grounds, because it enhances the reliability and validity of the research. The possibility of bias is reduced if the researcher can show that different methods yield results which complement one another. Moreover, the flaws attaching to any particular method will not attach to the research as a whole, and may even be overcome by another method (Hutter 1988).

The most important documents analysed in the study were the NHS contracts themselves. These were in the public domain (NHSME 1990), although they were not usually published by the parties. Staff were not always aware of their public nature, and a certain amount of negotiation was sometimes required in order to obtain access to them. The contracting process also generated a number of other documents, such as purchasing strategy plans and regular performance reports from providers. Many of these documents were also examined during the course of fieldwork. Contract negotiations took place partly through correspondence in which offers and counter-offers were made and details finalized. All three Health Authorities gave access to correspondence files.

These various documents were used in two ways. First, they were a vital source of data in themselves. Contracts contained the parties' formal statements of their accountability relationship. Providers' reports were their formal contribution to the monitoring stage of accountability. It was, however, important to be aware that the parties' statements might not reflect their practices. Secondly, therefore, documents could be used as

---

[24] This study found that clinicians played a less significant role in contracting than that implied by Audit Commission (1996).

a starting-point for interview questions designed to discover the degree of 'fit' between the documents and the parties' day-to-day activities.

Observation may take a number of different forms. At one extreme, the researcher using pure observation watches research subjects unobtrusively in order to see how they behave in particular situations (Adler and Adler 1994). At the other extreme, the participant observer joins the research subjects' activities and engages them in conversation in addition to watching their behaviour (Becker 1958). This study used an intermediate method of observation which was not covert but which did not involve participation in the activities being observed.

Observation was used primarily for contract monitoring meetings and contract negotiation meetings.[25] These were a rich source of 'observable' data. Observation was time-consuming, and could not be conducted in all three study areas. Instead, this aspect of the study was concentrated on Areas A and B. Authority B's contract monitoring meetings with its main acute and community providers were observed, as were most of the Authority's negotiations for the 1997–8 contracting round. Limited access was obtained to negotiation meetings between Authority A and its main acute provider. Meetings for monitoring and negotiation between several of the study's fundholding practices and the main acute and community providers in Areas A and B were also observed.

One of the problems with observation is that the presence of an observer may affect the behaviour of the research subjects. This can be minimized by 'staying in the field' for longer periods of time (Burgess 1984). This was problematic in this study because the activity to be observed was a small part of the research subjects' daily work, and because the remainder of their work could not sensibly be observed. Nevertheless, various strategies were employed for building a rapport with the participants. First, it was possible to attend certain types of meeting regularly from the outset of the study. This was particularly true of Health Authorities' frequent meetings with providers. Secondly, many of the participants were involved in interviews or could at least be engaged in informal conversations while waiting for meetings to begin. Thirdly, the analysis of contract documents and correspondence usually involved spending several days or even weeks in the research subjects' offices. These various factors helped to ensure that the presence of a researcher in meetings did not affect the participants' behaviour unduly. They discussed controversial

---

[25] Interviews were used to explore the role of meetings in the contracting process, in order to ensure that they were a significant forum for negotiation and monitoring.

or sensitive issues in a full and frank way. The need to get on with the meeting meant that the presence of an outsider was hardly noticed.

Observation and interviews complemented each other well (cf. Adler and Adler 1994). The interviews helped to validate the findings of observation by reducing the possibility that the interpretation of what took place at meetings was misguided or biased. Observation helped to validate the interview data, because it identified some instances in which an interviewee had deliberately or accidentally given a misleading answer to a question. For example, interviewees did sometimes exaggerate the degree of collaboration (or adversarialism) in their contract negotiations.

The interview was a central method of gathering information from those involved in the contracting process (cf. generally Fontana and Frey 1994). Some fifty formal interviews were conducted with key staff in Health Authorities, fundholding practices and providers. These interviews were supplemented by countless informal conversations when travelling to meetings or examining documents, for example. These were also a vital source of data.

In order to encourage a free flow of conversation and therefore information, each interview was semi-structured: it was approached with a list of topics to be covered in whatever order seemed appropriate. A closed questionnaire would not have accommodated the exploratory nature of the research. Many researchers find that interviewees welcome the chance to discuss their life or work (see, for example, Hutter 1988). This study found that most NHS managers (much vilified in the media) were glad of an opportunity to discuss the difficulties and challenges of their jobs. On occasions, they did seek to present a 'party line' about an issue, but further questioning often elicited more open responses.

Interviews raise a number of questions of self-presentation (Fontana and Frey 1994). Two strategies were used in this study. One was that of the 'learner', asking expert interviewees to explain their work to the lay outsider. Managers often responded well to this strategy. The second involved a claim to some theoretical and practical knowledge of NHS contracting, as a result of academic study. A busy GP might engage more readily with an expert researcher, raising difficult and interesting issues, than with someone requiring time-consuming explanations. In both roles, it was important to avoid prejudicing the interview by appearing to encourage or discourage certain lines of argument (Burgess 1984). With the permission of the interviewees, interviews were tape-recorded so that an accurate record could be kept. All the quotations in the text are taken from formal interviews. Fieldwork notes were kept of informal discussions.

Ethical issues

The Socio-Legal Studies Association's 'Statement of Ethical Practice' (SLSA 1993) was used as a source of guidance on research ethics. Two main ethical issues arose in the study.

One was the obligation to ensure that the research was based on the informed consent of the participants: 'This implies a responsibility on the socio-legal researcher to explain as fully as possible, and in terms meaningful to participants, what the research is about, who is undertaking and financing it, why it is being undertaken, and how it is to be disseminated' (SLSA 1993: para. 3.2). This was fulfilled by means of a carefully-drafted access letter. The key points were reinforced during informal conversations and at the beginning of interviews.

A second important obligation is that of ensuring that the identities of those participating in research are kept confidential (SLSA 1993: para. 3.3). The study has been written up with this obligation in mind. For example, the controversial topic of 'creative compliance' (McBarnet and Whelan 1991; 1997) will be described (in Chapter 8) without reference even to the area in which it took place, in case an attempt might be made to identify those responsible. Confidentiality must also be maintained within the research setting (Bryman 1988). It was inevitable (and accepted by the participants to whom it applied) that some staff would know that others were being interviewed, but care was taken to ensure that each interview was kept confidential. This was particularly important where both parties to a contract were involved in the research. But no direct requests for information in breach of confidence were encountered.

Methodological limitations

Any empirical study is bound to have limitations of research time, skills, access to information, and so on. Two significant limitations affected this study. One was that it proved impossible to examine conclusively the accuracy and honesty of the information supplied by providers to purchasers for the purposes of monitoring. This would have required the researcher to obtain parity of information with the provider. It would not merely have been possible to work with the staff producing the reports: the 'front-line' workers collecting the data might have had an interest in deceiving management as to their performance. Given the limited time allowed for empirical research, and the need to address a range of issues as well as monitoring, it was not possible to embark on this line of investigation.

Moreover, some data could be obtained by other means: providers did occasionally admit that the information they were supplying to purchasers was not accurate.

A second limitation was that it proved impossible to explore the other accountability mechanisms applicable to purchasers and providers in the same detail as the contracts at the heart of the study. This was because of the need to design a manageable empirical study and to complete it in the time available. But some relevant data were gathered during the study: purchasers' accountability to central government was commonly discussed in interviews, and some meetings were observed at which NHS Executive staff were present. These data were sufficient for a study in which the primary purpose was to investigate NHS contracts themselves.

Conclusion

Data from the case study are presented in the next three chapters. The evidence is explored with the aid of the accountability analysis presented in Chapter 4, and the hard and soft models of contractual relationship described at the beginning of this chapter. The findings are evaluated using ideas about 'good accountability': these are explained in each chapter as they become relevant. The three themes to be covered are: the interactions between NHS contracts and other mechanisms of accountability applicable either to purchasers or providers (Chapter 6); the nature of the accountability relationship between the parties and the due process issues thus raised (Chapter 7); and the issue of effectiveness, of ensuring that contracts did work well as mechanisms of accountability (Chapter 8).

6 Fitting In: The Role of Contracts in the Context of Other Accountability Mechanisms

At first sight, it may seem a little strange to begin a study of the accountability relationship from provider to purchaser by examining the other accountability processes applicable to the parties. But both the literature and pilot empirical work indicated that NHS contracts could not be understood in isolation. Their interactions with other accountability mechanisms raised key issues of effectiveness, efficiency and transparency.

The first part of this chapter examines interactions between the contractual accountability process and the accountability mechanisms applicable to *purchasers*. It raises the issues of delegation and discretion discussed in Chapter 3 in relation to purchasers and providers, but at the level of the relationship between purchasers and the centre. Although central government appeared to have delegated a substantial degree of authority to purchasers, it continued to call them to account for their financial performance and for the delivery of certain service standards. This enabled the government to exercise a considerable degree of control over the issues purchasers addressed in their accountability relationships with providers. The role of central government is contrasted with that of patients and members of the public. There was little evidence of purchaser response to their needs or requirements, largely because there were few effective mechanisms through which patients and the public could call purchasers to account. The data are evaluated using principles of effective accountability and transparency.

The second part of the chapter considers the extent to which purchasers attempted to use their contracts in order to micro-manage providers. As Chapter 3 explained, some commentators feared that contractualization would not in practice leave providers free to manage their operations in the most effective way, because purchasers would be tempted to interfere. Here, the study found that the problem was one of selective interference rather than the constant interference suggested in the literature and identified in the centre/purchaser relationship. Some principles of good role definition are derived from the data.

The third part of the chapter examines interactions between the contractual accountability process and the accountability mechanisms applicable to *providers*. In theory, contracts could be used to set standards on any aspect of a provider's performance. This created the potential for a substantial degree of overlap between the activities of NHS purchasers and other mechanisms of accountability applicable to providers, and between the activities of different NHS purchasers calling the same provider to account. The third part of the chapter presents data on how purchasers handled this overlap, and some thoughts about an appropriate normative response to the issue.

The accountability of purchasers: findings

The role of central government

The Next Steps literature discussed in Chapter 3 suggested that the attempt to hold agencies at arm's length from ministers would not be successful because ministers would be tempted to interfere in 'operational' matters. The creation of an internal market in the NHS implied a similar kind of delegation, although the relationship between purchasers and the centre was not clearly structured as a contract.[1] Decisions about the cost, quantity and quality of patient care would be taken by purchasers in the light of market conditions. But the NHS is usually a topic of considerable political sensitivity. This suggested that the government's delegation to purchasers might be more apparent than real. Despite the potentially broad scope of NHS contracts, the present study found that they were in practice focused almost entirely on two issues: the cost and quantity of care to be provided, and the time waited by patients for treatment. These were the issues on which purchasers were most energetically called to account by the government. Other studies have made similar findings: McHale *et al.* (1997) describe a high level of central control in their study of NHS dispute resolution, and use the label 'administered contract' to convey the limitations on the parties' freedom of action.

Two methodological caveats are in order before presenting this study's findings. First, 'central government' is used here as an umbrella term for the upper echelons of the NHS hierarchy (the NHS Executive and its regional offices) and the Department of Health. In a study focused primarily on purchasers, it was not possible to disentangle the respective influences of these different layers of the 'centre'. Secondly, it is important to note that the assessment of influences on behaviour is an inexact

---

[1] Health Authorities did agree 'corporate contracts' with the regional offices of the NHS Executive, discussed below.

science. Purchasers' explanations of their behaviour were cross-checked with first-hand observation of their actions and the evidence furnished by contracts and central guidance. But the explanations advanced here should still be seen as tentative.

Contracts invariably included a clear specification of the price, and some description of the activity[2] to be provided. Wherever possible, purchasers used 'cost and volume' contracts,[3] which involved complex predictions of the overall number of treatments to be performed, broken down into specific targets for each specialty. All the contracts studied also contained terms specifying maximum waiting times for outpatient appointments and inpatient procedures, sometimes with variations between specialties.

Both fundholders' and Health Authorities' contracts required providers to report their progress against activity and waiting time targets, usually on a monthly basis. Contracts often provided for a penalty if the data were late. Staff checked the reports for signs of actual or likely breaches of the targets, and used contract monitoring meetings to ask providers to explain or resolve any problems. The standards were rigorously enforced. Activity levels were enforced through a system of refunds from the provider for 'underperformance' (not reaching the activity level) and extra payments from the purchaser for 'overperformance' (exceeding the activity level). Providers obviously did not want to have to give refunds, since this might leave them without enough money to cover their fixed costs. But they had to be careful about overperformance too: purchasers might refuse to make additional payments if they had not consented to the extra work. All three Health Authorities in the study (and some fund-holders) used some form of relatively severe sanction for breaches of waiting times, usually a contractual penalty clause.

Why did purchasers focus so heavily on these issues? The concentration on activity and finance was, at one level, hardly surprising. The basic bargain is an important component of any contract. Without agreement on what is to be purchased and at what price, there is no contract in private law (Treitel 1999). Empirical studies of contractual relationships have found that the parties usually specify these elements clearly, however informal the rest of their contract may be (Macaulay 1963). Moreover, it was natural that purchasers should wish to ensure that they were 'getting what they had paid for' by enforcing the targets rigorously. This sentiment was

---

[2] NHS jargon for 'quantity of treatment'.

[3] See NHSME (1990) for a detailed discussion of contract types. Cost and volume contracts could not be used where the parties did not have reliable activity data, but the general trend was to move to cost and volume contracts once data collection systems had been improved.

particularly common among fund managers,[4] who devoted much of their time to querying providers' often inaccurate invoices.

But there was another important explanation for the focus on activity and finance. Purchasers of both types were required by the centre to remain within their annual budgets, and to achieve certain financial targets, notably the 'efficiency gain'.[5] In order to remain within budget, purchasers had to monitor activity levels carefully so that they did not incur additional liabilities which they could not meet. In order to achieve the efficiency gain, purchasers had to show that they had bought more activity for the same money (or the same activity for less money) than in the previous year.[6] Underperformance by a provider might jeopardize this.

The centre employed a number of formal and informal accountability mechanisms to enforce purchasers' financial obligations. Fundholding practices were accountable primarily to their local Health Authority. At the beginning of the year, practices were obliged to send the Health Authority details of their spending proposals, and at the end of the year, an annual report and accounts.[7] Each month, they were required to submit accounts[8] to the Authority, and details of the progress of the NHS contracts they had placed.[9] Practices were keen to keep their finances under control, because Authorities would monitor them more intensively if they showed any sign of exceeding their budgets. Health Authorities themselves were ultimately accountable to the Secretary of State, on whose behalf they exercised their functions.[10] They were obliged to provide annual audited accounts to the Secretary of State.[11] Their financial performance was also monitored on a routine basis by the regional offices of the NHS Executive. Few managers wished to incur the wrath of their NHS superiors: their performance-related pay, and even their jobs, could be under threat if they regularly failed to meet financial targets.[12]

---

[4] This term was common throughout the NHS to denote the person (not usually a GP) responsible for the administration of fundholding within a general practice.

[5] Providers also needed to achieve financial targets: they were under a statutory duty to break even each year and to achieve a return on their assets: National Health Service and Community Care Act 1990, s. 10. As a result, they usually supported purchasers' attempts to set clear targets on finance and activity.

[6] This was a Treasury requirement placed on the NHS as a whole. The rate was usually around 2 per cent (NHSME 1990).

[7] SI 1996/706, Schedule 2.

[8] The accounts must be audited: see s. 98 National Health Service Act 1977 and SI 1996/706.

[9] SI 1996/706, Schedule 2.   [10] SI 1996/708.

[11] National Health Service Act 1977, s. 98 (as amended).

[12] Threats expressed through the managerial hierarchy might be reinforced by the existence of the Secretary of State's formal powers to dismiss Health Authority or Trust boards (s. 85 National Health Service Act 1977, as amended).

Purchasers' accountability to central government also helped to explain the priority accorded to waiting times. In the Patients' Charter, the government made a much-publicized commitment to achieving and maintaining a set of maximum waiting times across the NHS as a whole (Department of Health 1991; 1995). The targets were laid down as a priority for the NHS in successive editions of the annual Priorities and Planning Guidance produced by the NHS Executive (for example, NHSE 1995*b*). Health Authorities were required to agree an annual 'corporate contract'[13] with their local regional office of the NHS Executive, under which they undertook to meet various targets, including a waiting time standard. They were required to report their performance each month. Fundholders were also affected by these pressures, to some extent.[14] They were obliged to report any patients waiting longer than the Charter maximum to the Health Authority. As with finance, most practices wished to avoid the more intrusive monitoring of their performance by the Health Authority which might ensue if they appeared to be in difficulties. Wealthier fundholders were able to contract for waiting times well below the Charter maximum,[15] so that the need to keep within the Charter was not a significant concern. But waiting times remained a high priority for these practices even though the central influence was less obvious. A number of the GPs interviewed said that the prospect of improving waiting times had been a major factor in their decision to join the fundholding scheme.

The role of central dictates can also be illustrated by reference to issues which were *not* high on the centre's list of priorities. Quality was one such issue. Health Authorities tended to disregard it altogether; fundholders set some quality standards but only in very specific circumstances.

All three Health Authorities' contracts contained large sections entitled 'quality'. The standards set concerned inputs, such as the number of trained nurses per shift, and processes, such as ensuring that outpatient clinics ran to time.[16] Providers were required to report quarterly or annually

---

[13] A management tool which was not legally enforceable (NHSE 1995*b*).

[14] Compare Audit Commission (1996) for a slightly earlier study of fundholder behaviour on this issue.

[15] Some fundholders (particularly those who had joined the scheme in its early years) appeared to have more generous budgets—more money per patient—than other fundholders or Health Authorities. This enabled them to pay for more treatments and thus to achieve shorter waiting times. For a review of the evidence on this issue, see Goodwin (1998).

[16] For a classification of different types of quality standard in health care, see Donabedian (1980). For an introduction to the controversy surrounding 'quality' in health care, see Morgan and Potter (1995), and in the public sector generally, see, for example, Gaster (1995); Kirkpatrick and Martinez Lucio (1995).

on their performance against quality standards. On the face of the contracts, monitoring through reports was intended to be accompanied by monitoring through inspection visits to the provider's premises, but in practice, only Authority C was conducting a regular programme of visits at the time of the study. Even here, visits had become less frequent. It was apparent that quality issues had been a higher priority during the period prior to the study, but were declining in importance when the study took place.

The rise and fall of quality in Health Authority contracts reflected a similar process at the central level. The initial focus on process and input standards was clearly linked to the Patients' Charter. Authorities had been encouraged to adopt and elaborate upon Charter standards in their contracts.[17] But the initial momentum of the Patients' Charter initiative had dissipated by the time of the study, five years after its initial publication.[18] Even for the NHS Executive, it had become a 'baseline requirement' rather than a current priority (NHSE 1995*b*). Moreover, prior to and during the study period, Authorities came under pressure to reduce their management costs. Because quality issues were receiving less attention from the centre, Authorities had targeted their quality departments when making cuts. Authority B, for example, had reduced its quality team from three full-timers to two part-timers with other responsibilities. Finally, some of the standards were controversial. This made it more difficult for quality managers in both Health Authorities and Trusts to insist on them in the absence of a strong central impetus. It was argued that the focus on easily measured process issues neglected or even conflicted with more difficult, but arguably more important, issues about clinical outcomes. The standards lacked legitimacy among clinicians and even among some quality managers. Authorities had little reason to enforce them if they were under no obligation to do so.

For fundholders, the position was rather different. With the possible exception of waiting times, they had never been under particularly strong pressure from the centre to use the Patients' Charter as the basis for their quality standards. Most practices were therefore happy to leave the enforcement of the Charter to Health Authorities, and to concentrate instead on their own quality agenda. The data on GPs' pursuit of quality standards showed a striking degree of commonality in their choice of priorities

---

[17] National 'league tables' were used to publicize performance: see NHSE (1998).
[18] Although waiting times were part of the Charter, they were usually treated as a separate issue. As explained above, they remained a high priority.

across the three different study areas.[19] Using contracts to set standards for communications from hospitals was a top priority for the vast majority of practices.[20] The standards specified deadlines for the receipt of letters from consultants detailing the treatment given to each patient. The sanction for non-compliance was that the treatment would not be paid for: practices cross-checked the letters they received from consultants with the invoices they received from the Trust, and refused to pay for items invoiced until the corresponding letters arrived.

Time and motivation conspired to make this issue a priority. In terms of motivation, poor communications were a long-standing grievance among GPs. Without knowing what treatment a patient had received in hospital, it was difficult for the GP to continue the patient's care appropriately on discharge. And the issue did not require a special investment of time or effort. The process of cross-checking against invoices served the dual functions of monitoring compliance with communications standards and ensuring that providers did not over-charge by invoicing practices incorrectly. Although it did occupy a substantial amount of fund managers' time, it was seen as worthwhile because it tackled both these issues.

In conclusion, central government's priorities exercised a considerable degree of influence, but not quite a stranglehold, over the contractual accountability process from providers to purchasers. Where purchasers were called to account for the achievement of central targets, they pursued those targets with vigour in their contracts. When central targets declined in importance, purchasers tended to pay them less attention. And most strikingly, it was relatively rare for purchasers to work on issues which were *not* central priorities. This was particularly true of Health Authorities. Fundholders did branch out on their own, but only when a relatively simple addition to the accountability process seemed likely to bring them a substantial benefit.

The role of patients and the public

Before evaluating the findings about the role of central government, it is instructive to compare and contrast them with those about the role of patients and members of the public. One model of the NHS administrative

---

[19] Compare Audit Commission (1996) for a slightly earlier survey of fundholders' approaches to quality standards.

[20] Other issues were also addressed in contracts, such as standards about the supply of drugs to patients on discharge, and requirements that patients should be seen by the consultant, rather than junior staff, at their first or second outpatient consultation.

structure might see purchasers as the agents of central government, charged simply with the implementation of central requirements. Under such a model, the views of patients and members of the public would be fed into the process, if at all, via central government. But the rhetoric surrounding the NHS reforms painted them in a rather different light. A considerable emphasis was placed on 'taking decisions close to the patient' (Department of Health 1989*b*; Hughes 1991). This suggested a model in which purchasers would respond to local needs and concerns when calling providers to account.

The data showed that Health Authorities gave only limited consideration to local concerns. Their response tended to be confined to situations in which such concerns *complemented* central requirements. For example, Authority C's quality managers worked on the accessibility of services to ethnic minority patients, in the light of a requirement in the Patients' Charter to make services accessible to different groups of patients, even though minorities were not expressly mentioned. The area had a relatively high proportion of ethnic minority residents and this was therefore an important local issue. By contrast, managers in Authority B felt unable to question or disobey a central requirement which was inconsistent with local needs. They were forced to spend more money on paediatric intensive care because of a national initiative, even though local provision was felt to be adequate and there was an ongoing programme of investment to ensure that the facilities were maintained:

I don't think our consultants here or us as purchasers would necessarily see paediatric intensive care as something we should be immediately putting more resources into. But we will be instructed that these services will be developed, therefore we will be expected to make a contribution towards the development of these services.

Where local needs posed a challenge to central requirements, they were not pursued.

The explanation for this seemed to lie in the relative weakness of the accountability mechanisms through which Health Authorities could be called to account by local people.[21] Although there were a number of such mechanisms,[22] none were capable of outweighing the influence exercised by the centre. First, Health Authorities were directed to consult on their purchasing plans (Department of Health 1994), but they approached this

---

[21] For critique, see generally Longley (1990; 1993).

[22] In addition to routine mechanisms, Authorities might also be the subject of a complaint by an aggrieved patient (Montgomery 1997*a*).

with varying degrees of enthusiasm and the study found no evidence of alterations to plans as a result of the views expressed. Secondly, this consultation process might have been assisted by the work of the Community Health Council (CHC) in each Health Authority area, a statutory body of lay people entitled to be consulted on certain aspects of an Authority's work.[23] CHCs might challenge Authority decisions as part of the consultation process. But again, the study did not find any evidence that decisions were changed because of CHC input. Thirdly, Health Authorities had a board comprised of non-executive as well as executive directors.[24] The non-executives might have been able to hold the executives to account for their decisions, and to act as advocates for the local community. The effectiveness of non-executive directors has, however, been shown to be limited (Day and Klein 1987; Ferlie *et al.* 1996). And since the reforms made boards less representative of local communities, by using 'business experience' as the main criterion for appointment (see Ferlie *et al.* 1996), non-executives were less likely to be well placed to act as community advocates. Authorities were therefore under very little pressure to pursue local concerns, and certainly had no reason to do so where this would not find favour with the centre.

As explained above, fundholders were one step removed from central government influence and did seem slightly more willing than Health Authorities to use the contractual accountability process to pursue their own agenda. Was there any evidence that they took action in response to the concerns of their patients? The data here showed a mixed picture. First, GPs were very aware, on a daily basis, of their patients' concerns. One of the reasons why waiting times were of importance to GPs was that they witnessed the suffering patients endured while waiting for treatment. Secondly, however, GPs used contracts to focus on issues which made *their* lives easier, as well as having benefits for patients. The focus on communications from hospitals helped patients because it enabled GPs to offer them appropriate care when they were discharged. But the reason given by most GPs for their emphasis on the standard was the trouble

[23] National Health Service Act 1977, s. 20 and Schedule 7; Community Health Councils Regulations 1996 (SI 1996/640); Montgomery (1997*a*). For critique, see Longley (1990; 1993). The Health and Social Care Bill before Parliament at the time of writing proposes the abolition of CHCs and the creation of Patient Forums and independent advocacy services.

[24] National Health Service Act 1977, Schedule 5 (as amended, Health Authorities Act 1995); Health Authorities (Membership and Procedure) Regulations 1996 (SI 1996/707). For discussion see Day and Klein (1987); Ashburner and Cairncross (1993); Ferlie *et al.* (1995).

poor communications caused *them*, rather than the need to improve the service offered to patients. Thirdly, practices rarely undertook any formal inquiries about the views of their patients. It was noticeable that where practices had conducted patient surveys, contracts were being used in more ambitious ways. One fund manager had discovered that patients were willing to travel quite long distances for quicker treatment, and had therefore decided to provide GPs with waiting time details for a larger number of hospitals in order to inform their referral decisions.

Although it could hardly be said that GPs were out of touch with the concerns of their patients, the formal external accountability mechanisms applicable to them were, again, relatively weak.[25] Like Health Authorities, GPs were directed to consult on their purchasing plans (NHSE 1995a), but the study found that they were not likely to engage in formal consultation. Of course, GPs may have felt that their informal contacts with patients were sufficient to give them a sense of local needs. But this was problematic. One difficulty was that GPs' perceptions might have been biased towards those who visited them regularly, rather than taking account of the needs of the population as a whole. Another was that informal consultation left GPs with a substantial discretion as to the selection and interpretation of relevant views, perhaps in contrast to a more formal, patient-driven mechanism of accountability.

It was certainly not true to say that patients and the public had no influence at all over the contractual accountability process. It seemed likely that their views, expressed informally to GPs, did affect contracts. Moreover, the staff involved in contracting did have some user perspectives to bring to bear on the process: the focus on ethnic minority issues in Area C was illustrative of this. But the weakness of the formal mechanisms of accountability to patients and the public, from purchasers of both kinds, did seem to be a problem. It meant that purchasers had no particular incentive to supplement—and certainly not to counteract—the demands of central government. The normative implications of these findings will be explored in the next section.

The accountability of purchasers: evaluation

The empirical findings suggested that delegation was a significant source of problems in the NHS. Purchasers had very little discretion to pursue

---

[25] Patients could make a complaint if they were dissatisfied with a purchasing decision (Montgomery 1997a).

local concerns in their contracts, because their actions were so heavily influenced by central priorities. This meant that few of the benefits of delegation—greater responsiveness to local needs, for example—were realized. There was evidently a conflict between the rhetoric of local autonomy which accompanied the reforms, and the reality of purchasers' behaviour. Any lessons about effective delegation which could be drawn from the data would be of significant value. 'Agencified' government depends heavily on the delegation of purchasing and other powers to separate centres of responsibility at arm's length from the core of government. This section explores ways in which the problems faced in the NHS might have been avoided.

Public law contains two core principles about delegation. The first is the maxim *delegatus non potest delegare*, which requires that discretions should be exercised by those to whom they have been entrusted and not delegated to anyone else. The second is the *Carltona* doctrine,[26] which provides that discretions entrusted to a minister may be exercised by civil servants within the department. As Freedland points out, this may either amount to an exception to the basic rule, a special case in which delegation *is* permitted, or it may fall outside the basic rule, in the sense that civil servants stand in the shoes of the minister so that there is no question of delegation at all (Freedland 1996). It is arguable that the recent developments of agencification (Freedland 1996) and contracting out (Freedland 1995) have ridden rough-shod over the *Carltona* doctrine. Both involve the exercise of discretions by officials at 'arm's length' from the minister—civil servants in agencies or staff in private firms—in contrast to the very senior departmental civil servant, the assistant secretary, whose decision was at stake in the *Carltona* case itself. As Freedland points out, 'It requires some ingenuity thus to treat somebody as standing in one's own shoes, yet at the same time to keep that person at arm's length' (Freedland 1995: 25).

This theoretical problem seems to have a practical counterpart. In relation to the nationalized industries, and more recently the Next Steps programme, it has been alleged that the government has created an appearance of delegation whilst in practice continuing to exercise a considerable degree of control over the delegates. Managers have complained that they have been promised the freedom to run their organization, but that it has been rendered largely nugatory by a stream of informal guidance, often driven by political imperatives rather than by the best interests of

---

[26] *Carltona v Commissioners of Works*, 1943 2 All ER 560.

the organization. But ministers remain accountable to Parliament and the public for the provision of services, and the temptation to intervene in response to public concern is often irresistible. This suggests that there is an urgent need to develop principles of good delegation, and that the *Carltona* doctrine is no longer sufficient.

Good delegation should involve both accountability and discretion. The delegate should be accountable for the performance of key aspects of his or her task, but there should be some elements of the task which are not determined by the principal over which the delegate can exercise some discretion. Accountability is essential to ensure that the principal is able both to control and to account for the actions of the delegate; discretion enables the delegate to use his or her managerial skills or local knowledge in the performance of the task. The present study could not be expected to put an end to the eternal quest for the balance between accountability and discretion. But it did provide some information about the conditions which had to obtain in order for purchasers to decide that they would pursue issues of their own choosing, even though they were subject to relatively strict accountability mechanisms to the centre. It might be possible for a government to promote these conditions in order to allow its delegates more discretion.

It was explained above, particularly in relation to GP fundholders, that they were willing to pursue their own priorities where they had both the time and the motivation to do so. There is little practical guidance to be derived from the notion of giving purchasers sufficient time to exercise autonomy. It might encourage the government to listen to, and act upon, complaints from delegates that they were overburdened with central guidance, but it cannot serve as a hard-edged principle. It would be difficult to calculate how much time particular central priorities were absorbing, or how much time purchasers would need in order to pursue an issue of their own choosing. Motivation seems rather more promising. There are a number of ways in which purchasers and other delegates might be motivated to work on their own priorities.

One technique would be to play on the self-interest of purchasers: they might be inclined to use the contracting process to pursue issues which would improve their own circumstances. The NHS reforms drew relatively successfully on this principle. Fundholding gave GPs the opportunity, for the first time, to call hospital clinicians to account. Many GPs seized the chance to tackle long-standing grievances even though the centre had no interest in those grievances. Communications were a striking example of this. But there were limits to the usefulness of the self-interest principle. Standards based on purchasers' self-interest did not necessarily improve patient care significantly or at all. Health Authority purchasers were so far removed from the process of delivering care that standards based on making their lives easier (ensuring the prompt and accurate supply of activity data from providers, for example) were unlikely to have much impact on patients. For GPs, the overlap was more significant, but nonetheless, there was no guarantee that standards set on this basis would benefit patients.

Another way of motivating purchasers to pursue issues other than central priorities in the contractual accountability process would be to force them to do so, paradoxically, through central accountability. Purchasers could be required to show that they had taken steps to identify and respond to local needs as an aspect of their accountability to the government. This approach had not been tried in the NHS at the time of the study. Although central guidance directed purchasers to consult on their purchasing plans, for example, they were not required to demonstrate to their NHS superiors that they had acted upon the results of consultation. But there is an obvious problem with this strategy: central government might not enforce consultation effectively where the findings were likely to conflict with its own priorities.

A third possibility is to institute an effective accountability mechanism under which purchasers could be called to account by interested parties other than the government: patients or members of the public, for example. The need to satisfy other taskmasters would give purchasers a good reason to pursue some priorities other than those laid down by the centre. Patients' views could be used to spell out in detail the local implications of central government's priorities, for example, in order to decide how best to spend funds earmarked for the reduction of waiting times. It would not, however, always be the case that central priorities and local needs were closely aligned. How might conflicts between them be resolved?

One option would be for local accountability to 'trump' central requirements in any case of conflict. But this would be difficult to implement in a service like the NHS, because it is funded from general taxation and because the government is accountable for its overall performance. Another option would be for central requirements to 'trump' local ones at all times. This might leave some room for local accountability, provided that the central requirements were not of a comprehensive, all-consuming nature. But the more purchasers were required to pursue central targets, the less significant local accountability would become. It is not difficult to imagine a situation in which purchasers would cease to put much effort into local accountability as a result. Finally, a mixed approach might be considered under which purchasers would be given some discretion to choose between the competing requirements of central and local actors. Some limits might be necessary—central budget requirements might be compulsory, for example—but otherwise, purchasers would be charged with resolving the tensions. This would give them a highly responsible and challenging role.

Designing accountability processes which leave those being called to account some discretion is a very difficult task. On the basis of the NHS data, it seems important to focus on two factors:

• ensuring that the delegates are given adequate time to pursue other issues;
• ensuring that some means is found of motivating them to use that time constructively.

These factors could usefully be the subject of further research in other contexts in which delegates have more discretion: on the basis of the NHS data, it is impossible to do more than speculate about what might happen if effective local accountability had to co-exist with accountability to the centre.

There is one further difficulty with the role of central government. Whatever the appropriate extent of that role, good delegation requires that it be *transparent*. Any particular decision about the provision of patient care might be the responsibility either of central government or of the purchaser. When MPs call ministers to account, they obviously need to know which decisions they have taken, and which they have delegated to purchasers. It should not be possible for ministers to evade responsibility by claiming that they have delegated a decision when, in fact, they have taken it themselves. The NHS data suggested that, as has been alleged in relation to other 'new public management' reforms, the government could be tempted to use the rhetoric of delegation to local agents as a way of concealing the true extent of its influence over, and therefore responsibility for, the service provided.

Central government was accountable for the NHS in a general way. Throughout the study period, the NHS was politically sensitive. The experiences of particular patients or hospitals due to shortages of beds in specific areas such as paediatric intensive care, or more generally during the winter months, were given a high profile in the media, forcing the government to respond with promises of extra resources and greater managerial effort to address the difficulties (see, for example, Brindle 1996;

Kennedy 1996). Towards the end of the study period, the general election campaigns of the major political parties focused on NHS issues, notably waiting lists or waiting times, and management costs (Webster 1998). The government was also subject to the usual channels of parliamentary accountability for the NHS, although these have some well-documented weaknesses (for example, Oliver 1991).

But this general political accountability did not necessarily mean that central government was clearly accountable for its influence over purchasers. They had formal freedom: there were no limits in the statute or guidance as to what could be covered in contracts. The rhetoric surrounding the reforms emphasized the delegation of decision-making and local discretion (Department of Health 1989*b*; NHSE 1994; and see Hughes 1991). Moreover, the very use of the contract mechanism gave the impression that the parties' accountability arrangements resulted from their own bargaining, in response to market forces. In practice, however, purchasers' priorities were strongly influenced by central guidance. This study has highlighted the extent of that influence. It was the major determinant of the topics covered in the contractual accountability process, particularly by Health Authorities. Moreover, it is arguable that this guidance was deliberately concealed. For example, although Health Authorities' purchasing plans were published and consulted upon, the NHS Executive's crucial Priorities and Planning Guidance (NHSE 1995*b*) was not openly available or subject to consultation. This might have given the appearance that some national priorities used in purchasing plans had been set locally. The extent of central influence over purchasers could have been made much more transparent in the NHS.[27]

Conclusion

Two important principles emerged from thinking about purchasers' accountability:

- if central government wishes to allow its delegates some freedom to pursue the issues they deem appropriate, it must ensure that they have the time and the motivation to do so. One important way of providing motivation is by making the delegates accountable to other interested parties, although this raises difficult issues about conflicts with accountability to the centre;

[27] See also the discussion in Longley (1990; 1993).

- the extent of central government influence over its delegates should be transparent to those who are calling both government and delegates to account, so that the government and its delegates can be made to explain the decisions and actions for which they are responsible.

The relevance of these principles to other internal contracts will be explored in Chapter 9.

Purchaser and provider roles: findings

One key aspect of the rhetoric surrounding contractualization, both in the NHS and elsewhere (in relation to agencies, for example) was that managers would be 'free to manage' their provider units within the framework set by contractual targets. But—as explained in Chapter 3—commentators were wary of this claim. They argued that it was difficult to define the roles of purchaser and provider precisely, and that even if some definition could be reached, purchasers would be tempted to over-step the boundaries of their allotted role.

The NHS guidance simply repeated the claim, without giving any clear indication of how it might be made to work in practice:

The contractual process will give hospitals . . . increasing freedom to manage the delivery of services as they think best. The changing role of [Health Authorities] from service managers to service purchasers will increasingly mean that they will concentrate on *what* services their residents need, without specifying in detail *how* every service is to be provided. (NHSME 1989: para. 2.11, emphasis in original)

A purchaser might still include a high level of detail in its description of the services required. And, in any event, there is no clear separation between 'what' and 'how': even a simple quality standard such as a waiting time target might go to the nature of the service or to the manner of its provision. Nor is it possible to resolve the issue using the hard and soft models. The purchaser may become involved in the details of service provision under either model. As Chapter 7 will demonstrate, hard purchasers involve themselves by negotiating highly detailed and specific standards in the contract; soft purchasers engage in a continuous process of close, detailed negotiations with the provider in order to work out the more general standards contained in their contracts.

The data showed that although Health Authorities and providers did experience problems in defining their respective roles, these problems were by no means as extensive as the literature seemed to predict. It might have been expected that the provider's position in relation to the purchaser would have been the same as the purchaser's position in relation to central government: the entirety of its activities would be dictated by the purchaser's requirements. But the problem at the purchaser/provider level is labelled 'role definition' here, rather than 'delegation', precisely because rather different issues arose in practice. Health Authorities did set quite long, complex contracts for providers containing detailed standards on finance, waiting times, quality, reporting, and so on. But in practice, they enforced only a limited selection of those standards. Moreover, they ignored many areas of providers' activities: for example, staffing issues, clinical quality, and buildings maintenance. Whereas purchasers could focus solely on central standards and still function as purchasers, providers could not have done their job of providing services to patients if they had concentrated solely on the issues raised by purchasers. As a result, providers did *not* complain that overall, they had inadequate discretion or that purchasers were trying to 'micro-manage' their operations. But it was clear that in specific instances, disputes did arise over the proper definition of the parties' roles.

Providers felt that some issues ought to be left to their discretion. One Trust manager gave what would generally have been regarded as a straight-forward example of where the line should be drawn:

They're quite at liberty to ask of any provider . . . what staffing levels are you going to put in to manage this facility, because that's part of the quality, isn't it, of the service that's being provided . . . we've had instances of where they've over-stepped that mark and got too involved in trying to specify which member and what grade of staff should provide a particular service, and we just politely tell them no, that's not your business. You set the specification, we'll decide how we're going to deliver the service and agree that with them.

Health Authority managers also agreed, in principle, that there should be limits, though the example given here is rather more controversial:

The Trusts would be very upset if we actually went along as a Health Authority and said we think that service is overfunded in your budget and you've got to cut it back. They would see that as that's their management. And I think we'd see it as their management.

In practice, the crucial issue was the provider's perception of the Health Authority's *motive* in becoming involved in the detail of service provision. The soft model treats close negotiations as a sign of high trust: the parties work together collaboratively to solve problems. But providers often perceived involvement in detail as an indication of low trust: the Health Authority had identified a failure on the part of the provider's managers and did not trust them to put it right. This led providers to resent the interference. The example given above about staffing arose in precisely this way. Problems had been identified with the service, and the Health Authority decided to try to solve them itself through an unusually prescriptive contract.

But there was another problem not mentioned in the literature. Providers might resent the *converse* situation: where the Health Authority refused to become involved in the details of service provision. Just before the study began, purchasers and providers had been encouraged to negotiate more collaboratively on finance.[28] Providers were supposed to share detailed cost information with purchasers well in advance of the deadline for contracts to be signed. But Health Authorities were aware that providers would find it difficult to meet the tough financial targets imposed by the centre. If Authorities scrutinized providers' finances in detail, they would be forced to acknowledge the legitimacy of providers' protests about the targets. And this would undermine Authorities' ability to insist that providers signed up to them. As one manager bluntly explained:

Certainly Trusts at times do get to the point of saying if it's so easy, why don't you tell us how to do it? And we avoid biting on that one.

Not surprisingly, providers resented this behaviour. They felt that purchasers used the notion of provider autonomy as an excuse for abandoning them when problems became intractable.

By contrast, the study did not identify any problems of role definition as between fundholders and providers. The findings here highlighted two important differences between fundholders and Health Authorities. First, fundholders tended to set a limited number of high-priority standards in their contracts. Of course, involvement in detail is not simply about the number of standards set, but the fact that fundholders did not attempt to draft the relatively comprehensive contracts used by Health Authorities significantly reduced the chances of a dispute about role definition. Moreover, providers acknowledged that issues such as waiting times and communications—the key GP priorities—were legitimate areas of purchaser concern. Secondly, providers and fundholders had no prior managerial relationship. As Chapter 2 explained, before 1990, providers were directly managed by Health Authorities. This meant that they were keen to safeguard their new-found independence against perceived interference by Health Authorities.

---

[28] Unpublished regional office guidance.

It is impossible to generalize about discretion. However detailed a contract (and Health Authority contracts, though voluminous, could have been much more detailed), the provider inevitably has some discretion over issues which are not mentioned, and over the interpretation of the contract's terms. Nonetheless, providers did feel that in certain specific instances, Health Authorities abused the flexibility of their role: they interfered when they believed that they had better management skills; they retreated when they knew they could not solve a difficult problem.

Purchaser and provider roles: evaluation

The problems raised by the data on role definition are difficult to resolve. Providers criticized purchasers both for interfering and for failing to interfere. There were no straightforward indicators in the data as to which attitude a provider might adopt in any given case. Because the problem of purchaser interference in provision was not as severe as the problem of central dominance over purchasers, the principles about delegation discussed above are not easily transferable to this context. Novel principles on role definition must be developed.

Central guidance on the separation of roles was in part to blame for the problem of role definition. By promising providers operational freedom, it gave credence to the notion that there were objectively separable roles of 'purchaser' and 'provider' waiting to be adopted by the parties. But the hard and soft models' silence on this issue suggests that roles are a matter for negotiation in every contract. The hard purchaser may choose to set detailed standards in the contract: this will result in detailed contract negotiations and monitoring. But the extent of that involvement depends upon the provider's agreement. The soft purchaser may choose to set detailed standards by engaging in ongoing, collaborative negotiations with the provider in which it elaborates the general standards included in its contract. Again, the extent to which this occurs depends on the provider's agreement.

This suggests that the key principles in this area are *negotiation* and *consistency*. The parties should attempt to agree a definition of their roles, and to act consistently within that definition in order not to disappoint one another's expectations. Negotiation should be particularly helpful in addressing the problem of unwanted purchaser interference. Providers could—as in the staffing example given above—refuse to agree to the purchasers' standards where they felt that those standards infringed their legitimate sphere of autonomy.

The value of consistency should guide the behaviour of both parties in relation to both the problems identified in the data. If a purchaser habitually adopts a 'hands-off' approach, it should continue to do so even if it feels that a provider is not coping well in a particular case (unless enforcement action is necessary because the provider is in breach). If the provider normally welcomes purchaser involvement in problem-solving, it should ask itself whether it is appropriate to resist that involvement in a particular case. Purchasers usually wanted to involve themselves in a particular issue, rather than in all aspects of the provider's management. It might therefore have been possible to make some concessions to this without losing all managerial control. Moreover, the data suggested that the problem of unwanted interference was connected to the prior managerial relationship between Health Authorities and providers. Providers might therefore find that they could be more relaxed about the issue over time. As staff who had been in place before the reforms moved on, for example, providers might not feel the need to assert their independence so strongly against Authorities. When providers wanted Health Authorities to collaborate, but found it difficult to persuade them to do so, the principle of consistency might also be invoked. That principle would suggest that Authorities should collaborate if they normally do so. Occasionally, an Authority might make a short-term gain by refusing to help the provider with an intractable problem. Consistency would suggest that the Authority should eschew this gain in the interests of avoiding disputes about roles and maintaining good relationships over the longer term.

Consistency is a familiar principle in public law: the doctrine of legitimate expectations attempts (albeit with qualifications and exceptions) to compel public authorities to follow their published policy, unless they have a good reason for changing their policy and engage in appropriate consultation before applying the new policy (see, generally, Craig 1999: 611–50). Of course, the notion of acting consistently is a guideline for purchasers and providers rather than a hard-edged rule: it may be difficult to determine a party's 'usual' approach to problems, or whether its behaviour in a given instance deviates from that approach. But it might at least form the basis for more explicit negotiations between purchasers and providers about role definition.

The rhetoric surrounding contractualization promised that providers would be autonomous but accountable to organizationally separate purchasers. But contractual relationships do not provide a magic solution to the perennial problems of accountability and discretion. The study did not find evidence of highly interventionist purchasing strategies in the NHS. Nevertheless, it was essential for the parties to negotiate their roles and to exercise a degree of forbearance if they were to avoid damaging disputes.

The accountability of providers: findings

Two types of accountability process applied to providers, in addition to any particular contract under investigation. First, providers were usually in contractual accountability relationships with several other NHS purchasers. Most sold their services to their local Health Authority and to a few neighbouring Authorities, and to numerous fundholding practices. Secondly, providers were subject to a range of non-contractual accountability processes. These included direct accountability to patients through complaints procedures, the accountability of clinical staff to their professional bodies, legal accountability for breaches of health and safety standards and for clinical negligence, and so on.

Purchasers were given two pieces of guidance in this area. First, the government's early documents on contracting described a detailed process of negotiation between Health Authorities and providers, but acknowledged that high transaction costs would ensue if this approach was used for every contract. It was therefore recommended that Authorities should negotiate in detail only with the providers in their area. When contracting with providers in neighbouring areas, they should adopt the terms negotiated by those providers' local Health Authorities (their 'host purchasers')[29] as far as possible (NHSME 1990). Secondly, the same guidance also suggested that purchasers should monitor other accountability mechanisms, where they existed (NHSME 1990). Thus, if a provider had a system of medical audit in place, the purchaser should include contractual terms requiring reports of its results, rather than attempting to duplicate it in the contract.

It was therefore expected that Health Authorities would make some effort to co-ordinate their activities and to avoid duplicating other accountability mechanisms, in the interests of saving transaction costs. The expectation that they would work together was reinforced by the fact that their substantive priorities were very similar, because they were so heavily influenced by central government. This would give them little reason to seek to stand out from the crowd. It was rather more difficult to predict

---

[29] The guidance uses the term 'primary client' instead of 'host purchaser', but the latter was the usual expression among interviewees.

the behaviour of fundholders. The initial guidance cited above was directed largely at Health Authorities. Fundholding was portrayed as giving greater flexibility to individual practices, and reforms designed to make it easier for patients to change GPs suggested that some competition between practices might be intended (Department of Health 1989*b*). Moreover, fundholders did pursue their own priorities, as demonstrated above, and although these overlapped, they were not identical.

Contractual accountability mechanisms

In fact, the study found that purchasers of both types routinely relied on or worked with other purchasers. Interestingly, the main reason for this was not any explicit concern to coordinate their efforts or to avoid wasteful duplication. Instead, it reflected a more basic desire on the part of purchasers to conserve their own time and resources.

Health Authorities used the 'host purchaser' approach set out in the government guidance. Indeed, they had little alternative: providers saw it as an essential tool in managing the contracting process, and generally refused to engage in separate negotiations with non-host Health Authorities. Authorities A and B in the sample welcomed the opportunity to save time. Authority C did not: its urban location meant that its contracts with neighbouring providers used a much higher proportion of its budget than did those for the other two Authorities.[30] Contract managers expressed some frustration at their inability to negotiate in detail with these providers. Authorities' reliance on their neighbours' contract documents was relatively passive: they did not attempt to influence their content or to check that they were being monitored. 'Hosts' therefore rarely acknowledged that their role included representing other purchasers as well as negotiating with providers for themselves.

Fundholders co-ordinated their accountability activities to a greater degree than was expected. Fundholding groups existed in all three areas, bringing together most, if not all, of the fundholding practices in each area. The most developed group in the sample was in Area A. The group appointed a team of representatives to work with each of the main local providers. The representatives negotiated basic contract documentation, including quality standards and prices. Individual practices could then negotiate their own activity levels (and any special requirements) within

---

[30] Very roughly, Authority C's biggest out-of-county contract was worth 20 per cent of its main local acute contract, whereas Authority B's biggest out-of-county contract was worth 2 per cent of its main contract.

this deal, or negotiate their own contract outside the group arrangement if the provider permitted it. During the life of the contract, the representatives met regularly with the provider to monitor overall activity levels and to discuss any problems raised by practices, such as breaches of quality standards. These arrangements did not always run smoothly: practices often disagreed on issues such as whether a proposed price rise was too high. But most continued to participate in the group for two reasons. First, it saved time, allowing hard-pressed fund managers to focus on concerns specific to their own practice. Secondly, it significantly increased practices' bargaining power: providers could ignore threats from one or two practices, but not from thirty acting in concert.[31]

Nonetheless, the initial prediction that the individualist market rhetoric of the reforms might limit fundholders' co-operation was borne out by the data in other areas. In Areas B and C, the groups were much less formal and had engaged in negotiating activity only in very specific circumstances (for example, where strength in numbers was needed to challenge a dramatic price increase by a provider). Although purchasers in some areas (and the centre (NHSE 1994)) had come to the realization that there were advantages to collaboration, purchasers' comments on the subject tended to have a 'confessional' element: it was feared that coordination might be seen as a sign of weakness rather than as a rational use of resources. As one fund manager put it:

We do a lot of work on the [activity and finance], which in a way is where the real meat is. Because quality issues, they've got to declare it [to the Health Authority] on their Patients' Charter reports,[32] . . . so to a large extent we're a little bit lazy, and we let them do that.

Purchasers wanted to save time, but did not feel that they could justify this within the NHS in terms of the pursuit of a deliberate goal of co-ordination with other contractual accountability mechanisms.

Non-contractual accountability mechanisms

Many of the non-contractual accountability mechanisms to which providers were subject addressed the quality of clinical care they offered to their patients: professional self-regulation, complaints procedures, negligence actions, and internal audits. Recently, the government has sought to tackle the perceived inadequacies of these mechanisms,[33] but

---

[31] See also Ch. 8.   [32] See NHSE (1998).

[33] The proposals are set out in Department of Health (1997) and implemented in the Health Act 1999. For discussion, see Ch. 2 and Davies (2000).

at the time of the study, they had not been subject to much criticism. They offered a useful forum in which to test the response of purchasers to the presence of other accountability mechanisms applicable to providers.

Neither Health Authorities nor fundholders tackled clinical quality issues in a systematic way in their contracts. Some effort was made by purchasers of both types, in response to the worsening financial climate, to make savings by eliminating the purchasing of particular procedures of doubtful clinical effectiveness, such as the removal of asymptomatic wisdom teeth. Health Authorities also made some use of standards 'parasitic' on providers' own accountability processes, which required providers to have complaints procedures and medical audit systems in place, and to report their results on a regular basis (NHSME 1990). But contractual quality schedules did not contain sets of standards about outcomes or even the process of clinical care.

There were a number of explanations for this omission. One was that clinical standards were not a central government priority, so purchasers had no real incentive to address them. Purchasers also lacked the necessary expertise: neither GPs nor Health Authorities' public health departments were well placed to set standards in highly specialized areas of clinical practice. And any intervention in clinical matters by purchasers would have been politically controversial, because of the challenge it would have posed to the medical profession's right to regulate itself (Allsop and Mulcahy 1996). But the main explanation for the absence of clinical standards in contracts seemed to be that purchasers thought them unnecessary. This did reflect the fact that there were other mechanisms of accountability for these standards. Even the more assertive fundholders in the sample saw their role as largely confined to non-clinical quality:

I think we should be using the power of purchasing to make sure that the quality is being improved and that people are being treated better as they go through—not treated clinically; I think clinically there's good quality all over the place, but treated as people better as they go through the system.

But purchasers' reliance on other accountability mechanisms took a relatively passive form. Fundholders did not evaluate them or examine their results in any way. Health Authorities purported to do so, through their 'parasitic' standards, but there was no clear evidence that they acted upon providers' reports in meetings or negotiations. Purchasers tended simply to assume that other accountability processes were functioning effectively.

The accountability of providers: evaluation

The question of interaction with other accountability mechanisms is particularly significant in the case of contract. Because contracts can contain any terms agreed by the parties, they offer considerable scope for duplicating or reinforcing other accountability mechanisms. There are a number of different techniques for reinforcement:

- the provider might be required to indemnify the purchaser against its failure to comply with the other accountability process (some standards in NHS contracts requiring the provider to comply with the general law seemed to fit this model);
- the purchaser might draw on the results of other accountability processes in its own accountability process (setting new quality standards for the provider on the basis of information gleaned from complaints procedures, for example);
- the purchaser might seek actively to reinforce other accountability mechanisms through the contract (this occurs where 'contract compliance' policies are used to enforce aspects of anti-discrimination law).

Duplication simply involves disregarding the presence of the other accountability mechanism and using the contract to set up a process with similar goals.

The presence of more than one contractual accountability mechanism, particularly where the various purchasers are part of the same organization, adds another layer of complexity. Here, purchasers could simply 'duplicate', instituting their own contractual accountability processes regardless of the presence of others. Or they could adopt group or agency approaches. A group of purchasers could 'pool' their individual accountability processes and work together to pursue the same goals. Under an agency approach, one purchaser could be selected to act on behalf of the others. The agency approach could blur into the group approach if the principals continued to supervise their agent closely.

Public law contains two basic doctrines which might help to regulate these various forms of contract compliance. One is the concept of 'improper purposes': as Chapter 1 explained, this has already been used to regulate local authorities' use of contracts for social ends.[34] A nuanced public law framework for contracts would be able to set out a list of aims which could be legitimately be pursued through contract.

[34] *R v Lewisham LBC, ex p. Shell*, 1988 1 All ER 938.

'Improper purposes' could then be used to prevent purchasers from using contracts inappropriately. The content of such a list is a complex political question and is beyond the scope of this book. The discussion here will rest upon a second public law doctrine: 'relevancy'. This provides a means of controlling the factors considered by public bodies before decisions are taken, and would make it possible to oblige purchasers to engage in a cost–benefit analysis of contract compliance before adopting it in a particular transaction. The remainder of this section explores the elements of that cost–benefit analysis.

The first factor which should influence the purchaser's decision as to whether to duplicate or reinforce a particular mechanism must be the relative efficacy of that mechanism and the purchaser's contract. If a purchaser found that the enforcement of health and safety standards in hospitals by specialist agencies was adequate, little would be achieved by including health and safety standards in the contract. But if the purchaser found that the enforcement of anti-discrimination law in hospitals was poor, it might be worthwhile for the purchaser to include a contract term requiring the provider to investigate the issue and comply with the law. Such a term would offer a means of enforcing the law without relying on individuals to bring claims. But it is also important for the purchaser to make an honest assessment of the efficacy of its own contract, as well as of the other mechanism. Chapter 8 will demonstrate that many NHS purchasers were in relatively weak bargaining positions and found it difficult to enforce their contracts against providers. This obviously limits the usefulness of contracts in reinforcing other mechanisms. Purchasers' own expertise is also relevant: even if weaknesses in clinical accountability mechanisms had been identified at the time of the study, it is not clear that purchasers would have had the knowledge to set detailed standards about clinical outcomes.

The concern with relative efficacy also has significant implications for a purchaser's decision as to whether or not to join a group or appoint an agent. In the NHS, it was clear that fundholders significantly improved their bargaining power when they acted together. Providers could resist or ignore the demands of one practice; the demands of thirty or forty practices had to be taken seriously. Agency approaches did not appear to make such a difference to bargaining power, partly because host purchasers rarely presented themselves as agents and partly because they already had significant purchasing power at their main local providers. The position could have been improved if host purchasers had involved their principals more closely in their activities.

But agency and group approaches could also bring problems. One was expertise: the agent or group negotiating team might not have the skills required to make the accountability process effective. Some Health Authorities in particular questioned the abilities of their neighbours, but were forced by the host purchaser system to rely on them. Agents or representatives should always be required to fulfil some minimum standards of competence.

Another potential disadvantage of groups or agents is that they reduce the participants' ability to pursue issues of particular concern. Group and agency approaches in the NHS did leave some space for individual negotiations on issues which *had* to be handled separately, such as the level of activity to be provided. But they tended to push purchasers towards a group of 'lowest common denominator' issues on which they could all agree. The pressure towards uniformity was reinforced by providers. They benefited from the co-ordinated approach because it saved time, and many feared that it would unravel if it was not rigorously enforced. Some providers therefore refused to offer variable waiting times for treatment, for example, even though purchasers might have preferred longer or shorter times on financial grounds. Thus, one crucial question for purchasers to ask themselves before joining a group is the extent to which their accountability requirements overlap with those of the other members of the group. The smaller the overlap, the greater the danger that the purchaser will lose the chance to pursue issues of particular concern to itself.

A further set of factors to be added to the equation is transaction costs. Duplication or reinforcement of other accountability processes, contractual or otherwise, represents a missed opportunity to reduce transaction costs by relying on those other processes. This is particularly true of duplication, which should be seen as a last resort when methods of reinforcement have failed. For example, a purchaser might reinforce health and safety law by requiring the provider to perform satisfactorily in statutory inspections. The purchaser should only duplicate—institute its own programme of standard-setting and site visits—if this reinforcement strategy does not succeed.

Agency approaches offered principals the chance to save time and resources by relying on the agent. Of course, the agent does not make a saving, but in the NHS, this was addressed by choosing the purchaser with the highest value contract with a particular provider to act as the agent. This purchaser would already have good reason to make a heavy investment of time. Group approaches probably also resulted in some time savings. They inevitably involved meetings to agree on the group's negotiating strategy, and extra work for those chosen to represent the group. But the majority of members did not have to participate in detailed negotiations. Moreover, both agency and group approaches offered significant reductions in transaction costs for providers. It was clearly quicker to negotiate with a fundholding group rather than with thirty individual fund managers, or with one Health Authority rather than three or four Authorities.

Purchasers need to examine several questions when faced with other accountability processes applicable to a provider:

- Does the other accountability process work effectively?
- If not, can the contract be used to reinforce or replace it?
- Would bargaining power be increased by grouping together with other purchasers?
- Would a group approach unduly hamper the pursuit of the purchaser's particular concerns?
- Are the transaction costs involved in duplication or reinforcement justified?

NHS purchasers were influenced by many of these issues but rarely considered them explicitly as key factors in the design of a good contractual accountability process. This was particularly worrying in the NHS because of the difficulty of enforcing NHS contracts, to be discussed in Chapter 8. Competition was weak in most parts of the NHS, so providers were not subject to strong market pressure to comply with their contracts. Enforcement therefore became a highly time-consuming activity. The conservation of purchasers' resources, and the enhancement of their bargaining power, were essential strategies for dealing with this problem. But, for the most part, purchasers failed to rationalize the issues clearly.

Conclusion

It is essential to view the contractual accountability mechanism in the context of other accountability mechanisms applicable to both parties to the contract. The discussion of purchasers' accountability in this chapter prompted the development of two important principles to guide the delegation of power to purchasers and more generally:

- if central government wishes to allow its delegates some freedom to pursue the issues they deem appropriate, it must ensure that they have the time and the motivation to do so. One important way of providing motivation is by making the delegates accountable to other interested parties, although this raises difficult issues about conflicts with accountability to the centre;

- the extent of central government influence over its delegates should be transparent to those who are calling both government and delegates to account, so that they can be made to explain the decisions and actions for which they are responsible.

When considering the definition of purchaser and provider roles, the parties should be guided by the fact that it is impossible to reach an objective definition of the roles of purchaser and provider. They should concentrate instead on *negotiating* their roles and attempting to behave *consistently*. This would help to address the problem of selective interference identified in the data.

The discussion of providers' accountability suggested principles about interactions with other accountability mechanisms. When faced with other accountability processes applicable to a provider, purchasers should engage in an explicit assessment of their proper role, based on the following questions:

- Does the other accountability process work effectively?
- If not, can the contract be used to reinforce or replace it?
- Would bargaining power be increased by grouping together with other purchasers?
- Would a group approach unduly hamper the pursuit of the purchaser's particular concerns?
- Are the transaction costs involved in duplication or reinforcement justified?

This chapter has tackled some complex and difficult issues: delegation, transparency, 'contract compliance', role definition. There was an urgent need, in the NHS at least, to address these issues more openly and explicitly. The principles set out in this chapter could at least be used to guide the debate, even if they do not provide definitive solutions to the various problems facing the contracting parties. Chapter 9 will explore the potential application of these principles to other types of internal contract.

7 Getting On: Accountability Relationships and Procedural Fairness

Why study accountability *relationships*? First, it would be easy to assume that 'calling to account' inevitably denotes aggressive questioning and sanctions. But the reality might be rather more complex, as it is for many regulatory agencies, involving a greater use of persuasive strategies. Accountability relationships and the factors which shape them warrant investigation in their own right. Secondly, a detailed understanding of relationships is essential when deciding how they should be regulated. Public lawyers commonly address relationships through the concept of procedural fairness, but this concept needs to be moulded to fit the relationship to which it is being applied. Mistaken assumptions about the character of a relationship might therefore give rise to inappropriate procedural norms.

The first part of this chapter examines contractual accountability relationships in the NHS, using (and developing) the analytical models introduced in Chapter 5. It will be remembered that the models reflected different levels of trust between the parties (high trust for the soft model; minimal trust for the hard model) and therefore denoted very different approaches to the accountability tasks:

Hard model:
- adversarial negotiations; comprehensive and precise standards
- monitoring through 'policing'
- enforcement through sanctions, particularly exit

Soft model:
- collaborative negotiations; broad, general standards
- monitoring through shared information or trusting the provider to comply
- enforcement through persuasion

It was predicted that NHS contracts would fit the soft model. Chapter 5 described a variety of factors, identified in the literature as indicators of the soft model, which seemed likely to be present in the NHS, such as long-term relationships. But this prediction was made with some caveats, such as the possibility that central government regulation might affect relationships regardless of the parties' preferences. Even given these caveats, the study's findings were strikingly at variance with the predictions. Very broadly, fundholders adopted similar, hard approaches to negotiations and contract drafting, but varied across the range from hard to soft when enforcing their contracts. Health Authorities tended to mix approaches even within the same contract, using both hard and soft standards and negotiating styles. But to describe their enforcement strategies, an 'intermediate' model[1] had to be developed.

The second part of the chapter addresses the issue of regulating contractual accountability relationships.[2] First, it is argued that the familiar public law concept of due process should be applied to such relationships, despite some theoretical difficulties. Secondly, ways of applying due process norms to contractual accountability relationships are explored. These norms must be adapted to fit the contractual context, and the different types of contract denoted by the hard and soft models.

Which model did purchasers adopt, and why?

The findings are most conveniently organized around the components of the contractual accountability process: standard-setting, contract drafting, and enforcement.[3] There will be some cross-referencing between the various components: using a particular model for one element has implications for the other elements.

Standard-setting

Negotiations are the main standard-setting forum in a contractual accountability process.[4] Standards are set directly when the parties agree the substantive terms of their contract, creating obligations for the provider. Standards are set indirectly when the parties agree the contract price. Although the payment of the price is an obligation for the purchaser, it acts as a financial target for the provider, and the process of negotiating it forces the provider to explain and justify its financial performance. Under the soft model of negotiation, the parties can be expected to share information and work collaboratively to ensure that

---

[1] There are some threefold classifications in the literature: Macneil (1978); Williamson (1979).

[2] Effectiveness is also a crucial consideration: it was possible that one model might prove to be more effective than the other. This issue is addressed in Ch. 8.

[3] Monitoring is not discussed here because the shape of monitoring was determined by practical factors such as the purchaser's access to data, and its resources, rather than by its relationship with the provider.

[4] Standard-setting can also take place during monitoring and enforcement as standards are interpreted and applied to specific situations.

the final agreement takes both their interests into account. Under the hard model, each party pursues its own interests during the negotiations, sharing as little information as possible and seeking the best deal it can get, regardless of the effects its behaviour might have on the other party.

Health Authorities

Authorities' approaches to negotiating their own standards varied quite widely. Authority B used the hard model when negotiating quality standards with its main providers. Managers drafted standards without consulting providers, and insisted that they agree to them. The providers disputed the content of some of the standards, but signed up because it was not worth provoking a dispute on low-priority[5] quality issues. Authority C adopted the soft model. Its staff produced draft proposals and consulted extensively with providers before agreeing a final specification.

The reason for the difference of approach seemed to lie in two factors. One was that the Authorities perceived their roles differently. Authority B's managers saw quality standards as a matter for the Authority: collaboration with providers would have limited its freedom to set out its own terms. Authority C's managers valued the provider's input: providers' comments ensured that the standards were realistic and perhaps increased the chances of compliance. A second factor was the relationship between the contracting parties' quality managers. Personal ties are an important feature of the soft model: once friendships have been established, collaboration on the professional level is more likely (Macneil 1974).[6] Authority B's managers did not have a good working relationship with their Trust counterparts, apparently for purely personal reasons, whereas Authority C's did.

When Authorities were negotiating central requirements, the position was very different. Hard strategies were the norm. Thus, for waiting times and other Patients' Charter requirements, Authorities simply insisted that the standards be included in contracts: providers had no choice. Similarly, during price negotiations, Authorities demanded a contract deal which would enable them to remain within their own limited budgets and to meet other central targets.[7] Price negotiations, in particular, demonstrate

---

[5] See Ch. 6.

[6] See Flynn *et al.* (1996) and Lapsley and Llewellyn (1997) for similar empirical findings.

[7] Notably the 'efficiency gain', a Treasury requirement that the NHS as a whole should either do more activity for the same money as the preceding year, or the same activity for less money. The figure was usually in the region of 2 per cent.

how strongly central requirements pushed the parties towards the hard model.

The typical approach to price negotiations was for each party to begin by calculating its preferred contract deal. The provider's sum would cover its projected costs; the purchaser's sum would allow it to remain within budget. The parties would engage in a bargaining process until a compromise could be reached between the two figures.[8] The process was essentially hard: each party pursued its own interests in getting a contract deal as close to its figure as possible. By the time of the study, the NHS Executive had adopted a policy of encouraging the contracting parties to share more information and to negotiate more collaboratively.[9] But attempts to implement this softer approach failed.

One difficulty was that purchasers and providers were unwilling to collaborate to the required degree. As Chapter 6 explained, sometimes providers sought to guard their new-found independence from Health Authority 'interference'; sometimes Health Authorities did not want to embroil themselves in complex funding issues. A second difficulty was that it was impossible to prevent hard elements from intruding into price negotiations. Under a genuinely soft approach, the parties would have the same goal of achieving a deal that remunerated the provider fairly for its work (Sako 1992). Soft negotiations on NHS contracts could not mask the fact that while the provider sought remuneration (fair or otherwise), the purchaser's aim was to keep prices down so that it could meet its central targets. For this reason, the purchaser could be forced to ignore an entirely legitimate argument from a provider that a particular contract deal would not cover its costs. Authorities therefore fell back on the hard approach.

Purchaser/provider relationships were damaged by these difficulties, even though purchasers were not themselves the source of the targets.[10] The following comment from a Trust manager was typical:

I think we've got a good relationship with them overall, in terms of service provision, and in talking to each other, but basically they want to give us less money every year, and get us to do more work every year, and you can imagine that at the end of the day that doesn't make for an easy relationship.

---

[8] Arbitration was a possibility in the event that they could not agree: see Ch. 2.

[9] Unpublished regional office guidance.

[10] Authorities did share some of the blame, in that they could reduce the efficiency requirement for particular Trusts by imposing a higher requirement on others. Most Authorities differentiated in a limited way, but obviously this approach brought its own difficulties.

It seemed to be impossible for Trusts to separate the centrally-determined aspects of their negotiations with Authorities from their relationships with them more generally. This reflected the extent to which central requirements dominated the contractual accountability process between Authorities and their providers. The expectation that Authorities' contracts would fit the soft model was, for the most part, proved wrong.

Fundholders

Fundholders' standard-setting tended to follow the hard approach. Their price negotiations had two key elements: price comparisons and 'deals'. Price comparisons were essentially hard: fundholders compared the current year's prices with the previous year's prices and demanded a reduction if the figures showed an 'excessive' rise. Fundholders also sought good 'deals'.[11] They commonly used 'cost and volume' contracts, under which they paid a contract price in respect of an agreed level of activity. If this level was exceeded, the provider undertook to offer some activity at a marginal rate, discounted to reflect the fact that the provider could afford to do a certain amount of extra work without incurring further fixed costs. A 'good deal' was one which offered cheap marginal rates, and set the agreed level of activity in such a way as to make it very likely that the practice would exceed that level and obtain some activity at a discount.

The process of obtaining a good deal showed fundholders at their hardest. Fund managers exercised a degree of cunning to secure the deal, by contracting for less activity than they were likely to need. One fundholder admitted:

You arranged your 110% of your contract to correspond with 90% of your predicted activity so that 90% of your predicted activity would take you up to 110% and then you would hope to get your 10% predicted activity at marginal rates.

Of course, providers tightened up on deals as time went on: they were able to tell that a practice was not contracting for sufficient activity, and demand that it agree to a more realistic level. Nevertheless, fund managers saw it as their job to pursue the best deal available, even if it could not be repeated. They had little regard for the effect of such contracts on the provider.

[11] As used here, the term does not refer to the 'one-off' initiatives described by Walsh *et al.* (1997: 100).

Why did practices adopt this hard approach? One reason was that it was relatively easy: most fund managers felt able to predict their likely activity for the purposes of a deal. But it did also reflect low trust. Fund managers felt that providers, characterized as large organizations with negotiating expertise, were well able to safeguard their own interests. Moreover, many gave examples of cases in which providers had undermined their trust by miscalculating prices or seeking to impose unreasonable increases.

When negotiating substantive standards, fundholders' approaches (usually in groups) were also hard.[12] The strategy was to demand compliance, reinforcing the demand with a threat of exit or some other sanction. A manager at the community Trust in Area A recounted a particularly adversarial meeting with local GPs:

> The GPs . . . swept in, sat down, and said right, unless you implement by April next year [a particular management structure for] community nursing, we are all going to go wholesale and buy from somebody else.

The very fact of a group approach could reflect a belief that the provider would not respond to individual requests, and that it was therefore somewhat recalcitrant. It was not surprising that this low-trust view was carried forward into the way in which the group's negotiating team approached discussions. Although hard behaviour damaged relationships with providers, practices continued to use the model because it was remarkably effective, as Chapter 8 will explain.

To sum up, both fundholders and Health Authorities used hard negotiating strategies, but for very different reasons. Authorities were forced to do so by the need to implement central standards, regardless of the wishes of providers. Fundholders adopted hard approaches partly for practical reasons, and partly because of low trust levels. On issues of real importance, the parties' immediate interests diverged, trust levels were low and the hard model prevailed.

Contract drafting

Different types of negotiations, and different relationships, result in different contract documents, according to the models.[13] A soft contract contains broad standards which can be worked out in more detail during

---

[12] *Individual* practices' negotiations on quality standards, where they occurred, sometimes used the soft model.

[13] Other factors, such as the extent to which the contract seeks to be comprehensive, can also be used to indicate one or other model. Space precludes a full discussion of these factors.

the course of performance. Because the parties trust one another, they are happy to leave matters to future negotiations. A hard contract relies on formal standards, preferably ones which can easily be measured for compliance: trust levels are low, so the parties are keen to specify their rights and responsibilities. In principle, it should not be possible to find both approaches combined in the same contract, because of the different trust levels they express.

Health Authorities

Interestingly, Health Authorities used both hard and soft drafting styles, selecting a style to fit the subject-matter of the standard in question. For finance and activity, the preference was to have standards which were as precise as possible. A manager explained:

I mean the first year of the contracts we had here were pretty woolly, the second year was slightly better, the third year was really the first year that we very much tightened up . . . they've certainly been refined year on year, and are not getting simpler. They are getting more complex in terms of finance and activity.

The general trend was to use more sophisticated contract types, such as the cost and volume contract, to replace the simple block contracts employed in the early years of the reforms.[14] Moreover, there was a high level of planning for contingencies in many contracts. Where cost and volume contracts were in place, it was felt to be important to agree on what the marginal rates for extra payments or refunds would be before the contract came into force. As one manager put it:

It's a question of agreeing these things before you start . . . rather than leaving it until later in the year when it looks like you might be overperforming or under-performing, because obviously whoever's going to benefit financially is going to negotiate a higher or lower rate according to where they are.

At one level, the interpretation of these findings must be that they reflected a lack of trust between the parties. Increasing precision was designed to safeguard the purchaser against the provider's pursuit of its own interests. At another level, however, a more subtle interpretation may be possible. With some specification of rights and responsibilities to give them a sense of security, the parties may have been hoping to build a trusting relationship. This could be done by ensuring that each party's position was clearly set out in the contract. In the NHS, it would have required

---

[14] See NHSME (1990) for further discussion of contract types.

an enormous leap of faith to rely on negotiations on the difficult and important issue of finance. Of course, if the contract became ever more specific, this might reasonably be taken as a sign of ever-declining trust. At the time of the study, however, many Health Authority contracts had reached a level of specificity with which both parties were reasonably satisfied. Moreover, there was no real suggestion in the data that trust had declined over the period during which the sophistication of contracts had increased. Thus, there was no straightforward link between precise financial standards in contracts and low trust levels.

Outside the realm of finance, Health Authorities used hard and soft contractual standards. Where the subject-matter of the standard lent itself to precise specification, the hard model was used. For example, Authorities set very specific targets for the supply of activity data and quality reports from Trusts, requiring them by a specific working day of the month, rather than using a vague term such as 'promptly'. This use of the hard model helped at least to safeguard, and even to build, trust between the parties, by reducing the potential for disputes about interpretation.

But various types of soft standard were also in use. One type was a broad, general term open to different degrees of compliance by providers, requiring further negotiations in order to apply it to particular circumstances. One of Authority C's contracts stated:

The Trust will ensure that there is a strong consumer focus to all services they [*sic*] provide . . . They should have in place systems to gain and evaluate consumer feedback, and mechanisms to ensure that the views of consumers are acted upon.

Another type provided that work would be done on a particular issue by the parties during the life of the contract. One of Authority A's contracts contained this term:

During 1996/7 the Trust will work with [the] Health Authority to continue to implement Changing Childbirth[15] recommendations and specifically to agree and implement an ongoing programme for the provision of breast feeding support and promotion.

Both types of standard acknowledged the parties' long-term relationship: not everything needed to be settled before the contract was signed.[16] They

[15] Department of Health (1993).
[16] A truly soft relationship is probably one of ongoing discussions with no formal point at which agreement is reached. But in the NHS, there was a sharper distinction between contract negotiations and the life of the contract because the parties were obliged by the NHS Executive to sign contracts by a certain date each year, and because annual budgets created a fixed point at which finances would inevitably change.

also reflected the difficulty of setting precise contractual standards on complex quality issues. It was easier to state a general principle in the contract and to work out its application in discussions.

But whilst all the Health Authority contracts sampled contained soft quality standards, not all Authorities could boast about their relationships with providers. This made it difficult for them to harness the benefits of the soft model. For example, one Trust had been asked to improve the management of pressure sores:

And we say 'Well, what do you want us to do?' 'Oh, just send us a six-monthly report.' 'Well, do you want us to include anything in particular in it?' 'Oh, no, just tell us what you're doing.'

Although the Trust was happy to be given some discretion, managers felt that the Authority was not taking the issue seriously: it had chosen the soft approach in order to avoid having to do any detailed work on the problem. As a result, the Trust did not feel motivated to comply. By contrast, soft standards were working well in Area C. The Health Authority held regular discussions with the provider to ensure that both were happy with the way in which the standards were being applied.

Fundholders

GPs' approaches to contract drafting invariably fitted the hard model. There was a gradual movement, similar to that in the Health Authority findings, towards more sophisticated contract types involving some activity measurement. Fundholders' quality standards were also drafted in a hard way. To some extent, this reinforces the point made above that the subject-matter of the standard was important in determining its drafting. Because fundholders tended to concentrate on issues such as waiting times and prompt communications, which could easily be specified in numerical terms, their standards were precisely drafted, regardless of whether their approach to negotiating and enforcing the standards was hard or soft.

Nevertheless, there was more evidence for fundholders than for Health Authorities to support the idea that hard standards did denote a lack of trust between the parties. Many such contracts 'hardened' over time, as practices encountered situations in which the provider disappointed their implicit expectations and gave them cause to abandon softer approaches. For example, some practices alleged that providers were deliberately failing to give patients a supply of drugs when they were discharged, in order to save money. They responded by including a contractual term (sometimes with a penalty clause) on the issue. Fund managers described this not as a means of giving both parties a sense of security (which seemed to be the case for Health Authorities) but as a game of 'cat and mouse', in which they sought to put a stop to each new cost-cutting scheme their providers invented.

Thus, Health Authorities used both models when drafting their contracts; fundholders tended towards the hard model. Low trust was an important factor in explaining usage of the hard model, but other considerations, such as the subject-matter of the standard, were also relevant.

Enforcement

At the enforcement stage, the hard model is characterized by a willingness to exit, to take the contract to another provider,[17] and the soft model by a willingness to persuade and even help the provider to tackle the breach. These pure versions of the models were rare in the NHS, in part because of the weakness of the institutional factors (the market and the 'legal' system) which would normally support the models in private sector markets. Many purchasers employed what will be termed an 'intermediate' model, in which they used sanctions other than exit, such as penalty clauses. The focus in this chapter is on the relationships associated with these different types of enforcement; their effectiveness is explored in Chapter 8.

Hard model

This approach was rare. Health Authorities' use of exit was highly constrained, as Chapter 8 will explain. But some of the more assertive fundholding practices in the sample were able and willing to use exit, particularly for breaches of high priority standards such as waiting times.

It may seem rather strange to consider the relationship implications of exit since, obviously, it terminates the parties' contract. But the data showed that these implications could vary. (This might be important in practice if, for example, the purchaser wished to return to the losing provider at some time in the future.) A provider in Area A had lost two fundholder contracts at the time of the study, because of poor waiting

---

[17] A purchaser might exit without finding the current provider to be in breach of contract, perhaps because another provider has offered a better deal, but such cases are not relevant here: this discussion focuses on exit as an enforcement response.

times caused by a high rate of emergency admissions. Managers reacted very differently to the two cases. One of the practices had a history of aggressive negotiations with the provider, and was highly critical of the waiting times problem. The provider characterized the practice as self-interested and unsympathetic. The other practice had been far more supportive, accepting the provider's excuse and emphasizing its reluctance to move the contract:

This practice . . . says . . . we can see it's all to do with emergencies . . . we would love to be able to keep work with you . . . but really, you know, if there are marked differences, then obviously we'll have to take that patient away.

The manner in which the exit was carried out—whether sympathetic or aggressive—was crucial to its effect on relationships. Once again, the data showed that the alleged link between the hard model and low trust was neither straightforward nor inevitable.

Soft model

For the reasons given in Chapter 5, it was expected that NHS contracts might fit the soft model. The data revealed, however, that clear cases of the soft model were rare. Many purchasers used sanctions, such as penalty clauses, which took them into the intermediate model.

There appeared to be three different sets of reasons for adopting the soft model. First, there were purchasers who found it to be an effective way of achieving compliance. Some fundholders sought to attain the status of a 'valued customer' of the provider, so that when problems arose, persuasion would be sufficient. By a carefully calculated use of exit and penalties, they had impressed on providers their seriousness about achieving high standards through their contracts.[18] For example, one practice had sent some of its patients to another provider when the local hospital had breached waiting time targets. On subsequent occasions when patients' waits were nearing the target, the fund manager telephoned the hospital and was able to obtain prompt dates for their operations. It was clear on the evidence that this did not indicate an adversarial, low-trust relationship. Instead, the provider treated the practice as a favoured customer, and strove to retain its business.

---

[18] This is similar to the 'negotiated compliance' behaviour of regulatory agencies: Ayres and Braithwaite (1992); Fenn and Veljanovski (1988). For empirical evidence see, for example, Hawkins (1984); Hutter (1988); Richardson *et al.* (1983); Rowan-Robinson *et al.* (1990). It also reflects the need for effective persuasion to be backed by threats, discussed in Ch. 8.

A second set of reasons for adopting the soft model was more political. Some fundholders were reluctant members of the scheme. Their reasons for joining varied: some had been pressured to do so by the Health Authority; others felt that while they remained outside the scheme, their patients were losing out. But once they had joined, they did not wish to make use of 'market' elements of the scheme that they felt were inappropriate in the NHS, such as exit or even intermediate sanctions. A couple of practices in the sample eschewed sanctions on this ground.

A third version of the soft model was the soft 'default' model. Some purchasers *appeared* to adopt the soft model where they did not bother with the contracting process. One practice in Area B fell into this category. The GPs felt that an individual practice could not change a provider's behaviour and that effort expended on contracting would be wasted. But it was arguable that the practice's version of the soft model (not using sanctions) was not that envisaged in the literature (more active persuasion). Instead, the practice tended to modify its expectations to what the provider was prepared to offer, failing altogether to enforce an accountability process against that provider.

The soft model's implications for relationships seem as obvious as the hard model's. It is premised on the existence of a high-trust relationship, and does not involve any activity that is likely to reduce the level of trust. Indeed, the purchaser's decision to persuade rather than to use sanctions could be thought to build trust. But all three versions of the model were problematic. The first version depended upon an underlying awareness on the provider's part that the purchaser might complain or use sanctions if persuasion failed (cf. Dore 1983). Some use of the intermediate model was often necessary in order to ensure its success.[19] The second and third versions did not appear to involve the full collaboration and joint working to address the problem implied by the pure model. Purchasers did not try to help; instead, they merely refrained from punishing the provider. These versions of the model were not necessarily linked to high-trust relationships.

Intermediate model

This model involved using sanctions but without bringing the parties' relationship to an end. Health Authorities tended to use the intermediate model for high priority standards, such as waiting times and the supply

---

[19] As Ch. 8 will show, the purchaser could not rely on competition to supply underlying threats.

of information for contract monitoring. Although Authorities used the soft model for low priority standards, such as quality, they felt that they needed some form of sanction, usually a contractual penalty clause (see NHSME 1990), for important issues. Sanctions were seen as a last resort when persuasion failed:

We would much rather talk it through and try and sort it out and agree an action plan to put the problem right, than take money out of the contract . . . but nonetheless . . . you've got to have some ultimate sanction.

There was a general sense that a contract which relied solely on persuasion to achieve compliance left the Authority exposed to the provider's whims.

Most fundholders also adopted an intermediate approach, using sanctions for high priority standards. Like Health Authorities, they used penalty clauses, but they had a range of informal strategies too. For example, where consultants failed to write to explain their treatment of particular patients, practices might refuse to pay the invoice for the treatment until a letter arrived. Another option was partial exit. Several practices had moved some patients to another provider in protest at poor communications or waiting times, moving them back when the losing provider's performance improved. Practices explained that their use of these techniques was designed to prompt providers to put more effort into complying with their contracts.

What were the relationship implications of the use of penalties by purchasers? Negotiating for a penalty clause to be included in the contract might imply that the purchaser anticipated problems and did not trust the provider to comply. Empirical studies of contracts between businesses have shown that such clauses are avoided for precisely this reason (Macaulay 1963). The findings tended to support this view. Providers often drew attention to the fact that contracts never contained incentives, and argued that their own willingness to work on improving performance was not enhanced by the presence of penalties:

They didn't act as a spur, and by penalising us, it wasn't going to be able to make us do something that we were really struggling to do any quicker than we would do by the sheer determination that we were going to try and get it right.

Nevertheless, purchasers included penalties because they were afraid of being left without a remedy in the event of a breach. The weakness of the institutional support for contracts, to be discussed in Chapter 8, contributed to this, because it meant that purchasers could not rely on the market or the legal system to safeguard their rights.

It might be expected that *invoking* a penalty would cause even more damage to relationships. But the data revealed a strong link between the effectiveness of penalties and their impact on relationships. Chapter 8 will demonstrate that penalties seemed to prompt compliance where the provider was clearly to blame for the breach, did not have a good excuse for its failure, and could easily put the problem right (Davies 1999*b*). One manager admitted that her Trust had been slow to modernize its management structure and should have anticipated purchasers' demands for change:

I would say probably that the Trust needed that kick, really, from our purchasers.

The relationship survived because the provider acknowledged that the purchaser's use of a sanction was fair.

But where penalties failed, relationships suffered. Authority C had used penalties to tackle breaches of waiting times at its main provider. The provider claimed that a high rate of emergency admissions made it impossible to meet the standards, and produced good evidence for its claims. The Authority's contract manager explained:

And we did it for a couple of quarters, and then [the Trust's Chief Executive] wrote across and said I'm really cheesed off with these penalties, because you know full well the problems we've got in terms of capacity, we're stuffed to bust with medical emergency admissions, we haven't got any beds, you won't give us any more money to open any more beds, you know, it's a bit over the top to keep penalizing us on these sorts of things. And we sort of said yes, fair do's, it's perhaps not an appropriate thing to carry on doing.

The damage to relationships was enormous. The provider's staff resented the Authority's behaviour and felt that their goodwill had been called into question. The Authority had been forced to stop applying the penalties, and to remove them from the next year's contract. Where penalties were used as a stepping-stone on the way to exit, as they were by some fundholders, it did not matter that they damaged relationships. The practice would simply respond by terminating the relationship altogether. But for Health Authorities and other fundholders, who lacked any real prospect of exit if their penalties failed, an incident such as this could be a source of extreme discomfort in a relationship they were bound to continue.

Enforcement was a complex issue. Health Authorities adopted a relatively uniform approach, using intermediate strategies on high priority issues and softer strategies on low priority issues. There was greater variety among fundholders: each practice tended to adopt the same approach in most situations, but that approach could be any one of the three possibilities. 'Pure' forms of the soft model were rarely encountered in practice because they depended, crucially, on the provider valuing the purchaser's custom. The use of sanctions could sometimes be necessary to achieve that 'valued customer' status. The hard approach terminated the parties' relationship for the time being, but interestingly, relationships of trust could be maintained if it was used fairly. The intermediate approach was the most problematic. Although sanctions did not damage relationships if they were fairly applied, they could destroy trust where the provider argued that it was not to blame for the breach. This caused particular difficulties where the purchaser was forced to remain in a relationship with the provider even after the sanction had been used. In short, fairness was the crucial factor in maintaining relationships here, whatever the model in use.

Conclusion

Summarizing the model adopted by each type of purchaser is a difficult task. Broadly, fundholders used the hard approach for most aspects of their negotiations and for contract drafting. Their behaviour varied most widely at the enforcement stage: hard, soft, and intermediate approaches were used by different practices. Fundholders' use of the hard model often reflected relatively low-trust relationships with providers. But trust did not explain everything: for example, some practices refrained from hard enforcement methods on policy grounds, believing that sanctions were not appropriate in the NHS.

Health Authorities' relationships were more mixed. They used both hard and soft methods of negotiation and drafting, and soft and intermediate approaches to enforcement. Several factors explained the findings. For example, the influence of central government was significant: central pressure to achieve certain standards pushed Authorities towards the hard model when those standards were at stake. But trust levels were also relevant. In relation to high priority finance and activity issues, for example, Authorities felt that they could not trust providers unless relatively precise standards were included in the contract.

The hard and soft models proved to be a useful addition to the armoury of analytical tools for accountability: they helped to explain many aspects of the findings. They were useful even where it was the *non-implementation* of a particular model that accounted for the findings. For example, soft enforcement was constrained by the need for effective underlying threats. But the discussion has highlighted the fact that some caution is required when applying the models. The links between particular features of the models and trust levels were more complex than the models themselves indicated. For example, a purchaser's apparently soft involvement in detail could denote low trust. It is therefore essential, when using the models, to *test* their assumptions about trust.

Procedural fairness in the good accountability relationship

How can these data on relationships be used to contribute to the development of a normative framework for internal contracts? One way in which public lawyers commonly think of relationships between the government and the governed is in terms of procedural fairness. It will be argued here that an accountability process should involve respect for procedural fairness norms. But there are complexities in applying these norms to internal contracts. This section begins with a theoretical discussion of due process in contractual accountability relationships, then reviews the theory in the light of the empirical evidence on NHS contracts.

Contractual due process in theory

Applicability

The rules of due process are, at the highest level, designed to ensure fairness in the government's interactions with citizens. The usual justifications for due process rules (Bayles 1990; Galligan 1996) are particularly strong in the case of accountability relationships, in which judgements are made about performance and, possibly, sanctions applied. On the instrumental level, fair procedures are those which help to ensure that the accountability process is effective (cf. Galligan 1996). They might include a requirement to gather sufficient evidence, for example, so that the caller to account's judgements about performance are as accurate as possible. On the non-instrumental level, fair procedures are an important means of ensuring that the person or body being called to account is given an opportunity to participate in the accountability process (Bayles 1990). Although this argument is perhaps morally less powerful in relation to a corporation, such as an NHS Trust, it is nevertheless relevant: unfair treatment of the organization may involve unfairness to individual members of staff.

Where the accountability process takes the form of a contract between two public bodies, however, some difficulties arise.[20] The argument that procedural protections are essential to regulate the relationship between the government and the governed is not relevant. But there is a case for extending the rules of procedural fairness into these relationships. First, there is some precedent for doing so. For example, *R v Secretary of State for Social Services, ex p. Association of Metropolitan Authorities*[21] involved a statutory obligation to consult organizations representing local authorities, which was found by the court to be mandatory.[22] Parliament created the obligation and the court had no difficulty in elaborating its meaning, even though it amounted, in effect, to enforcing a due process norm between public bodies. Secondly, the instrumental rationale for procedures, facilitating accurate decisions, remains applicable even within government. Thirdly, the 'new public management' reforms have created space for procedural rules in relationships between public bodies. Chapter 3 demonstrated that the replacement of managerial relationships with contractual ones requires a set of 'rules of the game' to govern the parties' interactions. Requirements that the parties should treat each other fairly are an obvious choice for inclusion in that set of rules.

Content

The principles of due process are not 'self-executing'. They must be tailored to the context in which they are to apply and to the values they are intended to serve (Galligan 1996). Here, the relevant procedure is the negotiation and operation of a contract, in accordance with either the hard or the soft model. The due process principles must fit both the concept of contract, and the different versions of it expressed by the models. What principles are appropriate?

In theory, contracts derive a high degree of legitimacy from the fact that the parties have agreed to the obligations they impose (Bayles 1990). But it may be impossible to implement this value to the full where the contract's role is to support an accountability process. This is because inequality of bargaining power—normally a worry in contracts (Collins 1997)—is a positive *requirement* of effective accountability: the caller to

---

[20] Ch. 3 explained that where a contract is enforceable in private law, the courts have been willing to imply some natural justice norms in limited circumstances. These cases are not relevant here because internal contracts are not legally enforceable.

[21] 1986 1 WLR 1.

[22] For an account of the juridification of central-local relations, see Loughlin (1996).

account should have the upper hand (Day and Klein 1987).[23] Where the
caller believes that the body being called to account is objecting unreasonably to particular standards, it should be able to impose those standards in the public interest.[24] This may be justifiable in accountability
terms (though assessing 'unreasonableness' may be difficult in practice), but it does not fit very comfortably into a *contractual* accountability
process. This acts as an important caveat to the models of procedural
fairness to be developed in this section. They apply to contractual
accountability relationships outside the extreme case in which the purchaser imposes standards on the unreasonable provider.

The hard and soft models involve different approaches to the central
value of consensus. Each model therefore requires its own version of procedural fairness. But the literature from which the models are derived is
not expressly concerned with fairness, so the challenge is to identify a
conception of fairness which fits most closely with each model, using an
analysis similar to Dworkin's 'interpretive' method (Dworkin 1986).

The soft model places a high value on consensus, both when the contract is being negotiated and during its life. Fair procedures in this context are those which promote agreement between the parties. This
suggests a particularly collaborative form of negotiation, in which the purchaser allows the provider full opportunity to comment on any proposed
standards, and shows that it is willing to take account of the provider's
representations.[25] Where problems arise during the life of the contract,
the purchaser is expected to hold meetings with the provider not only
to hear its excuses, but also to take joint responsibility with it for solving
those problems.

Fully participatory procedures bring with them particularly strong information requirements. Negotiations proceed on the assumption that all
relevant information is held in common: the parties cannot share the
responsibility for reaching an agreement which is fair to both of them
without full disclosure. Moreover, the purchaser's rejection of deliberate
monitoring activities is based on the assumption that the provider is entirely open with the purchaser about performance. It would therefore be

---

[23] See Chs. 4 and 8.
[24] The caller may not have power to do this, and other solutions—such as placing the
contract with a more willing provider—will often be more practical.
[25] A highly collaborative accountability process may be open to the claim that the caller
to account has been 'captured' by the body it is meant to be calling to account. There was
no real suggestion of capture in the data, with the possible exception of the 'default' soft
approach described above, but even this was rare.

unfair, under the soft model, for either party to conceal information from the other.

The emphasis on collaboration explains why the model's vague, general standards are not unfair, despite their failure to conform to the Rule of Law requirement that standards should be a clear guide to conduct (Fuller 1969; Raz 1977).[26] Fairness under the soft model requires that the provider be given regular opportunities to discuss the standards and negotiate their detailed application with the purchaser. This obviates the need for the provider to be able to predict how the standards will be used.

The hard model, by contrast, places limited value on consensus. Obviously, the parties must agree to the extent that they can sign a contract, but even the contract negotiation is not expected to proceed in a particularly collaborative way. Instead, the purchaser sets out its requirements and the provider must protect its own interests, where necessary, by raising objections and refusing to sign the contract. The model itself does not suggest any sharing of information, although it might be appropriate to graft onto it a minimum requirement, for example, that neither party should conceal any information that would materially affect the other party's consent to the contract.[27] This would help to ensure that each party's consent was voluntary. More controversially, it might be argued that the purchaser should be required to consult the provider on the proposed standards and to give it a reasonable opportunity to make representations, instead of simply demanding its assent. This would serve the instrumental goal of enabling the purchaser to learn from the provider's comments on the standards, and the non-instrumental goal of promoting participation. The extremes of the hard model might require some modification in the interests of fairness.

Once it has been agreed, the hard contract appears to fit a familiar procedure which might be labelled 'applying standards' (Galligan 1996). The value inherent in the procedure is that issues should be decided in accordance with the standards. A number of specific principles may be used to ensure that the standards are applied in a fair and effective way, most of which fit quite closely with the hard model.[28] First, the standards

[26] Under the hard model, this would be unfair: see below.

[27] The ordinary law of contract contains various rules, notably the doctrine of misrepresentation, which are intended to protect the genuineness of consent. See, generally, Treitel (1999) and cf. Collins (1997) for an argument that these rules might amount to a 'duty to negotiate with care'.

[28] The rule against bias is not discussed here. Its application is often modified or disregarded in administrative (as opposed to judicial) contexts.

to be applied should be set out clearly and in advance, to meet the Rule of Law requirement that those affected by rules should be able to use them as a guide to conduct (Fuller 1969; Raz 1977). A hard contract is likely to satisfy this requirement, in that the parties strive to include detailed, specific standards in the contract, and to avoid leaving issues for further negotiation. Secondly, the person applying the standards should seek to discover the facts as accurately as possible. The hard purchaser certainly strives for this, too, by policing the provider's activities, checking up on its accounts, and using independent information where available.[29] This requirement might also be used to justify a matching obligation on the provider to supply information to facilitate the application of the standards. But it would not be appropriate to require the openness of the soft model in this hard context. Instead, the provider might be obliged merely to supply specified information on demand. Thirdly, the person applying the standards should take into account any representations made by the provider. This is difficult to apply to the hard model. On the one hand, it is a highly important aspect of procedural fairness, particularly where sanctions are likely to be applied, serving the values of accurate decision-making and participation by the affected party (Galligan 1996).[30] On the other hand, the hard model may allow the purchaser to hold the provider liable regardless of its excuse. In these circumstances there is little point in the purchaser hearing the provider's representations. Thus, the element of adversarialism in the hard model cuts across apparently straightforward principles of due process. Again, the requirements of fairness may necessitate some modification of the hard model.

Contractual due process in practice

The empirical study permits an examination of some 'real-life' contracts against these due process principles, in order to develop the principles more fully. Three main problems could be identified in the data: imperfect implementation of the models, the mixing of models in the same contract, and the vexed question of fairness in the hard model.

Imperfect implementation was most obviously an issue in relation to the soft model. As explained above, 'persuasion' in the NHS usually denoted the absence of sanctions, rather than the presence of any very active

---

[29] Advocates of the soft model would argue that these methods are flawed.

[30] As Ch. 2 explained, the courts have been willing to imply natural justice into some contracts at common law, particularly where an individual is being judged and potentially punished.

involvement on the part of the purchaser. In particular, it was not clear that purchasers were willing to share the responsibility for problems or to help the provider to solve them. In a model which places a high value on collaboration, it was unfair of purchasers to 'disown' providers when problems arose.[31]

The use of both hard and soft approaches in the same contract also raised due process questions. Health Authorities tended to mix drafting styles, creating potential dangers of inconsistency and confusion. The problem of inconsistency might arise if an Authority using a mixed approach attempted to apply a soft standard in a hard way. This would be unfair to the provider, because it would not necessarily have been able to use the standard to guide its conduct: soft standards failed to meet the hard model's requirements of clarity and precision. The converse situation demonstrates the danger of confusion. A provider, confronted with a hard standard in a contract also containing soft standards, might expect that standard to apply subject to collaborative negotiations. It might be surprised to discover that the standard was not open to debate, but applied exactly as set out in the contract.

How might the requirements of procedural fairness be developed for a contract in which more than one model is in play? One possibility would be to argue that a mixed contract is inherently unfair: it is open to the problems identified above and should therefore be avoided. But this would restrict the parties' freedom of action: mixed standards were, arguably, a sensible response to concerns about varying levels of complexity and priority in the issues to be covered. Fairness in the mixed approach seems to require the observance of two key principles. First, it should be possible to separate the issues to be treated in a soft way from the issues to be treated in a hard way. Health Authorities did this when they used hard standards for finance and waiting times, which were dealt with by finance staff, and soft standards for quality, dealt with by quality staff. This division by subject-matter and staff minimized the risk of inconsistency in the application of the standards. Secondly, the purchaser should ensure that the provider is aware of how the mixed approach is to be used. This should address the danger that the provider might mistakenly assume, for example, that all the contract's terms were open to negotiation, despite the presence of some hard standards. But this would have required a much stronger awareness of the need to observe the principles of due process than was apparent in the behaviour of most NHS purchasers.

---

[31] See Ch. 6 for further detail on this point.

Perhaps the most significant problem highlighted by the data was the difficult issue of fairness in the hard model.[32] It was argued above that due process might require some modification of the extremes of the hard model. But there were numerous examples of cases in which NHS purchasers used the hard model without regard to fairness.

At the contract negotiation stage, hard purchasers imposed standards without engaging in any consultation with providers as to the content of the standards or taking account of providers' representations: Authority B's quality negotiations were a case in point. Moreover, there was some evidence that purchasers failed to share information which would affect the provider's agreement: for example, fundholders withheld information about the implications of particular financial deals.

Purchasers did sometimes argue that their decision to impose standards on a provider was justified by that provider's unreasonable refusal to agree. It was noted in the theoretical discussion, above, that this might be a good reason for disregarding the value of consensus in contractual accountability relationships. But it was difficult—even for a researcher with access to both parties—to assess whether or not purchasers' claims of unreasonableness were well founded. In relation to finance, for example, providers advanced apparently legitimate claims about their costs, which purchasers might have accepted had they not been constrained by their own budgetary targets. Even purchasers who proclaimed publicly that providers were unreasonable were often more sympathetic in private.

Some purchasers, particularly fundholders, also argued that hard behaviour at the negotiating stage was justified because providers were capable of taking care of their own interests and did not need procedural protections. In practice, however, purchasers did not engage in any explicit examination of bargaining power. Although fundholders lacked economic muscle relative to providers, Chapter 8 will demonstrate that they often had effective exit threats and the ability to enhance their power by grouping together. It was not clear that they were justified in *assuming* that their own position was weak.[33] In any event, although due process norms are often used as a way of protecting weaker parties from exploitation, their main rationale is that they facilitate the realization of whatever values are inherent in the procedure. In the case of the hard

---

[32] The intermediate enforcement model is included here because it seems closer to the hard model in terms of procedural fairness.

[33] Health Authorities had more obvious financial power, but less flexibility to exit, as Ch. 8 will demonstrate.

model, the relevant values are (limited) consensus and the accurate application of standards. It may therefore be appropriate to insist on fair procedures even if the parties themselves could bargain for them: arguably they are too fundamental to be left to the vagaries of negotiations.

During enforcement, hard purchasers did not always give advance warning of the penalties to be applied. Fundholders used a range of informal penalties, including refusals to pay invoices or partial exit, which were not set out in the contract. In practice, many providers did become aware of impending sanctions because fundholders did not resort to the sanction without threatening to do so first. But this occurred because it was a useful tactic for purchasers, rather than because they acknowledged the need for due process in their dealings with providers. Another fairness problem was that when using hard or intermediate enforcement, purchasers did not always give providers a hearing before using the sanction, or take notice of the representations they made. To punish the provider without giving it a chance to explain itself seemed of the essence of a procedural impropriety.

Again, purchasers offered some explanations for their hard behaviour. One claim was that a provider's response to a penalty would itself indicate whether or not the provider had a good excuse. If the provider put the breach right, this would be because its excuse was not genuine; if it continued to breach, this would be because the breach was unavoidable. But this argument seemed flawed on two grounds. One was that a provider might refuse to back down in the face of a penalty even if it did not have a plausible excuse for its breach. The other was that, as Authority C had discovered to its cost, relationships could be damaged by penalties even if they were subsequently withdrawn. A simple hearing to discuss the problem before resorting to penalties would have been a less risky method of evaluating the provider's excuses.

Some purchasers held providers liable for breaches regardless of whether or not they had a good excuse. In such cases, giving the provider a hearing would have been pointless. But these purchasers did not always make their stance apparent to providers when the contract began. Most purchasers were prepared to listen to excuses, thus placing a burden on those who did not do so to ensure that the provider was aware of their practice.

More fundamentally, fairness in the hard model raises the question of whether the unconstrained pursuit of self-interest is appropriate in a *public sector* market. On the one hand, it could be argued that promoting the pursuit of self-interest was the purpose of contractualization reforms. They played on public choice notions of bureaucratic self-interest by creating smaller agencies with divergent interests. Competition between these agencies would promote improvements in service quality and efficiency. Notions of fairness might impede the free play of competitive forces by giving weaker agencies an opportunity to justify their failures rather than face the market consequences of a poor performance. On the other hand, it could be argued that this type of self-interest is illusory. The various agencies' short-term interests did perhaps diverge: the purchaser's desire to stay within budget might not have been compatible with the provider's desire to break even. But purchasers and providers also showed signs of 'benevolence', and did not always pursue their 'own interests' at all costs.[34] This could suggest a longer-term view of self-interest, in which the parties to an ongoing relationship acknowledged that making a gain one year would make subsequent years' negotiations more difficult (implying either the soft model or a constrained version of the hard model). Moreover, it may suggest that a wider public interest was also at stake (implying at least a partial rejection of the public choice argument). On this view, procedural fairness—even in the hard model—could have played a central role in promoting that wider public interest, by ensuring that NHS contracts did not unduly disadvantage either party.

The application of the procedural fairness principles developed above to the NHS data is not a mechanical process: the principles require further refinement to take account of the complexities of the relationships encountered in practice. But perhaps the most significant point to emerge from the data is the importance of fair procedures: although purchasers did not give explicit consideration to them, it is clear that relationships would have benefited had they done so.

Conclusion

The internal contract should have a procedural dimension. Procedural fairness norms can help to maximize the effectiveness of the accountability process supported by such a contract, and to ensure that the parties treat each other with respect. But these norms must fit comfortably into the *contractual* relationship, taking account of the different forms that relationship might take under the hard and soft models.

---

[34] This study identified a number of examples: providers' maintenance of high clinical standards, for example, and purchasers' use of the soft model even where it was not in their immediate interests to do so. See also the discussion in Barker *et al.* (1997).

Some common assumptions about fairness had to be modified to fit the models: for example, it was acknowledged that standards did not need to be clear and precise—despite the usual Rule of Law requirement—under the particular circumstances of the soft model. And some aspects of the models had to be modified to meet the demands of fairness: in particular, the hard model's extremes of concealing information and punishing without warning were rejected on due process grounds. The study's conclusions on fair procedures under each model can be summarized in the following way:

Soft model:
- collaborative negotiations (as far as the need for some purchaser domination allows); an obligation on both parties to share information during negotiations; no requirement to set out clear standards in advance (but no ban on doing so where the parties feel that clarity is desirable)
- an obligation on the provider to share information for the purposes of monitoring
- an obligation on the purchaser to take account of the provider's explanations and excuses at the enforcement stage, and to take joint responsibility with the provider for solving the problem which has led to the breach of standards

Hard model:
- consultative negotiations with no deliberate concealment of relevant information; clear and precise standards set out in advance as a guide to conduct
- an obligation on the provider to supply relevant information on request for the purposes of monitoring
- an obligation on the purchaser to give advance warning of any sanctions to be applied, and to give the provider a hearing at which to offer its explanations and excuses

Public lawyers would normally expect all accountability mechanisms to involve respect for procedural fairness. This is most obvious in mechanisms such as complaints procedures, in which individuals may be criticized and punished for falling short of required standards, but it is also relevant where the mechanism is a contract. This study has begun to address some of the difficulties of achieving a fit between familiar procedural principles and contractual processes of accountability; further research is needed to test the ideas presented here in other internal contracts.

8 Winning Out: Making the Accountability Process Effective

NHS contracts were not particularly effective as mechanisms of accountability. Purchasers struggled to set the standards they required and to ensure that providers complied with them. A number of factors contributed to purchasers' weak positions. These are explored in the first part of the chapter. Of course, these factors are highly context-dependent, but nonetheless, they help to highlight some of the issues that might need to be examined in relation to other internal contracts. The second part of the chapter suggests some possible generalizations from the NHS data, and topics for further research.

Before turning to the data, it is essential to understand what is meant by 'effectiveness'. In a contractual accountability process, effectiveness should be judged both during contract negotiations and during the life of the contract. During negotiations, the purchaser's goal should be to set the standards it believes to be in the public interest, normally by agreement with the provider but with the possibility of imposing standards where the provider's objections are unreasonable. Once the contract has been agreed, the purchaser's primary goals should be to obtain information in order to monitor performance, and to secure compliance with the standards set, with the subsidiary goal of obtaining a reasonable explanation in the event of a breach.

These general goals could be expressed in more specific terms for the NHS purchaser. During contract negotiations, NHS purchasers focused on the obligations they were setting for the provider, and the obligations they were accepting for themselves. They sought to set various standards for providers, particularly on the high priority issues discussed in Chapter 6: waiting times, information, and so on. They also sought to ensure that the contract price they would have to pay amounted to a 'good deal': offering reasonably-priced services and enabling them to remain within their budgets. During the life of the contract, purchasers sought compliance with its terms: this could involve making sure that breaches did not occur at all, attempting to prevent threatened breaches, and seeking to resolve breaches when they did take place. In the latter event, the subsidiary goal of obtaining a reasonable excuse from the provider came into play, unless the purchaser was applying a 'strict liability' approach. And of course, none of this would be possible if the purchaser did not discover breaches of contract in the first place. Purchasers required accurate and honest information from providers about the progress of the contract in terms of activity levels, and about their compliance with high-priority standards, such as waiting times. But what factors affected purchasers' success in achieving these various goals?

Findings and explanations

The data revealed five main factors that affected purchasers' ability to institute an effective accountability process through their contracts: the degree of competition in the market and the efficacy of sanctions other than exit; the availability of conciliation and arbitration; the impact of pressure from central government to achieve certain targets; the degree of effort and energy purchasers brought to their task; and the parties' relative access to information. The explanations should, of course, be treated as tentative: most of the cases studied involved a combination of factors, making it impossible to assert clear cause-and-effect relationships between a particular factor and purchaser success or failure.

Discussion of the hard and soft models will take second place to the consideration of these factors because, for the most part, the factors constrained purchasers' ability to implement either model to the full. Although the study was intended to evaluate the relative efficacy of the models, this goal had to be modified in the light of the much more complex reality revealed by the data.

Competition and sanctions

Both the hard and the soft models of enforcement were dependent on the presence of effective underlying threats, and in particular, on the threat that the purchaser might take its contract elsewhere if the provider refused to agree to certain standards or breached those standards during the life of the contract. The hard purchaser might well carry out its exit threats. The soft model's reliance on exit was indirect. For persuasion to be effective, the provider had to value the purchaser's custom. The provider was unlikely to do so where the purchaser had no alternative contracting partner and was bound to continue the contract regardless of the provider's behaviour. This point became apparent from cases in which purchasers succeeded in implementing the soft model. One fundholding practice had referred its patients to another provider when it became apparent that its local provider would not be able to treat them within the contractual waiting time. On subsequent occasions, a telephone call to the provider to alert it to patients nearing the waiting time limit had been sufficient to encourage the provider to give those patients a date for their operations. Persuasion worked because the provider knew that it was reinforced by an implicit threat of exit.[1] Purchasers who tried to persuade without threatening were rarely successful.

In practice, however, purchasers faced a variety of constraints on their ability to exit. One major problem for Health Authorities was that they had a duty to ensure that core services were provided to their patients (NHSME 1989; 1990). There was a natural flow of emergencies to local hospitals which was difficult to change, and contracts had to be in place to pay for them. There was more flexibility in relation to non-emergency work, but this was only a part of Authorities' contracting portfolios.

Even more importantly, purchasers did not always have a wide choice of providers. Area C offered the greatest choice in the study, being situated in a large conurbation with its own district general hospital and numerous neighbouring providers, including a large teaching hospital. Areas A and B had one major provider at the centre, which had to compete only for the custom of patients who lived on the borders. This meant that exit was most easily available to purchasers of both types in Area C, and to fundholders on the borders of Areas A and B. Where the purchaser was situated close to the local provider, exit was not a realistic option. One GP gave a startling illustration of the point:

Even where the waiting list has been a year [at the local provider] and six weeks [at a provider an hour's drive away], about 90% of the patients did not wish to travel for that investigation, which basically says that people don't—in this area, because of the geography, there isn't a suitable alternative for most services.

Of course, it was possible that patients were more willing to travel than purchasers believed. Nevertheless, purchasers' behaviour meant that providers' contracts were relatively secure. The study confirmed the view of many commentators that the NHS 'market' was one of limited contestability at the margins, rather than full competition (for example, Barker *et al.* 1997; Walsh *et al.* 1997).

There is, however, one important caveat to this finding. Providers were sometimes more afraid of exit than they needed to be. Obviously, this

---

[1] Cf. Dore (1983) on soft contracts in competitive markets. The approach is similar to 'negotiated compliance' in regulation (see, for example, Hawkins 1984).

could work to purchasers' advantage. In Area B, the community Trust attempted to impose a substantial price increase on fundholders. One fund manager confessed:

We did then threaten them with going [elsewhere], but it's extremely difficult with community services to actually move who you're going to have as your provider.[2] So that was a bit of an empty threat in a way.

Nevertheless, the Trust had been quite strongly affected by the threat. One manager described it as 'real' and explained that he had 'managed to talk them round'. Thus, the exit threat could be a useful weapon, particularly for fundholders, though it had to be used with caution: there was always a risk that a provider might call the purchaser's bluff by refusing to make concessions.

Because of the weakness of competition, purchasers often employed intermediate sanctions, such as penalty clauses or partial exit, once the contract had been signed. The data showed that these sanctions could help to secure compliance with the contract, but only when certain conditions were satisfied (see, further, Davies 1999*b*). The provider had to perceive the sanction as a significant harm, and had to be able to remedy the problem relatively easily. One provider in the study had lost substantial sums of money because it failed to invoice fundholders on time.[3] It responded by instituting a complex system of checks to ensure that as much activity as possible was billed promptly. The penalty worked because the problem could be resolved through these administrative changes, and because the sanction was significant: it deprived the provider of remuneration for the work it had done.

By contrast, purchasers' use of partial exit in response to breaches of waiting time standards illustrated some of the problems with penalties. First, providers claimed that long waiting times were attributable to a complex set of factors, such as staff shortages and unpredictable demand for emergency treatment. These issues were much more difficult to address than administrative errors. Secondly, partial exit was not seen as a significant sanction, particularly in relation to waiting times. Where demand exceeded supply, some reduction in demand enabled the provider to manage its workload more easily. As one Trust manager explained:

---

[2] Flynn *et al.* (1996) found similar evidence that fundholders were reluctant to move community contracts, preferring local provision by trusted staff.

[3] National rules stipulated that fundholders could refuse to pay invoices that failed to arrive within six weeks of the end of the month in which the activity took place (Richardson and Taylor 1995).

We're trying to do something about it . . . [but] I said to [GPs] if you wish to, you know, send them to [a neighbouring provider], feel absolutely free. Because it takes the pressure off our waiting list, and our [consultants] will never be under-employed.

Moreover, providers felt that they could withstand the loss of some contracts where the sums involved were not substantial. A single fundholder's contract would not necessarily make much impact on a large provider:

GP fundholders certainly threatened to take work away, and some of them did, but that's like a sting on the side of an elephant, to an extent.

This cast doubt on the argument of commentators such as Barker *et al.* (1997: 96) that contestability at the margins could be an adequate substitute for competition. Providers were unperturbed precisely because most contracts were safe.

Exit and lesser sanctions were thus problematic in the NHS. This made it difficult for purchasers to secure agreement to the standards they wanted to set, or to secure compliance with the standards once they had been agreed. Often, providers did comply—where they thought that the standards were appropriate, for example—but this left purchasers exposed to providers' whims and reversed the balance of power required for effective accountability.

Conciliation and arbitration

The NHS conciliation and arbitration arrangements[4] had two potential roles. One was to resolve disputes about contract performance.[5] The other was to prevent contracting parties with dominant bargaining positions from exploiting weaker parties during contract negotiations.[6] What was the impact of the possibility of conciliation[7] on purchasers' ability to use contracts effectively?

Conciliation was an unattractive prospect for the parties during negotiations. Its use was strongly discouraged by the NHS Executive's regional offices: purchasers and providers were told that it would be seen as a sign of management failure, a threat that was taken very seriously

---

[4] National Health Service and Community Care Act 1990, s. 4; National Health Service Contracts (Dispute Resolution) Regulations 1996 (SI 1996/623). See Ch. 2, and Hughes *et al.* (1997).

[5] 1990 Act, s. 4(3).   [6] 1990 Act, s. 4(4).

[7] The study found no examples of statutory arbitration, so 'conciliation' is used to denote the informal conciliation and arbitration process operated by regional offices.

by all concerned.[8] This had deterred Authority B and its providers altogether. Nor was there evidence of fundholders going to conciliation. Authorities A and C had invoked the process, but were quick to point out that they had done so only as a last resort. Secondly, those who had used conciliation were dissatisfied. Although the intention had been to employ pendulum arbitration (NHSME 1989), regional offices had developed a practice of awarding some items to one party and some to the other in order to achieve an overall compromise. The parties saw this as a 'fudge' rather than a genuine attempt to engage with and resolve their dispute.

Paradoxically, however, purchasers could turn the unattractiveness of conciliation into a bargaining advantage. When the purchaser had a better case or a stronger nerve than the provider, it could threaten conciliation in order to manipulate the provider's desire to avoid involving the regional office. Authority C had extracted significant concessions from one provider by refusing to accept a dramatic price rise and suggesting conciliation. The provider did not have a good justification for the price rise and did not feel that it was worth pursuing the matter to conciliation because the total value of the contract was not significant. Of course, in other cases, the balance of advantage might lie with the provider.

The pressure to avoid conciliation seemed to be even more effective during the life of the contract. The study unearthed only one example of its use. As a result, purchasers experienced two significant problems. First, purchasers found that their contracts lacked normative force. Of course, many contractual terms were routinely met: those with which providers would comply in the normal course of events, or in response to other regulatory regimes. But simply including a term in the contract did not guarantee compliance. One GP said this about a contractual term requiring prompt clinical letters:

> You get a proportion that are, but there's a proportion that aren't, and the sort of comment is 'Well, we just can't manage that. We'll try and work on it.' But there isn't any great sense of 'It's imperative'.

Interviews with providers reinforced this finding. One of the more extreme examples occurred when one Trust could not[9] meet a contractual deadline:

---

[8] Interview data. See also NHSME (1990); Hughes *et al.* (1997).

[9] The Trust in question was an ambulance Trust which had undertaken to publish its prices by a certain date. Its argument was that compliance was impossible because the government had changed the date of the Budget. It did not wish to issue prices until after the Budget, so that any rise in fuel costs could be reflected in its prices.

They said you can't do this, it says in here, you can't do it. I said well, tough. So all I did was just Tippex it out and put a new date in.

This sense that contracts were not 'binding' could be attributed, at least in part, to the weakness of 'legal' remedies in the NHS.[10] Contractual obligations did not bind because there were no real consequences of a failure to comply with them: there was no threat of 'legal' action in the form of NHS conciliation or arbitration. Nor, as explained in the previous section, did purchasers have any very effective threats of exit or other sanctions.

The second problem experienced by purchasers during the life of the contract was that in the absence of conciliation, they had no means of resolving disputes with providers about compliance. Where they could not take their business to another provider, they could find themselves trapped in a relationship in which there was an ongoing dispute. For example, the provider might argue that a particular clause could not be met, but the purchaser might believe it to be entirely reasonable. Conciliation could have provided a way of resolving such problems. This point was illustrated by the one conciliation case examined in the study. Authority C had sought to invoke a penalty clause when a provider failed to supply activity data on time, but the provider had refused to pay. At conciliation, the regional office awarded the Authority a payment, though less than it would have been entitled to under the contractual formula. Although neither party was entirely satisfied with this compromise, it did enable both to claim a partial victory. It solved the immediate dispute and provided a starting-point for a renewal of trust between them. Of course, the evidence from the private sector is that businesses are reluctant to litigate (Macaulay 1963), but unlike NHS purchasers, they are more likely to have the option of exit.

The NHS Executive seemed to take the view that an accessible dispute resolution procedure would simply have encouraged the parties to disagree. But the absence of such a procedure created problems for purchasers seeking to set the standards of their choice, to enforce their contracts, and to resolve disputes about enforcement. If anything, it seemed to render the contractual accountability process *less* effective.

Central pressure

Chapter 6 demonstrated the dominant role of central government priorities in the contracting process. Did the fact that a standard was

[10] This reinforces the conclusions of studies emphasizing the role of institutions in the contracting process (Deakin *et al.* 1997).

reinforced by central pressure help purchasers to negotiate and enforce it effectively?

During negotiations, central pressure helped to make some standards 'unquestionable'. For example, Patient's Charter standards and the 'efficiency gain' (a tough financial target) were taken as read by the parties and included in contracts almost without the need for any negotiation, even though providers often complained bitterly that the targets would be difficult to meet. Moreover, central pressure also enhanced providers' awareness of the need to comply with the standards. As one manager vividly explained:

There would be punishments, penalties, if the Patients' Charter standards weren't recorded and we didn't monitor them and submit that information. Heads would roll.

But central pressure could sometimes be a 'false friend' to purchasers. The data showed that where providers could not easily comply with the standards, they might be tempted to cheat. One of the community providers in the sample submitted false reports in relation to the Patients' Charter standard on appointment times for district nurses. It reported a high rate of compliance with the requirement that patients should be given appointments within two-hour time bands, but in practice, simply told patients whether the nurse would call in the morning or the afternoon, giving a precise appointment time when patients requested one. The nurses felt that this was an adequate service, and the provider chose to submit false reports rather than to change their behaviour. A more subtle response was 'creative compliance' (McBarnet and Whelan 1991; 1997). This involved interpreting the standard in a way which made it easier to meet. Allegations of this were common in relation to the Patients' Charter requirement that patients should be given an initial assessment within five minutes of arrival in the accident and emergency department. It was claimed that although the standard was meant to apply to an assessment of the patient's condition by a trained nurse, many Trusts were counting a contact with the receptionist as sufficient. This made it easier for short-staffed departments to meet the standard.

Why did providers respond in this way? First, the targets were often genuinely difficult to meet: providers found it hard to tackle rising waiting times when they had no extra funds to employ more staff, for example. Secondly, they were under enormous pressure to meet the targets. Purchasers attached penalty clauses to breaches of central targets, and the NHS Executive published providers' results in annual league tables

(NHSE 1998). And thirdly, both purchasers and the NHS Executive ignored providers' excuses. Purchasers did so because they were themselves required by the NHS Executive to secure compliance with the standards at all costs.[11] The NHS Executive disregarded excuses in the sense that the published league tables gave providers no opportunity to explain breaches: to say that long waiting times were due to a high rate of emergency admissions, for example. Providers did not see why they should be made liable for breaches where they were not at fault—strict liability is not a concept readily accepted by non-lawyers—and felt that it was unfair that they had no opportunity to explain themselves.[12] As the discussion of information, below, will demonstrate, providers were much more likely to admit to their own failures where they were permitted to give excuses.

Central pressure helped to make purchasers' contract negotiations effective, but could be counterproductive during the life of the contract. It seemed both unfair and ineffectual to adopt a 'strict liability' approach at *both* stages: at no time did providers have a chance to point to legitimate reasons why they might not be able to meet the contract's terms.

Purchaser effort

Much of the analysis thus far has focused on circumstantial factors over which purchasers had little or no control. But the data showed that purchasers could make a difference to the effectiveness of the accountability process by their own efforts. One of the most striking examples of this was the power of fundholding groups: although providers sometimes ignored the demands of individual practices, they found it much more difficult to disregard the demands of several practices acting in concert. The discussion here will concentrate on examples which do not depend on the perhaps rather unusual situation of multiple purchasers in the NHS, and which may therefore be more readily generalizable to other contexts.

The data suggested that where purchasers did not put much effort into the contracting process, its effectiveness was reduced. Health Authorities tended to set large numbers of contractual standards, but focused their monitoring and enforcement efforts on high-priority issues such as finance and waiting times. Providers felt that they could ignore low priority standards: the main provider in Area B made little effort to work

---

[11] There was some suggestion that the pressure on purchasers was so great that they were prepared to 'turn a blind eye' to, or even encourage, cheating by providers.

[12] This demonstrates the importance of procedural fairness, discussed in Ch. 7.

to the Authority's quality standards because it was not clear that the standards would be monitored or that the purchaser would act on breaches. These findings cast doubt on whether there was any value in including low priority standards in contracts.

A special investment of effort on the part of the purchaser could, by contrast, yield striking results. This was most noticeable in relation to the soft model. Many fundholders complained of a 'communication gap' between providers' contract managers and the clinicians responsible for delivering services. Practices would agree a standard with the managers, but then find that it was breached because clinicians either did not know about it or did not agree with it. Not unreasonably, many practices saw this as an issue for providers themselves to address. But at least one had come up with an innovative solution: to require the lead clinician of every department to sign the practice's contract. The fund manager believed that compliance was improved by ensuring that clinicians, as well as managers, were aware of the contract's requirements:

> If you make them all sign up then yes, they come back with fiddly bits like . . . one of them picked up some very small point relating to his specialty . . . but it makes them read it . . . it's worth it, because it means that they do tend to then perform what they've said they'll perform.

Using persuasion effectively required this level of effort. The practice had entered into the spirit of the soft model, and had sought to build a genuinely close relationship with the provider. But cases in which the soft model was implemented in this way were rare, because of the amount of energy it required.

It is important not to conclude from this that purchasers were always to blame for failures. Purchasers' efforts were not always rewarded: the discussion of sanctions, above, illustrates this. And many staff—particularly GPs—felt that they did not have sufficient time to put more effort into the contracting process. It would probably have been unreasonable to expect high levels of enthusiasm and involvement from everyone.

Access to information

Information is vital to effective accountability. The purchaser needed to know whether the provider's negotiating position was reasonable, whether it was complying with the contract once agreed, and whether its excuses for breaching the contract, if any, were valid. But for the most part, providers had all the advantages in terms of access to information.

There were occasions on which purchasers had superior information and benefited from it. Fund managers deployed their knowledge of their own likely activity needs in order to secure good financial deals from providers, in which they would obtain some activity at a discount. One fund manager had obtained £55,000-worth of activity for £10,000 by agreeing to a contract with a high activity level but very cheap marginal rates (only 25 per cent of the provider's published prices). The provider agreed because it thought that the practice would be unlikely to exceed the activity level by very much. But the fund manager knew that the practice's list was expanding rapidly as new housing estates were built in the town, and predicted, correctly, that the practice would easily exceed the agreed level. The only disadvantage of this hard use of superior information was that the benefits accruing to purchasers were not usually sustainable over the longer term. The fund manager admitted: 'So they didn't see us coming last year—unfortunately they have done this year!'

It was, however, usually the case that providers had superior information, both about their potential ability to meet standards proposed by the purchaser during negotiations, and about their actual performance during the life of the contract. This did not mean that providers were unwilling to disclose information to purchasers. In fact, there were various incentives for them to do so. At the contract negotiation stage, providers were understandably keen to draw attention to proposed standards which they would be unlikely to meet.[13] They sought to ensure that these standards would not be included in the contract. During the life of the contract, providers had financial incentives to supply information. Where the contract was for a particular level of activity, providers had to demonstrate that they were performing to that level in order to get paid. And most purchasers applied some form of penalty where the provider failed to produce activity or waiting time reports by the contractual deadlines. Most strikingly, providers were even prepared to admit to breaches of their contracts if they were given a chance to make excuses. Many staff simply wanted to be honest, and more specifically, to educate purchasers about the difficulties of achieving the standards they set. One manager welcomed site visits for this reason:

They need to come here and get a feel for what we're doing and what the place is like, to understand perhaps some of the difficulties, the areas why we're not

---

[13] In a more competitive market, providers might have been less willing to admit to potential problems for fear of not winning the contract.

able to achieve . . . we can't do it all, but as long as you explain why you can't do it . . .

Providers hoped that purchasers would respect them for their openness and would understand that they were endeavouring to comply with their contracts.

But how could purchasers be sure that the information they received from providers was reliable? Where the parties have a genuinely soft relationship, this is not a problem because the purchaser trusts the provider and is inclined to accept its excuses. One fund manager explained his policy on the negotiation of outpatient waiting times:

We were determined to only have in quality clauses that were realistic. It's pointless having in three weeks if we know they're only going to do nine. We'd rather have in one that they feel they can achieve.

This demonstrated a high level of trust: the purchaser accepted that the provider would give an honest assessment of what was realistic. But soft relationships were uncommon.

Under the hard model, the purchaser is suspicious of the provider's claims and seeks to verify them, using independent sources of information wherever possible.[14] Fundholders had some data of their own about referrals which enabled them to carry out checks on providers' activity and waiting time reports. Health Authorities, by contrast, lacked independent information against which to verify providers' accounts.[15] Sometimes, they could tease out inconsistencies at meetings, but for the most part, they were reliant on the provider's accuracy and honesty. In one striking incident, Authority C had written to all its GPs asking them to stop referring to a particular provider, because the provider's reports indicated high activity levels exposing the Authority to a liability to make extra payments. A few weeks later, the Authority had been forced to send another letter to GPs explaining that the contract was in fact on target, and that the earlier reports were attributable to the provider's computer error. If purchasers could not detect accidental errors, it was hard to see how they might detect the deliberate falsehoods discussed in relation to central standards, above.

[14] Assessing the effectiveness of purchasers' attempts to cross-check providers' information raised methodological difficulties, discussed in Ch. 5, which act as an important caveat to the discussion here.

[15] In theory, non-fundholding practices could have supplied this information, but most lacked the sophisticated computer systems which would have been necessary to maintain the relevant records. (Fundholding practices received special grants to procure such systems.)

The situation was exacerbated by the fact that purchasers could not usually resolve disputes caused by information asymmetry. At the contract negotiation stage, accountability theory suggests that the caller to account should be able to impose standards where the body being called to account is objecting to them without good cause. But the study found that purchasers were only able to impose standards on providers where those standards were dictated by central government. And few purchasers had the alternative of taking their business to another provider. During the life of the contract—in the absence of easy access to conciliation— there was no authoritative means of deciding which party's view of a breach was correct. Purchasers and providers engaged in ongoing debates about whether or not particular standards were realistic. Such debates were a constant source of tension in relationships and, of course, meant that purchasers did not secure compliance with the standards they had set.

In short, purchasers obtained a reasonable quantity of information from providers, but had great difficulty in assessing its quality where they did not trust the provider. This limited their ability to set the standards they believed to be in the public interest, and to enforce those standards where providers seemed to be recalcitrant.

Conclusion

At the standard-setting stage, purchasers' main goal was to agree a contract which included the standards they wished to set for the provider's performance. But they faced three obstacles. First, whichever model they used, they lacked a means of making providers responsive to their demands. Often, they could not make a plausible threat of exit if their requirements were not met. Conciliation did not offer a way of addressing this problem. Secondly, where the purchaser consulted the provider on proposed standards, it could be difficult to scrutinize the provider's input, because of the disparity of information between the parties. Thirdly, with the exception of standards required by central government, there were no clear examples of purchasers being able to impose standards on a provider where they believed that the provider's objections to the standards were unreasonable. Of course, there were exceptions to this negative picture. For example, fundholders could obtain concessions where the provider was afraid that they might exit, and Health Authorities could do so where the issue at stake was not worth disputing. Nevertheless, purchasers were often in a weak position.

During the life of the contract, purchasers' main goal was to secure compliance with the standards set: to enforce their contracts effectively. Again, they experienced difficulties. Providers did meet many contractual terms as a matter of course, but NHS contracts did not carry a strong sense of obligation. Providers were aware that breaches were unlikely to lead to conciliation or to the loss of the contract. This undermined purchasers' attempts to enforce the contract through the soft model as well as through the hard model: both depended (indirectly or directly) on the presence of effective underlying threats. Purchasers' enforcement efforts using the intermediate model—to which they often resorted in an attempt to alleviate the weakness of their position—depended on their ability to cause a significant harm to the provider by their sanction. Purchasers did have more success in their subsidiary goals of obtaining information for monitoring and obtaining explanations for breaches. But providers' superior access to information was again apparent: purchasers found it difficult to verify providers' accounts where they were not inclined to believe them.

Effectiveness: wider lessons

Effectiveness is self-evidently a question that must be judged afresh in relation to each accountability process. But some of the factors that seem to reduce or enhance the effectiveness of one such process may be relevant to other processes, particularly where a similar technique—such as a contract—is being employed. It is therefore worth considering what measures might be taken to address the problems identified in relation to NHS contracts, and the wider implications of those measures. The discussion reflects the second strand of public law thinking identified in Chapter 3: that which is concerned with facilitating effective government action in the public interest.

Competition and sanctions

The extent to which internal contracts take place in a competitive market may vary considerably, as Chapter 2 suggested. Although agencies are, in theory, potentially subject to market testing, Foster and Plowden (1996) suggest that this is much more likely to be applied to their support services rather than to their functions as a whole. Many framework documents may therefore be agreed in non-competitive conditions. By contrast, DSOs were required to compete with private providers for contracts under CCT, and are still required to compete with, or at least benchmark their performance against, other providers under 'best value'. The NHS findings might therefore be relevant to some, but not all, of the other types of internal contract.

One solution to the problem of weak competition which might have suggested itself on an initial survey of the literature was the soft model of contractual relationship. The soft model's reliance on building a close and trusting alliance in which the purchaser persuades and helps the provider to comply with the contract seems to offer a way of achieving compliance without exit or exit threats. But the NHS data highlighted the fundamental flaw in this view. Providers tended to respond positively to persuasion only where they felt that the purchaser was a valuable customer whose requirements merited attention. The most obvious way for a purchaser to secure this status was to emphasize the possibility that it might take its business elsewhere if the provider did not comply. A purchaser might be able to persuade effectively even where exit is impossible: for example, a Next Steps agency might be concerned about the adverse publicity it might attract if it failed to meet its targets. But on the NHS evidence, the soft model seemed to work best where the purchaser had an underlying threat of exit.

NHS purchasers commonly opted for what was dubbed the 'intermediate' model of enforcement, in which they used sanctions other than exit to enforce their contracts. This might provide a useful model to be generalized to other internal contracts.[16] The NHS data suggested two key principles for purchasers to observe if their sanctions were to be effective. First, the sanction must appear to the provider as a significant harm. This point may seem obvious, but it was noticeable that in the NHS, purchasers' views of what counted as a tough sanction did not necessarily correspond to providers' perceptions. It might also be difficult to satisfy: a provider might refuse to sign a contract containing very harsh sanctions.[17] Secondly, the purchaser must be confident that the provider is to blame for the breach and can put it right. It was important to avoid using sanctions where they were unlikely to prompt compliance, because of the damage to relationships unsuccessful sanctions could cause.

---

[16] Of course, penalty clauses are not generally enforceable in private law (Treitel 1999), so some caution would be required in generalizing these findings beyond the case of unenforceable internal contracts.

[17] NHS providers usually had no choice but to contract with their local Health Authority, but some did refuse to contract with fundholders where they felt that their demands were unreasonable.

Observance of the principles of procedural fairness suggested in Chapter 7, particularly the principle of giving the provider a hearing before imposing a sanction, could help to reduce this risk. The provider may also be more inclined to agree to a contract including penalties where it feels assured that they will be fairly applied.

Conciliation and arbitration

The findings on conciliation seem, at first glance, to be the most NHS-specific aspect of the data. The other internal contracts discussed in Chapter 2 are not enforceable at all, so it is difficult to discern what general lessons might be derived from a *sui generis* dispute resolution mechanism. But the NHS experience deserves a closer look.

The NHS data suggested that one role for a dispute resolution mechanism—even an internal one—might be to help the parties to treat their contracts as binding. NHS managers were aware that (in addition to the absence of effective exit threats) there were no 'legal' sanctions for failing to comply with contracts. Moreover, even where conciliation was used, the regional offices' practice of awarding compromise solutions, rather than clear judgements on the merits, made the parties' agreement seem irrelevant. The findings confirmed the predictions made on this point in Chapter 3.

A further point that became apparent from the NHS data was the need for an accessible dispute resolution mechanism for the parties to a long-term contract, particularly where exit was not an option. This might be relevant in several contexts: agency framework documents, PSAs, and local authority contracts for which there is little external competition. As in the NHS, long-term relationships in these contexts could be soured by a dispute over one aspect of the delivery of a highly complex service.[18] An accessible dispute resolution mechanism might act as a safety-valve in such cases.[19] If both parties were willing to accept a third party's determination, they could then put the incident behind them and strive to rebuild their relationship. This does not necessarily mean that litigation is the answer: as Chapter 3 explained, the expense and formality of going

---

[18] Often, the breach might be insufficiently serious to justify termination of the contract: for example, where the term in question was one of a multitude of contractual quality standards.

[19] Note that the NHS conciliation system was also designed to act as just such a safety-valve during contract negotiations between parties who had no alternative but to agree a contract.

to court is problematic in itself, and the reluctance of contracting parties to litigate is well-documented (Beale and Dugdale 1975; Macaulay 1963). NHS managers did not want access to the courts but did suggest that easier access to conciliation would have been helpful:

We don't view conciliation and arbitration as setting us up as enemies . . . what it means is, the system has defeated us, we have nowhere else to go, we have tried every single thing we can try . . . and we need an outsider.

All the indications were that a permanent dispute resolution mechanism for internal contracts—provided that it was informal and approachable[20]—would be a desirable development.

Central pressure

It seems likely that 'central' pressure will always be a factor in internal contracts. It creates particular tensions in local government because of the potential for conflict with local accountability. But even internal contracts at the highest level in central government are bound to be influenced by Treasury financial norms, the possibility of NAO scrutiny, and accountability to Parliament (particularly Select Committees) for public services.

In the NHS, the fact that certain targets emanated from the upper echelons of the service helped purchasers to achieve agreement to them: providers were aware that they were non-negotiable. But central pressure increased the risk of cheating or creative compliance where providers found the standards difficult to achieve. Providers were tempted to conceal their breaches because they faced relatively harsh penalties whether or not they were at fault. One possible response to this would be to argue that it was acceptable to enforce the standards strictly because providers had agreed to them. But this argument is undermined by the fact that providers had no choice but to accept the standards during negotiations. At no stage did providers have a chance to explain that the standards might be, or were, impossible to meet.

One of the common responses to creative compliance is to draft standards more precisely in an attempt to close up loopholes. But in their study of accountancy regulation, McBarnet and Whelan (1991; 1997) make clear that regulators should resist the urge to do this. They argue that detailed standards offer *more* opportunities for creative interpretation and

---

[20] For an introduction to the large literature on ADR, see Freeman (1995); Smith (1996).

evasion. Instead, regulators should employ broad principles which are harder to twist and which are therefore more likely to catch deviant behaviour. In the NHS, however, the primary problem was not one of deviousness on the part of providers, but of the difficulty of meeting the required standards: many (though perhaps not all) providers would have complied had they been *able* to do so.

It therefore seems that the solution lies not in drafting, but in the negotiation and enforcement of the standards. If providers had been given the opportunity to explain poor performances—perhaps by including their excuses in the NHS Executive's published league tables—they might have been more willing to admit to breaches of the standards. Purchasers could then have engaged in debate with providers as to what could be done to improve their level of compliance. Of course, it would have been difficult for purchasers to evaluate providers' excuses, due to the problem of information asymmetry, but this seems to be a lesser evil than failing altogether to uncover breaches. Alternatively, purchasers and providers could have been permitted to negotiate the exact detail of the central standards, giving providers an opportunity to voice objections before agreeing to standards which could then be strictly enforced. Under either solution, there is a need for greater central flexibility: however important a particular standard may be, imposing it and enforcing it strictly may not be the best way to achieve compliance. Of course, cheating can never be entirely eliminated, but central flexibility could help to mitigate the problem.

Purchaser effort

It stands to reason that the amount of effort devoted to the accountability process by the caller to account will make a difference to its success. The enthusiastic and innovative caller to account is likely to achieve more than the indifferent conservative. But how can this be translated into practical recommendations?

The obvious difficulty is that effort is impossible to quantify. In theory, there must be an optimal effort level. In practice, however, it could not be said that a fundholder needed to invest a particular number of hours per week in the accountability process, employing the time in particular ways, in order to achieve optimal accountability. Nevertheless, there should be room for some debate, in any accountability process, as to whether that process is adequately resourced. In the NHS, for example, purchasers (particularly Health Authorities) were instructed to cut management costs and one of the ways in which they had done so was by reducing the number of staff employed to monitor quality standards. This limited the value of contracts as accountability processes for the quality of care delivered by providers. Perhaps this was an acceptable trade-off, but there should at least have been a debate about the accountability implications of the budget cuts.

In addition to the general need to resource accountability processes, the study highlighted a more particular point in relation to the resourcing of contractual accountability processes. There seems to be a tendency in contractual settings to assume that the bulk of the purchaser's effort should be devoted to the negotiation and drafting of the contract.[21] Once the contract is signed, the accountability process will be 'up and running' and will require much less attention. The reasons for this are both practical and political. Contract negotiation is perhaps a more precise, recognized skill than contract management. And by emphasizing that there is no need for intensive contract management, the government is able to highlight the administrative savings generated by contractualization (see, for example, NHSME 1990: para. 5.26). But the NHS experience suggested that it was wrong to neglect contract management. Securing compliance with the contract, particularly in a long-term relationship unaffected by competitive pressures, is a labour-intensive process. Contract *management* is a vital task.

It was also apparent from the NHS data that purchasers, particularly fundholders, varied widely in their skills and enthusiasm. It would have been unreasonable to expect all purchasers to be highly committed to the scheme. But there is much to be said for finding ways of sharing good practice. The Audit Commission made some effort to do this in the NHS and local government, and a similar role might be performed externally by the NAO, and internally by the Cabinet Office and the Treasury, in relation to central government. This would help to ensure that innovations which have been tried and tested by enthusiasts can then be employed by 'average' purchasers.

Access to information

Information asymmetry is a general problem in contractual relationships (see, generally, Williamson 1979). The provider of a product or service is likely to have much better information than the purchaser about costs, standards, performance and so on. The problem is exacerbated in

---

[21] For example, NHSME (1990), an early guidance document for NHS purchasers, is dominated by a discussion of the process of contract negotiation and issues of drafting.

internal contracts because many such contracts are for the provision of a service to third parties, members of the public, rather than to the purchaser itself. Monitoring is more difficult where the purchaser is not the client.

The hard and soft models suggest different ways of tackling the problem. Under the hard model, the purchaser should strive to check the information supplied by the provider. The NHS data showed that Health Authorities could use discussions with providers to tease out flaws and inconsistencies in written reports even though they did not have independent information. Purchasers could also employ expert assistance: the fundholding group in Area A had pooled resources in order to pay an information expert to scrutinize activity reports from providers. Under the soft model, the purchaser has no need of such checks because it is in a close relationship with the provider. Information is shared and the parties trust one another's honesty. This was a neat solution where it could be instituted successfully. Multiple 'monitoring' methods were as important as they were under the hard model, but for the purpose of building and maintaining the parties' close relationship, rather than as a way of checking up on the provider. But the real problem with both models is that they required an enormous investment of effort. In the NHS, this reduced the likelihood that any except the most enthusiastic purchasers would implement them to the full. It also made it impossible to state, on the NHS data, whether one model was more effective than the other.

Interestingly, it is not clear that access to information would have been any less problematic had the NHS market been more competitive. If providers had been threatened with the loss of their contracts, they might have been even more tempted to conceal information, particularly about breaches, from purchasers. Economic theory suggests that where the problem of information asymmetry is severe, it will be more efficient to integrate the purchaser and the provider into the same firm (Williamson 1979). It is hard to tell whether the problems encountered by NHS purchasers qualified as 'severe' for these purposes. Moreover, the problem of information asymmetry must be weighed against the advantages of market exchange which would be lost through vertical integration. The issue of whether the NHS was appropriate for contractual governance is beyond the scope of this study.

Conclusion

This study has identified several important recommendations which might help to promote effectiveness in contractual accountability processes:

- Where competition is weak, it is difficult to implement either the hard or the soft model to the full. To be effective, intermediate approaches need to employ sanctions which the provider perceives as significant, in cases in which the provider is clearly to blame for the breach and can put it right. But some caution is required: providers may refuse to sign contracts if the purchaser seeks to impose draconian enforcement measures.

- A dispute resolution mechanism may help to make contracts seem binding, and may render contracts more effective by addressing intractable disputes about aspects of compliance in long-term relationships.

- Central pressure on purchasers and providers to achieve particular targets needs to be moderated so that there is room for a debate about the possibility of meeting the targets. Otherwise, providers might be tempted to cheat.

- Effective accountability requires an investment of resources. In a contractual setting, this investment should apply to contract management as well as to contract negotiations. Purchasers should be encouraged to share good practice.

- Information asymmetry is difficult to address but *might* perhaps be mitigated by strategies suggested by the hard and soft models. Both strategies require heavy investments of effort by purchasers.

In conclusion, it is perhaps worth emphasizing the importance of ensuring that the caller to account in a contract can perform its functions effectively. NHS purchasers' experiences shaped their perceptions of what could be achieved through contracting. Those who had achieved much, through a combination of their own determination and favourable circumstances, were enthusiastic. One fundholder commented: 'Having the money does make a big difference, because . . . they have to understand that they are there to do a job for us, and that the patient doesn't live in hospital.' Not surprisingly, those whose experiences had been less favourable took a very different view. The following comment was from a lead GP who had little choice (for geographical reasons) but to contract with one of the least responsive providers in the sample:

If I were to go to the provider and say I want to contract in a certain way, they really can't handle that . . . so we don't really have to be very imaginative in terms of contracting, because it's a waste of time.

A failure to achieve the goals of accountability, because the caller to account lacks the required authority, may lessen that caller to account's willingness to work at the accountability process. This produces a vicious circle in which little effort is made and little is achieved. This is inevitably soul-destroying for those it affects, and leads to an obvious reduction in accountability. Effectiveness is too crucial to be left to chance.

9   Conclusions and Prospects

This chapter does not present a draft Internal Contracts Bill, ready for enactment. It does summarize the study's proposals for the regulation and enforcement of internal contracts through public law. But it is important to acknowledge that these proposals raise as many questions as they answer. One major question is the extent to which proposals based on experience in the NHS might be generalized to some or all of the other internal contract settings explored in Chapter 2. The second section of this chapter will address this question, drawing on the available empirical evidence and identifying issues in need of further investigation. There is also a much broader question of whether the study's proposals might be of relevance to some or all of the government's contracts with private parties, which were examined in Chapter 1. The third section of this chapter will briefly explore the empirical and theoretical aspects of this question. The chapter will conclude by setting out the research agenda arising from this study: this involves both testing the generalization of its results and refining and developing its approach.

Towards a public law of internal contracts

This study has attempted to show that the success of contractualization could be enhanced by creating a public law normative framework for internal contracts, based on the policy of using them as fair and effective mechanisms of accountability. This section summarizes the study's specific proposals for new norms, and revisits the arguments used to justify the choice of public law as the route for development.

The study's proposals

1. *The purchaser should give explicit consideration to the interaction between its contract and the other accountability processes applicable to the provider.*

Providers are invariably subject to mechanisms of accountability other than the purchaser's contract. It may be appropriate for the purchaser simply to duplicate these other mechanisms or, at the other extreme, to disregard certain issues in the contract because they are addressed through the other mechanisms. The study identified several factors relevant to the purchaser's decision:

- Does the other accountability process work effectively?
- If not, can the contract be used to reinforce or replace it?
- What are the savings to be made by relying on the other accountability process?
- Are the transaction costs involved in duplication or reinforcement justified by considerations of effectiveness?

If the other accountability process under consideration is a contract, two further factors are relevant to the purchaser's decision as to whether or not to join forces with other purchasers:

- Would bargaining power be increased by grouping together with other purchasers?
- Would a group approach unduly hamper the pursuit of issues of particular concern to the purchaser?

2. *The parties should reach a negotiated agreement about their respective roles and should attempt to behave consistently.*

Contracts do not offer a simple solution to the problem of defining the parties' roles: the purchaser may attempt to regulate the provider's activities in detail under either the hard or the soft model of contractual relationship. The parties should not be led to believe that there is an 'objective' definition of their roles, and should instead be encouraged to reach a negotiated agreement on the issue. Once such an agreement has been reached, the parties should act consistently. If the purchaser habitually collaborates with the provider or seeks to regulate its activities in detail, it should continue to do so even when faced with difficult problems. If the purchaser tends to leave the provider a large measure of discretion, it should continue to do so even if the provider appears to be performing poorly, unless enforcement action becomes necessary. And if the provider normally welcomes purchaser involvement, it should endeavour not to resist that involvement when problems arise. If the provider wishes to secure itself discretion on a particular issue, it should do so by negotiation.

3. *Effective delegation requires that purchasers should be given the time and the motivation to pursue issues of their own choosing in contracts.*

One of the claims made for contractualization in the NHS was that purchasers would be given some freedom to respond to local needs as well as being accountable to the centre for their purchasing activities. The study identified time and motivation as key factors in giving purchasers discretion and encouraging them to use it. Whether a purchaser has adequate time to pursue a particular issue is obviously difficult to determine. But although this factor cannot be used as the basis for a hard-edged rule, the government might take account of it if, for example, purchasers complained that they had insufficient time to pursue their own agenda.

Motivation is, however, more productive of specific norms. The study suggested three possible ways of encouraging purchasers to pursue local priorities:

- by relying on their own self-interest to introduce standards other than those set by the centre where those standards would make their lives easier in some way
- by using central accountability to require them to pursue some local priorities in their contracts
- by making them subject to an effective mechanism of accountability to the local community through which they could be called to account for their pursuit of local issues.

The last option seemed most appealing, but would require the development of norms to resolve clashes between central and local demands. More research is needed on this issue.

The requirements of transparency should also be observed in this context. In the NHS, purchasers had various formal indicia of autonomy, even though in practice their behaviour was heavily influenced by central requirements. Both purchasers and central government were accountable to patients and the public. But if outsiders cannot discern the respective responsibilities of purchasers and central government, they will not be able to call either to account. It is therefore essential that the relationship between purchasers and the centre should be transparent.

4. *Purchasers should observe the requirements of natural justice in their relationships with providers.*

(a) *Purchasers should respect the central value of consensus, except where the provider is objecting unreasonably to some aspect of the accountability process.*

Contracts derive their legitimacy from the fact that the parties consent to the obligations they impose. Suitable norms of fairness for contracts are therefore those which promote consensus in the parties' relationship. But effective accountability may override this norm in some circumstances. It requires (as Chapter 4 demonstrated) that the caller to account should have superior bargaining power, and should be able to impose standards on a provider in the public interest where that provider is being recalcitrant. The other norms of procedural fairness, described below, take effect subject to this principle.

(b) *Where the parties have a soft relationship, they should observe corresponding norms of procedural fairness:*

- collaborative negotiations (as far as the need for some purchaser domination allows); an obligation on both parties to share information during negotiations; no requirement to set out clear standards in advance (but no ban on doing so where the parties feel that clarity is desirable)
- an obligation on the provider to share information for the purposes of monitoring
- an obligation on the purchaser to take account of the provider's explanations and excuses at the enforcement stage, and to take joint responsibility with the provider for solving the problem which has led to the breach of standards

(c) *Where the parties have a hard relationship, they should observe corresponding norms of procedural fairness:*

- consultative negotiations with no deliberate concealment of relevant information; clear and precise standards set out in advance as a guide to conduct
- an obligation on the provider to supply relevant information on request for the purposes of monitoring
- an obligation on the purchaser to give advance warning of any sanctions to be applied, and to give the provider a hearing at which to offer its explanations and excuses

Where a contractual relationship straddles both models, it is important for the purchaser to observe two key fairness principles. One is that the issues to be dealt with in a hard way should be clearly separable from those to be dealt with in a soft way: in the NHS it was common for finance managers to use hard standards for finance issues, and for quality managers to use soft standards for quality issues, thus achieving separation by staff and subject-matter. The other is that the provider should be made aware of how standards are to be used: whether or not an excuse for a breach might be accepted, for example.

5. *The internal contracting system should be designed in such a way as to promote effectiveness.*

(a) *There should be an accessible mechanism for the resolution of the parties' disputes.*

This simple recommendation was ignored in the NHS with disastrous consequences. It contributed (together with the weakness of competitive pressures) to a general sense on the part of providers that contracts were not binding. And it meant that purchasers and providers had no way of resolving their disputes when circumstances trapped them into long-term relationships.

The concept of 'accessibility' suggests a number of subsidiary criteria, discussed in Chapter 3, which the dispute resolution mechanism should fulfil. First, no stigma should attach to its use. The parties should not be laid open to allegations that they have failed as managers if they are unable to resolve problems themselves, for example. Secondly, the mechanism should be cheap to use: one of the disadvantages of permitting litigation on internal contracts would be the costs it would inevitably involve. These costs would render the mechanism inaccessible to the parties and would expose them to criticism for wasting public funds. Thirdly, it should be informal and as non-adversarial as possible. Disputes are most likely to arise when the parties to an internal contract have no choice but to contract with one another. The mechanism should therefore be designed to *rebuild* relationships. Fourthly, the mechanism should be run by suitably qualified experts, since internal contracts may raise highly complex, polycentric issues. The NHS conciliation and arbitration scheme might provide a model here provided that the restrictions on access to the scheme were removed.

(b) *Central pressure on purchasers and providers to meet particular targets should admit of the possibility of debate about the practicalities of achieving those targets.*

The study showed that while central pressure could encourage providers to agree to standards, it tempted them to cheat if the standards could not be achieved. The imposition of standards on providers, without the possibility of debate, *both* during contract negotiations and during the life of the contract, was counterproductive.

(c) *Purchasers and providers should be given adequate resources to conduct the contractual accountability process.*

As with the discussion of adequate time above, it is difficult to quantify the precise resource needs of accountability. This principle cannot be hard-edged. But it does draw attention to the need for a debate about the costs of accountability. There can be no accountability without some investment, but there is little to commend an accountability process which costs more than the activity being accounted for. A balance must be struck between these two extremes. And in the contracting context, resources must be allocated to contract management as well as to the more obvious and glamorous task of contract negotiation. It is simply not the case that contracts can be 'left to run' once they have been signed.

6. *Purchasers should adopt strategies which are likely to maximize the effectiveness of their contracts as processes of accountability.*

In a competitive market, the hard and soft models suggest different strategies for enforcing the purchaser's requirements. The hard model involves an aggressive negotiating stance, and a willingness to move the contract to another provider if standards are not met. The soft model indicates a collaborative approach to negotiations and a persuasive approach to compliance, bolstered by underlying threats that the purchaser may move elsewhere if the provider undermines its trust. The models also suggest different strategies for overcoming the perennial problem of information asymmetry in contracts. Under the hard model, the purchaser cross-checks the provider's information against as many other sources as possible, particularly any which are independent of the provider. Under the soft model, the purchaser seeks to build a trusting relationship with the provider in which substantial amounts of information are shared. Because NHS purchasers did not, for the most part, contract in clearly competitive conditions, the present study did not gather sufficient data to comment on the relative efficacy of these two models. Further empirical research on this issue in other contexts might produce more specific recommendations.

The NHS study can, however, be used to suggest principles of effectiveness in less competitive market situations. Here, the best option is the intermediate model, in which the purchaser uses sanctions other than exit—such as penalty clauses or partial exit—in order to enforce its requirements. This model could be effective when it was used carefully, with regard to the following principles:

- the sanction must be perceived as significant by the provider; otherwise it may be ignored
- but the purchaser must not seek to use too draconian a sanction because the provider might refuse to sign the contract
- the purchaser must ensure that the provider is to blame for the breach and can put it right before applying the sanction; otherwise the penalty will fail to achieve compliance and the provider will resent its imposition.

Of course, it may be difficult to determine whether or not the provider is to blame for a breach, but the purchaser should at least put in place a fair procedure—a hearing or an obligation on the provider to offer written explanations—to help it to make an accurate judgement.

It was also possible for purchasers to improve their bargaining positions through their own efforts, in some circumstances. More skilled NHS purchasers were able to combine a tactical use of penalty clauses with a considerable investment of effort in the soft model in order to get providers to pay attention to their requirements. If more effective measures had been taken to share good practice among different purchasers, others might have been able to replicate these successes.

The underlying assumptions revisited

These proposals have been developed on the basis of two key assumptions: that regulation and enforcement are appropriate concepts for internal contracts, and that public law might be a fruitful source of ideas for new norms. Both these assumptions were defended in theoretical terms in Chapter 3; here they will be reassessed in the light of the empirical evidence.

Regulation and enforcement might seem inappropriate if internal contracts were viewed as symbolic statements of the government's aspirations for public services. No real consequences would flow from a provider's failure to comply with them, nor would there be any restrictions on a purchaser's ability to alter their terms. It was suggested in Chapter 3 that this argument did not accord with the reformers' original intentions, nor did it provide a satisfactory *ex post* interpretation of the reforms, particularly given the cost of implementing them.

The empirical evidence reinforced the view that this argument was misplaced. Most of the managers interviewed during the course of the study did not perceive NHS contracts as purely aspirational documents. Purchasers in particular acknowledged that contracts would not always be met or enforced, but they behaved in ways which suggested that they expected contracts to be binding. They tried to agree standards which were realistic for providers, they were disappointed when providers did not meet the standards and did not offer a reasonable excuse, and they were frustrated when they could not enforce standards against 'recalcitrant' providers. It might, of course, be argued that this proves nothing: that the interviewees were simply responding to the market rhetoric which accompanied the reforms and would have acted differently if the contracts had been presented as symbolic documents. But although this might have lessened their sense of frustration, it still seems problematic as a solution. It would not have made contracts any more effective at changing behaviour: indeed, by reducing managers' expectations of what could be achieved through contracting, it might have weakened contracts still further. And it is even more difficult to see how the expenditure of time and energy on the contracting process (which the study found to be quite considerable) could be justified for the purposes of symbolism. Given that staff were willing to adopt some of the attitudes associated with a contracting system, it was unfortunate that the government did not reciprocate by implementing that system more fully.

As Chapter 3 explained, there were two possible routes for the regulation and enforcement of internal contracts: public law or private law. Relationships between public bodies are normally regulated by public law, but contractual relationships involving the government are normally regulated by private law with a small body of supplementary public law rules. The choice of route was therefore far from straightforward. Since the study was not designed to compare the public and private law routes, it is not possible to *resolve* this debate here. But the empirical evidence supported the choice of public law in two significant ways.

First, the evidence showed that the problems predicted in Chapter 3 did materialize in practice. Purchasers and providers did need an accessible mechanism for the resolution of their disputes. Purchasers did need the power to penalize providers for failing to comply with their contracts. And providers needed the protection offered by the norms of natural justice. It was argued in Chapter 3 that public law seemed to have significant advantages over private law in dealing with these problems. If the data had shown that the problems did not occur in practice, the attractions of the public law solution would have been greatly reduced. But in fact the opposite was the case.

Secondly, the NHS data identified some other problems faced by the contracting parties for which it is difficult to imagine private law solutions. One such problem was that of 'contract compliance': the extent to which the government should use its contracts to reinforce other mechanisms of accountability. In private law, the purposes for which a contract is used, and the terms it contains, are primarily a matter for agreement between the parties. The courts have various powers to strike down terms which are unfair, but since these powers are intended to protect consumers confronted with standard form contracts, it seems unlikely that they would be readily applicable to internal contract settings. Public law, by contrast, is more willing to control the purposes for which the government acts.

The doctrine of improper purposes permits a comparison of the reason for giving the government a particular power, with its use in a particular instance. It is true that the precedents for the use of this power in contracting contexts offer only limited encouragement to the advocates of contract compliance,[1] but this could be remedied by clear statutory guidance on what should count as a 'proper purpose' in contracting. Public law is also able to control the factors taken into account by public bodies through the doctrine of 'irrelevant considerations'. As Chapter 6 explained, this would provide a way of ensuring that purchasers engaged in a cost–benefit analysis of the use of contract compliance in particular instances. Thus, although a public law of contract would require considerable development, the general principles of public law do at least act as suitable doctrinal pegs on which to hang more specific norms.

More fundamentally, this study has tackled the central methodological problem identified in Chapter 3. Public and private law approaches to internal contracts could not easily be compared because the public law approach was much less well defined than the private law approach. But the study has now given considerable content to the notion of a public law of internal contracts. It cannot claim to be comprehensive: it has drawn only on accountability as its guiding policy. Nonetheless, it has provided a firmer foundation for comparisons. The idea of public law rules for internal contracts can no longer be dismissed simply by saying that it is too vague even to be discussed.

Wider implications 1: internal contracts

Any attempt to generalize empirical findings must inevitably be speculative. It cannot be claimed that research on other internal contracts would necessarily yield the same results as did research on NHS contracts. But it is possible to review the available evidence on other internal contracts in order to suggest issues which warrant further investigation. The discussion will focus on framework documents in Next Steps and local authority contracts under CCT, because it is possible to draw on published empirical studies of these areas. As yet there is little evidence on PSAs or on the extent to which 'best value' has brought about changes in local authority internal contracting.

The investigation in Chapter 6 of the division of roles between purchasers and providers was prompted by the Next Steps literature. This

---

[1] *R v Lewisham LBC, ex p. Shell*, 1988 1 All ER 938.

literature, discussed in detail in Chapter 3, suggested that—given the experience with the nationalized industries—ministers would not respect the autonomy of agencies, and would instead interfere in 'operational' matters. The NHS study identified a rather different version of this issue. Sometimes purchasers' interference was unwelcome because it suggested a lack of trust in the provider to resolve a problem; at other times purchasers' unwillingness to become involved was resented because it suggested a desire to avoid helping with difficult issues.

One question raised by these findings is whether the problem in the Next Steps context was one of constant interference or selective interference. It is difficult to judge on the available evidence. At least some agencies appear to have acquired a substantial degree of independence. The practice of allowing agency chief executives to answer written parliamentary questions (Evans 1995) has limited one opportunity for ministerial involvement in agency affairs. But commentators agree that the key issue in agency independence is the extent to which the agency's work is politically sensitive (Greer 1994; Zifcak 1994). Greer (1994: 88) gives the interesting example of ministerial involvement in the apparently operational issue of the design of local social security offices, because staff safety and client privacy were politically controversial. Some major agencies—the Prison Service, for example[2]—may be politically sensitive all or most of the time; others may become politically sensitive from time to time when problems arise or political priorities change. This suggests that some agencies may experience constant interference, and others may experience the NHS problem of selective interference. This issue would certainly warrant further investigation.

In local authority contracting, there was some evidence of the constant interference predicted by the Next Steps literature. Some contracts, particularly for 'blue-collar' services, were highly detailed and prescriptive. Vincent-Jones (1994*b*: 222–3) describes a contract for building cleaning in which different tasks (polishing, mopping and so on) were described in minute detail for different types of surface. But this might not hold for all contracts: those for 'white-collar' professional services, such as legal and personnel work, might be more analogous to NHS contracts. Given the complex, professional nature of the work, the contract might focus on finance and process standards rather than substantive standards about the service itself (see Walsh *et al.* 1997: 64). Again, this would create risks

---

[2] On which see Foster and Plowden (1996); House of Commons Public Service Committee (1996).

of selective rather than continual interference. Local authority contracts also involve a further element of complexity because of the potential for 'interference' from elected members as well as from the officers concerned with the day-to-day management of the contract. It appears that some DSOs welcomed the opportunity to shelter behind their contracts in order to avoid interference (which might result in unjustified preferential treatment for areas represented by more vocal members), but members resented any attempt to use contractualization to make it difficult for them to address their constituents' grievances (Walsh *et al.* 1997: 128–39). This raises a further possibility of selective interference.

Another striking feature of the NHS data presented in Chapter 6 was the extent to which purchasers' actions were dominated by centrally determined priorities, despite a rhetoric of delegation to the local level. It seems likely that this issue would also be significant in relation to local government. Walsh *et al.* (1997: 64) comment: 'In most of our case study sites, there were tensions between the way that the authorities concerned wanted to approach contracting and the constraints imposed on their actual approach . . . as a result of the highly prescriptive framework for contracting for local government services.' Their study identifies at least two problems. First, because of the need to be fair to all bidders, authorities were forced to introduce relatively formal purchaser/provider splits. This made it difficult to maintain trusting relationships with DSOs where they won contracts. Secondly, in order to prevent accusations that they had favoured the DSO, authorities felt obliged to award contracts to private providers who offered a cheaper price even if the difference in bids was slight and there were doubts about the quality of the private provider's service.

These difficulties arose because of the stringent *process* constraints placed on authorities by the CCT legislation. Interestingly, the new 'best value' regime relaxes these constraints—by removing the element of overt compulsion—but appears to impose significant *substantive* constraints. As Chapter 2 explained, one of the four elements in the five-yearly best value service reviews[3] is a comparison of the service against local and national performance indicators.[4] National service standards are not new in local government—under CCT the Audit Commission produced annual league tables of authorities' services—but under best value, the national service standards are much more fully integrated into the legislative scheme.

---

[3] 1999 Act, s. 5; Local Government (Best Value) Performance Plans and Reviews Order 1999 (SI 1999/3251), Article 5.

[4] 1999 Act, s. 4; Local Government (Best Value) Performance Indicators Order 2000.

This raises the possibility—obviously requiring further research—that local government internal contracting under best value could become as heavily dominated by central priorities as was NHS contracting. This would not sit comfortably with authorities' democratic accountability to the local electorate.

At the most general level, the NHS study's findings on relationships and fairness are likely to be relevant to all internal contracts. In local government, it might have been expected that internal contractualization would result in soft relationships, because the parties' contracts would be relatively long-term and they would have prior personal relationships. In practice, however, the position was more complex, as it was in the NHS. Authorities tended to draft their contracts relatively strictly, in case the tendering process resulted in the award of the contract to a private provider with which they did not have an established, trusting relationship (Walsh *et al.* 1997: 135). If the authority then tried to invoke the strict terms of the contract against the DSO, it might set off a 'low-trust spiral'[5] in the relationship (Vincent-Jones 1997: 157–9). This suggests that the NHS study's proposals about how to behave fairly when mixing the hard and soft models—for example, by ensuring that the provider understood which elements of the contract would be strictly applied and which were subject to negotiation—might be of assistance in this context too.

More generally, the NHS study also suggested principles of fairness to apply to relationships at the hard and soft extremes. There was evidence of both types of relationship in other internal contracts. In local government, much seemed to depend upon the way in which the authority separated the purchaser and provider functions internally. Vincent-Jones (1997: 154) found that high levels of trust and co-operation (resulting in soft relationships) could be maintained where purchasers and providers either remained within the same department or had at least some common managerial structures. Where authorities had tried to introduce a formal separation of the two roles, conflicts tended to arise because the parties were tempted to behave opportunistically rather than to work collaboratively towards shared goals. On the available data it is difficult to tell exactly how the parties behaved towards one another under either the soft or hard models in this context, but the very presence of the models suggests that the NHS study's principles of procedural fairness might well have some application.

---

[5] The terminology originates with Fox (1974).

The effectiveness of any particular internal contract is pre-eminently a matter for empirical investigation. But the various factors identified on the basis of the NHS data might provide a good starting-point for that enquiry. Internal contracts vary, as noted in Chapter 2, in the extent to which they take place in a competitive market. Public Service Agreements may contain a competitive element, as departments seek a larger slice of the funding 'cake'. In local government, contracts are in theory awarded after a competitive process, but in practice, there may be little or no competition for some contracts. And agency framework agreements may be negotiated in the absence of any genuine competition for the agency's functions. Some of the effectiveness problems attributable to lack of competition might therefore arise in other internal contracts too.

In the NHS, various types of self-help strategies (most commonly, penalty clauses) were used in an attempt to encourage providers to comply with their contracts. This possibility has been explicitly excluded in relation to PSAs: they are intended to fit the soft rather than the intermediate model. But self-help strategies do feature in other contexts. Even in CCT, the element of competitive pressure was periodic rather than constant, so authorities found it necessary to use penalties to ensure that contractors met quality standards during the life of the contract. For example, deductions might be made from a DSO's monthly fee if its work failed the authority's inspections (Vincent-Jones 1994*b*: 224). The NHS study's recommendations on the fair and effective use of penalties might be of assistance here. In some contracts, authorities collected relatively robust information about default by conducting their own inspections (accompanied by a contractor representative) (Vincent-Jones 1994*b*: 224). In others, authorities' monitoring was less effective: allowing individual schools to decide whether or not rooms were being kept clean did not provide sufficiently objective data on which to base the application of penalties (Walsh *et al.* 1997: 135). Thus, this study's proposal that purchasers should investigate the circumstances—usually by giving the provider a hearing—before levying penalties might be relevant.

One of the points of contrast (noted in Chapter 2) between NHS contracts and other internal contracts was that the NHS regime made provision for arbitration in the event of a dispute. In practice, the possibility of arbitration made little difference to the parties' behaviour: they were strongly discouraged from using the mechanism. Interestingly, there is some evidence of a similarly negative approach to dispute resolution in local government. Vincent-Jones (1994*b*) explains that disputes in internal CCT contracts were arbitrated either by senior officers within the local authority or by a third party if they were particularly serious. But his case-study authority was beginning to discourage arbitration, perceiving the process to be costly and time-consuming (Vincent-Jones 1994*b*: 225). The NHS data suggests that this strategy is questionable: where the parties have a genuine dispute, it may be better to give them an accessible means of resolving that dispute and rebuilding a trusting relationship.

It is important to emphasize the point made at the outset: that the NHS findings have no *automatic* relevance to other internal contracts. But the available evidence suggests that the proposals made on the basis of the NHS findings might be more widely applicable. They might indeed form the basis for a public law regime for internal contracts as a group. Further research on this issue is urgently required.

Wider implications 2: external contracts

This book's proposals for public law norms for internal government contracts raise the wider question of whether or not the government's *external* contracts with private firms should be the subject of a similar public law regime. Obviously, this issue is too complex to be resolved here, but it is worthy of some consideration in order to identify the broader research agenda arising from this study. Two key issues must be explored: whether the parties to external government contracts might encounter similar problems to those identified for NHS contracts, and if so, whether it might be appropriate to use public law to address those problems.

Practical relevance

Space precludes an exhaustive survey to test the relevance of the NHS proposals to all the various types of external contract described in Chapter 1. Instead, this section will explore a handful of examples in procurement and PFI to which this study's proposals do seem to have some application. There are bound to be numerous counter-examples: Chapter 2 identified various ways in which internal contracts might differ from their private law counterparts. Thus, the argument in this section is not that the NHS proposals would fit all external contracts; rather, it is that there is some evidence to suggest that further research on this issue might be warranted.

It was argued in Chapter 6 that purchasers should consider whether their contractual accountability process was likely to result in the duplication of other accountability mechanisms, contractual or otherwise. If so, they should assess the balance of advantages between saving time and instituting their own accountability process on a particular issue. These principles are currently of considerable relevance to procurement in central government. Procurement has traditionally been delegated to departments. This means that even supplies which are required by all or most departments—utilities, for example—are purchased separately. The recent Gershon Review (HM Treasury 1999*b*) found that some departments paid up to 66 per cent more for electricity and 140 per cent more for gas than those departments which had secured the best prices. The Review therefore recommended the creation of the Office of Government Commerce (OGC), with various responsibilities including that of procuring supplies on behalf of several departments where their requirements can be aggregated. Departments will continue to conduct their own procurement where their requirements are more specialized, though they will be obliged to follow a common procurement process (designed by OGC) when doing so. Aggregation has two advantages: it avoids the unnecessary duplication of effort inherent in several departments negotiating separately on price and quality standards, and it enables the government to obtain better value for money by enhancing its bargaining power. These are exactly the advantages secured by the use of fundholding groups, and to some extent, 'host' purchasing arrangements, in the NHS.

In Chapter 7, issues of procedural fairness were considered. Interestingly, although the government's procurement and PFI guidance does address procedures for contract negotiation and management, it does not focus explicitly on procedural *fairness* (see, for example, HM Treasury 1997*a*; Treasury Taskforce (undated)). Nonetheless, there are indications that the study's proposals would be of relevance. The hard and soft models used in the NHS study were derived from the more general socio-legal literature on contractual relationships between businesses (Fox 1974; Macneil 1974; Sako 1992). The likelihood that government contracts would give rise to a similar range of relationships is confirmed by guidance on contract management (HM Treasury 1997*a*: para. 4.5) which sets out two extremes, labelling them 'partnership' and 'distant relationship'. The choice between the extremes is said to be governed by factors similar to those identified in the socio-legal literature (for example, Williamson 1979), such as the nature of the relationship and the ease of measuring performance. Moreover, the guidance indicates that the two extremes denote different types of behaviour during the contracting process. For example, a contrast is drawn between an 'open' management style in which the provider shares its cost information and the purchaser discloses its budget, and a 'formal' management style in which the parties are reluctant to share this information (HM Treasury 1997*a*: 4.14). This links closely with the procedural fairness principles suggested on the basis of the NHS data: where the parties have a soft relationship, they should be willing to hold information in common; where the relationship is hard, they should at least respond to reasonable requests for information.

Perhaps even more significantly, there is a strong suggestion in the PFI guidance in particular that many of the government's contractual relationships will, in practice, be mixed or intermediate (Treasury Taskforce (undated)). The guidance acknowledges that PFI relationships are long-term, and that a 'partnership' approach is most likely to ensure the contract's continuing success: 'The aim should therefore be to establish a relationship in which both sides are open, share information fully and work together to solve problems' (Treasury Taskforce (undated): para. 3.1.8). Nevertheless, the guidance also makes clear that the purchaser's primary goal is to secure compliance with the contract, insisting on its strict contractual rights where appropriate (Treasury Taskforce (undated): para. 2.1.1). This indicates the adoption of an approach which is not wholly soft: despite the general emphasis on trusting relationships, the government reserves its right to use contractual sanctions in the event of significant breaches. Thus, the principles of procedural fairness developed for mixed or intermediate relationships in the NHS might be of some assistance. For example, it was suggested on the basis of the NHS data that purchasers should ensure that contractors knew which standards might be applied in a hard way without any negotiation, and that contractors were given a hearing before sanctions were used. Both these suggestions might help PFI purchasers to maintain the delicate balance between partnership and insistence on their contractual rights.

In Chapter 8, several important recommendations were made concerning the effectiveness of internal contracts. At first sight, it seems that these recommendations are unlikely to be of relevance to external contracts: it is generally assumed that the government has superior bargaining power. As Chapter 1 noted, for example, the government is able to use its contracts to pursue non-commercial ends because contractors are willing to sign up to a range of terms in order to secure lucrative government business. But on closer inspection, it is clear that the government does not always obtain the performance it requires from its contracting partners.

One major problem is delay. The most recent NAO annual report on defence procurement found that most projects were not expected to enter service on the date planned (NAO 2000*b*: 8–11). Improvements in the procurement process itself might address some problems: ensuring that agreements to collaborate with other countries to develop new weapons are robust before the project begins, for example. But two-thirds of the total delay reported is caused by technical problems: the inability of the contractor to deliver the promised solution on time (NAO 2000*b*: 10). The government seems to lack any effective means of forcing the contractor to comply with the agreed timetable. But delay is not the only problem: in extreme cases, government projects may fail altogether. The contract to develop a Benefits Payment Card and associated computer systems had to be cancelled because the project fell behind schedule and those elements which were delivered did not meet the purchaser's requirements (see, generally, NAO 2000*a*). The NAO identified a number of flaws in the purchaser's strategy. For example, the purchaser could have done more to require bidders to demonstrate their competence before the contract was awarded (NAO 2000*a*: 9). More generally, however, the collapse of the deal illustrates the weakness of the government's position: when the government tried to claim that the contractor was in breach, the contractor responded by demanding a higher price and a longer timetable than those agreed in the contract (NAO 2000*a*: 27).

The NAO's role in improving value for money inevitably leads it to emphasize the various steps purchasers could take in order to engage in more effective procurement. But the NAO's proposals do not address the underlying problem: the weakness of the government's bargaining power. Once a complex, long-term contract has been awarded, the government may become dependent on the supplier: it is difficult to change to another IT provider once new software is partially installed. As a result, the supplier may be tempted to invest minimal effort in the performance of the contract. Moreover, this problem may affect contractors' behaviour at the tendering stage. They may make over-ambitious claims in order to win the contract, knowing that they will not be subject to effective pressure if they fail to live up to those claims during the life of the contract.

In the NHS, purchasers employed various kinds of contractual sanctions to address problems of compliance with their long-term contracts. This approach is also used in external government contracts: the monthly payment in PFI contracts usually contains a number of performance-related elements, so that the contractor only receives the full amount if the facilities are available and fully maintained (HM Treasury 1997*b*: para. 3.20). But the NHS data highlighted some of the problems with this approach.

If the contractor did not perceive the sanction as significant, or could not easily put the breach right, the sanction would be ineffective and might cause considerable damage to relationships. These points might help the government to make more effective use of intermediate sanctions in other contexts.

But there are two caveats. First, as noted in Chapter 3, the government's use of sanctions in external contracts is constrained by the common law distinction between penalties and liquidated damages. In effect, a clause which cannot be construed as a genuine pre-estimate of a party's likely losses will not be legally enforceable (see, generally, Treitel 1999: 929–37). This may limit the government's ability to use sanctions which are perceived by the provider as a significant harm. Chapter 3 suggested that it might be appropriate to relax these restrictions in the special circumstances of government contracts. Secondly, NHS contracts differed from the procurement contracts described above because they were not, for the most part, *awarded* under competitive conditions. This made it easier for purchasers to secure agreement to penalty clauses. But where private firms are able to sell their services to other purchasers, the government may need to be cautious: excessively harsh penalties may make firms reluctant to accept government business.

To sum up, the NHS study's findings do not seem to be wholly at odds with what is known about at least some external government contracts. This does not mean that they would necessarily fit all such contracts: they might not be relevant to contracts of employment or 'contracts' with regulatory bodies, for example. Indeed, one crucial issue for further research is the extent to which it is appropriate to consider external contracts as a single category. Moreover, of course, the suggestions made in this section are speculative and require confirmation through empirical research. But they do at least indicate that this research might be worth conducting.

The theoretical obstacles

Even if it could be established empirically that some or all of the norms suggested here would be of assistance in regulating some or all external government contracts, there would still be a number of theoretical obstacles to be overcome before a public law of contract could be developed. Some of these obstacles will be mapped out here because they form an important part of the research agenda arising from this study. Space precludes a detailed analysis of their merits.

The internal contracts which have been the main focus of this study are not currently enforceable in public or private law. Advocates of reform are therefore faced with a relatively simple choice between the two. As Chapter 3 explained, the public law solution is attractive, given that both parties are in the public sector; that it may be possible to develop a more suitable normative framework through the creative application of public law; and that enforcement through the courts would be inappropriate. But external contracts are, for the most part, enforceable in private law, supplemented only to a limited extent by public law doctrines. The choice between public and private law regulation of government contracts is therefore raised in a much more stark and controversial form in relation to external contracts. As Chapter 1 explained, the question is not simply which mode of development offers the most interesting creative possibilities, but also where to locate the public/private divide.

Dicey (1885) famously argued that private law was the best means of protecting the ordinary citizen against the excesses of the government. Any special system of public law would inevitably grant privileges to public officials. Some modern writers, notably Harlow (1980), oppose the development of a public law of contract on this ground. Some aspects of this study's proposals might be vulnerable to this objection. It was argued that the parties to internal contracts should not be given the option of taking cases to court but should have access to an ADR mechanism. This suggestion might be of relevance to external contracts: litigation on such contracts is rare (Turpin 1989) and is avoided by various forms of negotiation and arbitration which might usefully be merged into a single forum. But this would involve removing (as far as possible) contractors' *existing* rights of access to the courts. This might at least give the appearance of privileging the government: it might be difficult to persuade contractors that the forum was sufficiently impartial to protect their interests.[6] Other aspects of this study's proposals do, however, meet the concern about privilege. The argument that carefully tailored natural justice norms should be extended to all stages of contract negotiation and management would offer significant protection to contractors. It demonstrates that there is no *inevitable* link between a public law solution and privileges for the government: the issue depends entirely on the content and design of the public law regime.

---

[6] In order to comply with the Human Rights Act 1998, it would be essential to ensure that the mechanism was an 'independent and impartial tribunal established by law' within Article 6 of the European Convention on Human Rights.

Another theoretical obstacle to the development of public law rules for external contracts might be dubbed the *O'Reilly v Mackman*[7] problem. The *O'Reilly* case brought the very concept of public law into disrepute among some commentators because of its clumsy attempt to turn the application for judicial review into an exclusively public law procedure (see, for example, Allison 1996: 90–100; Oliver 1999: 71–93). It resulted in a large body of boundary-mapping litigation, as the courts struggled to classify cases as 'public' or 'private' and as litigants sought to use the procedure which offered them the greatest number of tactical advantages (see, generally, Craig 1999: 754–83). If a body of special public law rules existed for contracts, similar problems would arise.

The internal contracts discussed in this book were relatively easy to classify because they each formed part of a specific programme of contractualization within the public sector: best value, Next Steps and so on. Problems of classification are not, however, inconceivable even in this context. For example, if the government concluded an agreement with a self-regulatory organization, it might be arguable that this agreement should be treated as an internal contract if the self-regulatory organization could be classified as a public body.[8] The internal contracts arbitrator would need to decide whether to extend the regime to agreements outside recognized contractualization programmes, and if so, on what criteria. External contracts raise more difficult problems of classification, for two reasons. First, the contract in question would not necessarily form part of a recognized contracting 'programme', of the type encountered within the public sector. As a result, the public or private nature of the contract would probably be made to turn solely on the classification of the purchaser[9] as public or private. English law contains several different tests for determining whether or not a body counts as 'public': under the European public procurement regime,[10] under European Union law more generally,[11] under the Human Rights

---

[7] 1983 2 AC 237.

[8] As noted in Ch. 1, the courts have classified some self-regulatory organizations as public for the purposes of judicial review: *R v Panel on Take-overs and Mergers, ex p. Datafin*, 1987 QB 815. But not all self-regulatory organizations are so classified: see, for example, *R v Disciplinary Committee of the Jockey Club, ex p. Aga Khan*, 1993 1 WLR 909. For discussion, see Craig (1999: 774–8).

[9] In some circumstances, public bodies may provide services to the private sector, but their role is usually that of purchaser.

[10] See, for example, r. 3 of the Public Supply Contracts Regulations 1995 (SI 1995/201).

[11] The leading case (in the context of the direct effect of directives) is *Foster v British Gas* (ECJ Case C–188/89), 1990 ECR 3313.

Act 1998[12] and for the purposes of judicial review in domestic law (on which see Craig 1999: 754–83). All these tests are notoriously uncertain in their application. Secondly, uncertainty as to the applicable law would be particularly unattractive to private firms. Despite the prospect of lucrative government business, many firms would be unwilling to take the risk of additional litigation on the applicable law in the event of a dispute.[13] Within the public sector, where profits are not at stake, such uncertainty would be inconvenient but not prohibitively so. Again, however, these problems may not be insoluble. One option, which has some practical appeal even if it is intellectually unsatisfying, would be to enact a statutory list (following the example of the Parliamentary Commissioner Act 1967) of the bodies whose contracts were subject to public law rules. Of course, the content of the list would have to be determined, but this would be a matter for Parliament rather than for contractors and public bodies themselves.

An argument in favour of public law norms for external government contracts would be highly controversial. It would need to be supported by empirical evidence as to the types of problem, if any, encountered by the parties to these contracts, and specific proposals as to how public law rules might solve those types of problem. Its proponents would need to demonstrate that public law offered better options for norms and for enforcement than did private law. And they would need to find ways of overcoming objections: demonstrating that their proposals did not simply privilege the government over contractors, and defining the scope of application of those proposals. None of these tasks are simple. But they raise fundamental issues about the development of a modern, comprehensive body of public law, and about the crucial distinction between public and private law. Further research on these issues would be of considerable significance.

The way forward

The research agenda arising from this study has five significant components. The first two, discussed in this chapter, use the NHS data as the

---

[12] Section 6 of the Act appears to distinguish between public bodies, all of whose functions are covered by the Act, and private bodies performing public functions, whose public functions are covered by the Act. As yet it is unclear how the courts will apply this distinction (see, generally, Craig 1999: 563–7).

[13] The importance of certainty in this area is illustrated by the enactment of the Local Government (Contracts) Act 1997 in response to the decision in *Crédit Suisse v Allerdale BC*, 1997 QB 306.

starting-point for further empirical research. One involves testing the NHS proposals for their applicability to other internal contracts, in order to determine whether or not they would provide a suitable basis for an Internal Contracts Act. The second is an investigation of the possibility that the study's findings might have a wider relevance to the government's external contracts with private firms.

The other three components develop and supplement this book's methodology. It has focused on one guiding policy within public law: the development of contracts as fair and effective mechanisms of accountability from provider to purchaser. The third component of the research agenda is therefore the application of other public law principles and policies to internal contracts. For example, the doctrine of legitimate expectations might be used to give members of the public a right to be consulted before the terms of an internal contract could be changed by the parties. Fourthly, further research is required to test this study's choice of public law as the best source of norms for internal contracts. The proposals provide a useful forum for debate between those who advocate the maintenance and development of a distinctive body of public law, and those who emphasize the extent to which public law shares the same values as private law. Fifthly, there is a need for comparative work. Contractualization is not unique to the UK. Different versions of the 'new public management' manifested themselves in many developed countries. It may therefore be possible to learn from the ways in which other legal systems regulate and enforce internal contracts.

A sceptic might ask whether this body of research would have any practical value. Internal contracts (and, to a considerable extent, external contracts) are a sphere of substantial discretion for the government. However attractive the substantive proposals, no government is likely to volunteer for legal regulation unless it is placed under considerable pressure to do so. Moreover, it is not clear where such pressure might come from: the parties to internal contracts are all in some sense 'governmental' bodies and are unlikely to press for change. And although Parliament, through Select Committees in particular, has expressed concern about contractualization, it has not considered the possibility of solving the policy's problems through legal regulation. But this is precisely why there is a need for further academic work on government by contract. A lively debate in the literature should produce detailed, robust proposals which might in turn engender a debate among policy-makers.

To advocate further work on a normative framework for government contracts is not, of course, to say that contractualization as a policy should command unquestioning approval. Many commentators have drawn attention to its shortcomings. Its emphasis on the setting of performance targets may lead to a focus on quantifiable issues which fail to take account of the complexities of public service provision. Its emphasis on enterprise and competition may undermine the public service ethos among staff, reducing their commitment to public interest values and increasing opportunities for excessive risk-taking and even fraud. But contractualization policies, both internal and external, have been adopted and developed by governments of *both* main political parties. This makes it difficult to imagine the abandonment of government by contract: it is clearly no longer the preserve of Conservative administrations. Since contractualization is apparently here to stay, drawing attention to its weaknesses is no longer enough. A new kind of scholarship is needed: one which accepts the inevitability of contractualization and makes positive and detailed proposals for reform.

This book has been a first attempt to meet that need. It has developed a public law framework for the regulation and enforcement of internal contracts as fair and effective mechanisms of accountability. It has also identified a challenging agenda for future research. Internal government contracts are now a major mode of policy implementation and service delivery. Many of the anxieties caused by their increasingly innovative and widespread use are attributable to the weakness of the surrounding legal regime. Not everyone will agree with this book's proposals for reform. But if they inspire a lively debate, the book will have succeeded.

Bibliography

ADLER, P. A., and ADLER, P. (1994), 'Observational Techniques', in Denzin and Lincoln (1994).

ALLEN, P. (1995), 'Contracts in the National Health Service Internal Market', *Modern Law Review*, 58: 321–42.

ALLISON, J. W. F. (1996), *A Continental Distinction in the Common Law: a Historical and Comparative Perspective on English Public Law* (Oxford: Clarendon Press).

ALLSOP, J., and MULCAHY, L. (1996), *Regulating Medical Work: Formal and Informal Controls* (Buckingham: Open University Press).

ARROWSMITH, S. (1992), *Civil Liability and Public Authorities* (Winteringham, South Humberside: Earlsgate).

—— (1996), *The Law of Public and Utilities Procurement* (London: Sweet & Maxwell).

—— (1997), 'The Way Forward or a Wrong Turning?: An Assessment of European Community Policy on Public Procurement in Light of the Commission's Green Paper', *European Public Law*, 3: 389–411.

ASHBURNER, L., and CAIRNCROSS, L. (1993), 'Membership of the "New Style" Health Authorities: Continuity or Change?', *Public Administration*, 71: 357–75.

ATIYAH, P. S. (1986), *Essays on Contract* (Oxford: Clarendon Press).

AUDIT COMMISSION (1995), *Briefing on GP Fundholding* (London: HMSO).

—— (1996), *What the Doctor Ordered: a Study of GP Fundholders in England and Wales* (London: HMSO).

AYRES, I., and BRAITHWAITE, J. (1992), *Responsive Regulation: Transcending the Deregulation Debate* (Oxford: Oxford University Press).

BALDWIN, R., and CAVE, M. (1999), *Understanding Regulation: Theory, Strategy and Practice* (Oxford: Oxford University Press).

—— and MCCRUDDEN, C. (1987), *Regulation and Public Law* (London: Weidenfeld & Nicolson).

BAMBERG, G., and SPREMANN, K. (eds.) (1989), *Agency Theory, Information, and Incentives* (New York: Springer-Verlag).

BAMFORTH, N. (2000), 'Public Law', in P. Birks and F. Rose (eds.), *Lessons of the Swaps Litigation* (London: Mansfield Press).

BARKER, K. (1993), 'NHS Contracts, Restitution and the Internal Market', *Modern Law Review*, 56: 832–43.

—— CHALKLEY, M., MALCOMSON, J. M., and MONTGOMERY, J. (1997), 'Contracting in the National Health Service: Legal and Economic Issues', in Flynn and Williams (1997).

BARRON, A., and SCOTT, C. (1992), 'The Citizen's Charter Programme', *Modern Law Review*, 55: 526–46.

BAYLES, M. D. (1990), *Procedural Justice: Allocating to Individuals* (Dordrecht: Kluwer Academic Publishers).

BEALE, H., and DUGDALE, T. (1975), 'Contracts Between Businessmen: Planning and the Use of Contractual Remedies', *British Journal of Law and Society*, 2: 45–60.

BEATSON, J. (1995), 'Public Law Influences in Contract Law', in J. Beatson and D. Friedmann (eds.), *Good Faith and Fault in Contract Law* (Oxford: Clarendon Press).

BECKER, H. S. (1958), 'Problems of Inference and Proof in Participant Observation', *American Sociological Review*, 23: 652–60.

BLACKSTONE, W. (1765–9), *Commentaries on the Laws of England* (Oxford: Clarendon Press).

BRINDLE, D. (1996), 'Warning of "Meltdown" in NHS Market as Trusts Resist Squeeze', *The Guardian*, 7 May.

BROWN, L. N., and BELL, J. S. (1998), *French Administrative Law*, 5th edn. (Oxford: Clarendon Press).

BRUCE, A., and McCONNELL, A. (1995), *Changing Regimes of Accountability in Local Government and the NHS* (Glasgow: Policy Analysis Research Unit, Glasgow Caledonian University).

BRYMAN, A. (1988), '"Inside" Accounts and Social Research in Organizations', in A. Bryman (ed.), *Doing Research in Organizations* (London: Routledge).

BURGESS, R. G. (1984), *In the Field: an Introduction to Field Research* (London: Allen & Unwin).

CABINET OFFICE (1998a), *Better Quality Services: a Handbook on Creating Public/Private Partnerships through Market Testing and Contracting Out* (London: HM Government).

—— (1998b), *Next Steps Report 1998* (Cm 4273; London: TSO).

CAMPBELL, D., and FISKE, D. (1959), 'Convergent and Discriminant Validation by the Multitrait—Multimethod Matrix', *Psychological Bulletin*, 56: 81–105.

CAMPBELL, D., and VINCENT-JONES, P. (eds.) (1996), *Contract and Economic Organisation: Socio-Legal Initiatives* (Aldershot: Dartmouth).

CANE, P. (1996), *An Introduction to Administrative Law*, 3rd edn. (Oxford: Clarendon Press).

COFFEY, D., NOLAN, P., SAUNDRY, R., and SAWYER, M. (1997), 'Regulatory Change in the British Television Industry: Effects on Productivity and Competition', in Deakin and Michie (1997).

COLLINS, H. (1997), *The Law of Contract*, 3rd edn. (London: Butterworths).

—— (1999), *Regulating Contracts* (Oxford: Oxford University Press).

COMMITTEE ON THE CIVIL SERVICE (1968), *The Civil Service: Reports of the Committee, 1966–68* (Cmnd. 3638; London: HMSO).

CRAIG, P. P. (1999), *Administrative Law*, 4th edn. (London: Sweet & Maxwell).

DAINTITH, T. (1979), 'Regulation by Contract: The New Prerogative', *Current Legal Problems* 32: 41–64.

—— (1994), 'The Techniques of Government', in J. Jowell and D. Oliver (eds.), *The Changing Constitution*, 3rd edn. (Oxford: Clarendon Press).

—— and PAGE, A. (1999), *The Executive in the Constitution: Structure, Autonomy, and Internal Control* (Oxford: Oxford University Press).

DAVIES, A. C. L. (1999*a*), 'Accountability: A Public Law Analysis of National Health Service Contracts', D.Phil. Thesis (University of Oxford).

—— (1999*b*), 'Using Contracts to Enforce Standards: the Case of Waiting Times in the National Health Service', in McCrudden (1999*a*).

—— (2000), 'Don't Trust Me, I'm a Doctor: Medical Regulation and the 1999 NHS Reforms', *Oxford Journal of Legal Studies*, 20: 437–56.

DAY, P., and KLEIN, R. (1987), *Accountabilities: Five Public Services* (London: Tavistock).

DEAKIN, S., LANE, C., and WILKINSON, F. (1997), 'Contract Law, Trust Relations, and Incentives for Co-operation: a Comparative Study', in Deakin and Michie (1997).

—— and MICHIE, J. (eds.) (1997), *Contracts, Co-operation, and Competition: Studies in Economics, Management, and Law* (Oxford: Oxford University Press).

—— and MORRIS, G. S. (1998), *Labour Law*, 2nd edn. (London: Butterworths).

DENZIN, N. K., and LINCOLN, Y. S. (eds.) (1994), *Handbook of Qualitative Research* (California: Sage).

DEPARTMENT OF HEALTH (1989*a*), *Caring for People: Community Care in the Next Decade and Beyond* (Cm 849; London: HMSO).

—— (1989*b*), *Working for Patients* (Cm 555; London: HMSO).

—— (1991), *The Patients' Charter* (London: HMSO).

—— (1993), *Changing Childbirth* (London: HMSO).

—— (1994), *Managing the New NHS: Functions and Responsibilities in the New NHS* (London: Department of Health).

—— (1995), *The Patients' Charter*, 2nd edn. (London: HMSO).

—— (1997), *The New NHS: Modern, Dependable* (Cm 3807; London: TSO).

—— (1998*a*), *A First Class Service: Quality in the New NHS* (London: Department of Health).

—— (1998*b*), *Modernising Social Services: Promoting Independence, Improving Protection, Raising Standards* (Cm 4169; London: TSO).

—— (1999), *Supporting Doctors, Protecting Patients: a Consultation Paper on Preventing, Recognising and Dealing With Poor Clinical Performance of Doctors in the NHS in England* (London: Department of Health).

—— (2000), *Regulating Private and Voluntary Healthcare: Developing the Way Forward* (London: NHS Executive).

—— (2001), *Assuring the Quality of Medical Practice: Implementing Supporting Doctors, Protecting Patients* (Leeds: Department of Health).

DEPARTMENT OF THE ENVIRONMENT (1991), *Competing for Quality: Competition in the Provision of Local Services: a Consultation Paper* (London: Department of the Environment).

—— (1996), *Compulsory Competitive Tendering: Consultation on Proposals for Changes to the Framework* (London: Department of the Environment).

DEPARTMENT OF THE ENVIRONMENT, TRANSPORT AND THE REGIONS (1998*a*), *Local Government and the Private Finance Initiative: an Explanatory Note on the Private Finance Initiative and Public/Private Partnerships in Local Government* (London: DETR).

—— (1998*b*), *Modern Local Government: In Touch with the People* (Cm 4014; London: TSO).

—— (1999), *Local Government Act 1999: Part I: Best Value* (Circular 10/99; London: DETR).

DICEY, A. V. (1885), *Lectures Introductory to the Study of the Law of the Constitution* (London: Macmillan).

DONABEDIAN, A. (1980), *The Definition of Quality: Approaches to its Assessment* (Ann Arbor: Health Administration Press).

DORE, R. (1983), 'Goodwill and the Spirit of Market Capitalism', *British Journal of Sociology*, 34: 459–82.

DOWNES, T. A. (1996), 'Rethinking Penalty Clauses', in P. B. H. Birks (ed.), *Wrongs and Remedies in the Twenty-First Century* (Oxford: Clarendon Press).

DOWNS, A. (1967), *Inside Bureaucracy* (Boston: Little, Brown).

DWORKIN, R. (1986), *Law's Empire* (London: Fontana).

EFFICIENCY UNIT (OFFICE OF PUBLIC SERVICE AND SCIENCE) (1988), *Improving Management in Government: the Next Steps* (London: HMSO).

ENTHOVEN, A. C. (1985), *Reflections on the Management of the National Health Service: an American Looks at Incentives to Efficiency in Health Services Management in the UK* (London: Nuffield Provincial Hospitals Trust).

EUROPEAN COMMISSION (1996), *Public Procurement in the European Union: Exploring the Way Forward* (Brussels: European Commission).

—— (2000), *Proposal for a Directive of the European Parliament and of the Council on the Co-Ordination of Procedures for the Award of Public Supply Contracts, Public Service Contracts and Public Works Contracts* (COM (2000) 275 final; Brussels: European Commission).

EVANS, P. (1995), 'Members of Parliament and Agencies: Parliamentary Questions', in P. Giddings (ed.), *Parliamentary Accountability: a Study of Parliament and Executive Agencies* (Houndmills: Macmillan).

FENN, P., and VELJANOVSKI, C. (1988), 'A Positive Theory of Regulatory Enforcement', *Economic Journal*, 98: 1055–70.

FERLIE, E., ASHBURNER, L., and FITZGERALD, L. (1995), 'Corporate Governance and the Public Sector: Some Issues and Evidence from the NHS', *Public Administration*, 73: 375–92.

—— —— —— and PETTIGREW, A. (1996), *The New Public Management in Action* (Oxford: Oxford University Press).

FERNÁNDEZ MARTÍN, J. M. (1996), *The EC Public Procurement Rules: a Critical Analysis* (Oxford: Clarendon Press).

FISS, O. M. (1984), 'Against Settlement', *Yale Law Journal* 93: 1073–90.

FLYNN, R., and WILLIAMS, G. (eds.) (1997), *Contracting for Health: Quasi-Markets and the National Health Service* (Oxford: Oxford University Press).

—— —— and PICKARD, S. (1996), *Markets and Networks: Contracting in Community Health Services* (Buckingham: Open University Press).

—— —— —— (1997), 'Quasi-Markets and Quasi-Trust: The Social Construction of Contracts for Community Health Services', in Flynn and Williams (1997).

FONTANA, A., and FREY, J. H. (1994), 'Interviewing: The Art of Science', in Denzin and Lincoln (1994).

FOSTER, C. D. (1992), *Privatization, Public Ownership and the Regulation of Natural Monopoly* (Oxford: Blackwell).

—— and PLOWDEN, F. J. (1996), *The State under Stress: Can the Hollow State be Good Government?* (Buckingham: Open University Press).

FOX, A. (1974), *Beyond Contract: Work, Power and Trust Relations* (London: Faber & Faber).

FREDMAN, S., and MORRIS, G. S. (1989), *The State as Employer: Labour Law in the Public Services* (London: Mansell).

FREEDLAND, M. (1994), 'Government by Contract and Public Law', *Public Law*: 86–104.

—— (1995), 'Privatising Carltona: Part II of the Deregulation and Contracting Out Act 1994', *Public Law*: 21–6.

—— (1996), 'The Rule against Delegation and the Carltona Doctrine in an Agency Context', *Public Law*: 19–30.

—— (1998), 'Public Law and Private Finance: Placing the Private Finance Initiative in a Public Law Frame', *Public Law*: 288–307.

FREEMAN, M. (1995), *Alternative Dispute Resolution* (Aldershot: Dartmouth).

FRIDMAN, G. H. L. (1996), *The Law of Agency*, 7th edn. (London: Butterworths).

FRIED, C. (1981), *Contract as Promise: a Theory of Contractual Obligation* (Cambridge, Mass.: Harvard University Press).

FUKUYAMA, F. (1995), *Trust: The Social Virtues and the Creation of Prosperity* (London: Hamish Hamilton).

FULLER, L. L. (1969), *The Morality of Law*, rev. edn. (New Haven: Yale University Press).

—— (1978), 'The Forms and Limits of Adjudication', *Harvard Law Review* 92: 353–409.

GALLIGAN, D. J. (1986), *Discretionary Powers: a Legal Study of Official Discretion* (Oxford: Clarendon Press).

—— (1996), *Due Process and Fair Procedures: A Study of Administrative Procedures* (Oxford: Clarendon Press).

GAMBETTA, D. (ed.) (1988a), *Trust: Making and Breaking Cooperative Relations* (Oxford: Basil Blackwell).

—— (1988b), 'Can We Trust Trust?', in Gambetta (1988a).

GASTER, L. (1995), *Quality in Public Services: Managers' Choices* (Buckingham: Open University Press).

GIDDINGS, P. (2000), 'Ex p. Balchin: Findings of Maladministration and Injustice', *Public Law*: 201–4.

GLENNERSTER, H., MATSAGANIS, M., and OWENS, P., with HANCOCK, S. (1994), *Implementing GP Fundholding: Wild Card or Winning Hand?* (Buckingham: Open University Press).

GOETZ, C. J., and SCOTT, R. E. (1977), 'Liquidated Damages, Penalties and the Just Compensation Principle: Some Notes on an Enforcement Model and a Theory of Efficient Breach', *Columbia Law Review*, 77: 554–94.

GOODWIN, N. (1998), 'GP Fundholding', in J. Le Grand, N. Mays, and J.-A. Mulligan (eds.), *Learning from the NHS Internal Market: a Review of the Evidence* (London: King's Fund).

GREER, P. (1992), 'The Next Steps Initiative: an Examination of the Agency Framework Documents', *Public Administration*, 70: 89–98.

—— (1994), *Transforming Central Government: the Next Steps Initiative* (Buckingham: Open University Press).

GRIFFITHS, R. (1988), *Community Care: Agenda for Action* (London: HMSO).

HARDEN, I. (1992), *The Contracting State* (Buckingham: Open University Press).

—— (1993), 'Money and the Constitution: Financial Control, Reporting and Audit', *Legal Studies*, 13: 16–37.

—— and LEWIS, N. (1986), *The Noble Lie: the British Constitution and the Rule of Law* (London: Hutchinson).

HARLOW, C. (1980), '"Public" and "Private" Law: Definition without Distinction', *Modern Law Review*, 43: 241–65.

—— and RAWLINGS, R. (1997), *Law and Administration*, 2nd edn. (London: Butterworths).

HARRIS, B. V. (1992), 'The "Third Source" of Authority for Government Action', *Law Quarterly Review*, 109: 626–51.

HART, H. L. A. (1968), *Punishment and Responsibility* (Oxford: Clarendon Press).

HART, K. (1988), 'Kinship, Contract and Trust: the Economic Organization of Migrants in an African City Slum', in Gambetta (1988*a*).

HARTLEY, K., and HUBY, M. (1986), 'Contracting-Out Policy: Theory and Evidence', in J. A. Kay, C. P. Mayer, and D. Thompson (eds.), *Privatisation and Regulation: the UK Experience* (Oxford: Clarendon Press).

HAWKINS, K. (1984), *Environment and Enforcement: Regulation and the Social Definition of Pollution* (Oxford: Clarendon Press).

—— (ed.) (1992), *The Uses of Discretion* (Oxford: Clarendon Press).

HIRSCHMAN, A. O. (1970), *Exit, Voice, and Loyalty: Responses to Decline in Firms, Organizations, and States* (Cambridge, Mass.: Harvard University Press).

HIRST, P. (1995), 'Quangos and Democratic Government', *Parliamentary Affairs*, 48: 341–59.

HM GOVERNMENT (1991), *The Citizen's Charter: Raising the Standard* (Cmnd. 1599; London: HMSO).

HM TREASURY (1991), *Competing for Quality: Buying Better Public Services* (Cm. 1730; London: HMSO).

—— (1993), *The Private Finance Initiative: Breaking New Ground* (London: HM Treasury).

—— (1995*a*), *Government Accounting: a Guide on Accounting and Financial Procedures for the Use of Government Departments*, consolidated edn. (London: HMSO).

—— (1995*b*), *Private Opportunity, Public Benefit—Progressing the Private Finance Initiative* (London: HM Treasury).

—— (1997*a*), *Central Unit on Procurement Guidance No. 61: Contract Management* (London: HM Treasury).

—— (1997*b*), *Partnerships for Prosperity—the Private Finance Initiative* (London: HM Treasury).

—— (1997*c*), *Review of the Private Finance Initiative (Public/Private Partnerships), by Sir Malcolm Bates* (London: HM Treasury).

—— (1998*a*), *Modern Public Services for Britain: Investing in Reform: Comprehensive Spending Review: New Public Spending Plans 1999–2002* (Cm 4011; London: TSO).

—— (1998*b*), *Steering a Stable Course for Lasting Prosperity: Pre-Budget Report November 1998* (Cm 4076; London: TSO).

—— (1998*c*), *Public Services for the Future: Modernisation, Reform, Accountability: Comprehensive Spending Review: Public Service Agreements 1999–2002* (Cm 4181; London: TSO).

—— (1998*d*), *Procurement Policy Guidelines* (London: HM Treasury).

—— (1999*a*), *Modern Government, Modern Procurement* (London: HM Treasury).

—— (1999*b*), *Review of Civil Procurement in Central Government, by Peter Gershon* (London: HM Treasury).

—— (1999*c*), *Second Review of the Private Finance Initiative, by Sir Malcolm Bates* (London: HM Treasury).

—— (2000), *Public Private Partnerships: the Government's Approach* (London: TSO).

HODGSON, K. (and HOILE, R. W.) (1996), *Managing Health Service Contracts* (London: W. B. Saunders).

HOOD, C. (1991), 'A Public Management for All Seasons?', *Public Administration*, 69: 3–19.

—— (2000), *The Art of the State: Culture, Rhetoric and Public Management* (Oxford: Clarendon Press).

HOUSE OF COMMONS PUBLIC SERVICE COMMITTEE (1996), *Ministerial Accountability and Responsibility* (Second Report for Session 1995–6, HC 313; London: HMSO).

HOUSE OF COMMONS SELECT COMMITTEE ON HEALTH (1999), *Primary Care Groups* (Second Report for Session 1998–9, HC 153; London: TSO).

HOUSE OF COMMONS SOCIAL SERVICES SELECT COMMITTEE (1988), *The Future of the National Health Service*, (Fifth Report for Session 1987–8, HC 613; London: HMSO).

HUGHES, D. (1991), 'The Reorganisation of the National Health Service: the Rhetoric and Reality of the Internal Market', *Modern Law Review*, 54: 88–103.

—— MCHALE, J. V., and GRIFFITHS, L. (1996), 'Contracts in the NHS: Searching for a Model?', in Campbell and Vincent-Jones (1996).

—— —— —— (1997), 'Settling Contract Disputes in the National Health Service: Formal and Informal Pathways', in Flynn and Williams (1997).

HUNT, D. (1995), 'Worthwhile Bodies', *Parliamentary Affairs*, 48: 192–206.

HUNTER, R., and LEONARD, A. (1997), 'Sex Discrimination and Alternative Dispute Resolution: British Proposals in the Light of International Experience', *Public Law*: 298–314.

HUTTER, B. M. (1988), *The Reasonable Arm of the Law? The Law Enforcement Procedures of Environmental Health Officers* (Oxford: Clarendon Press).

HVIID, M. (1996), 'Relational Contracts and Repeated Games', in Campbell and Vincent-Jones (1996).

JACOB, J. M. (1991), 'Lawyers go to Hospital', *Public Law*: 255–81.

KAPLAN, P. R. (1977), 'A Critique of the Penalty Limitation on Liquidated Damages', *Southern California Law Review*, 50: 1055–90.

KENNEDY, D. (1996), 'Dorrell Orders New Intensive-Care Beds for Children', *The Times*, 30 May.

KIRKPATRICK, I., and MARTINEZ LUCIO, M. (1995), *The Politics of Quality in the Public Sector* (London: Routledge).

KLEIN, R. (1995), *The New Politics of the NHS*, 3rd edn. (London: Longman).

KRONMAN, A. T., and POSNER, R. A. (1979), *The Economics of Contract Law* (Boston: Little, Brown).

LAPSLEY, I., and LLEWELLYN, S. (1997), 'Statements of Mutual Faith: Soft Contracts in Social Care', in Flynn and Williams (1997).

LEONARD, J. (1990), 'The Impact of Affirmative Action Regulation and Equal Employment Law on Black Employment', *Journal of Economic Perspectives*, 4(4): 47–63.

LEVITT, R., WALL, A., and APPLEBY, J. (1995), *The Reorganized National Health Service*, 5th edn. (London: Chapman & Hall).

LONGLEY, D. (1990), 'Diagnostic Dilemmas: Accountability in the National Health Service', *Public Law*: 527–52.

—— (1993), *Public Law and Health Service Accountability* (Buckingham: Open University Press).

LORENZ, E. H. (1988), 'Neither Friends nor Strangers: Informal Networks of Subcontracting in French Industry', in Gambetta (1988a).

LOUGHLIN, M. (1992), *Administrative Accountability in Local Government* (York: Joseph Rowntree Foundation).

—— (1996), *Legality and Locality: The Role of Law in Central-Local Government Relations* (Oxford: Clarendon Press).

MACAULAY, S. (1963), 'Non-Contractual Relations in Business: a Preliminary Study', *American Sociological Review*, 28: 55–67.

MCBARNET, D., and WHELAN, C. (1991), 'The Elusive Spirit of the Law: Formalism and the Struggle for Legal Control', *Modern Law Review*, 54: 848–73.

—— (1997), 'Creative Compliance and the Defeat of Legal Control: the Magic of the Orphan Subsidiary', in K. Hawkins (ed.), *The Human Face of Law: Essays in Honour of Donald Harris* (Oxford: Clarendon Press).

MCCAHERY, J., PICCIOTTO, S., and SCOTT, C. (1993), *Corporate Control and Accountability: Changing Structures and the Dynamics of Regulation* (Oxford: Clarendon Press).

MCCRUDDEN, C. (ed.) (1999a), *Regulation and Deregulation: Policy and Practice in the Utilities and Financial Services Industries* (Oxford: Clarendon Press).

—— (1999b), 'Social Policy and Economic Regulators: Some Issues from the Reform of Utility Regulation', in McCrudden (1999a).

—— (1999c), 'International Economic Law and the Pursuit of Human Rights: a Framework for Discussion of the Legality of "Selective Purchasing" Laws under the WTO Government Procurement Agreement', *Journal of International Economic Law*, 2: 3–48.

—— (1999d), 'Human Rights Codes for Transnational Corporations: What Can the Sullivan and MacBride Principles Tell Us?', *Oxford Journal of Legal Studies*, 19: 167–201.

McEldowney, J. (1991), 'The National Audit Office and Privatisation', *Modern Law Review*, 54: 933–55.

—— (2000), 'The Control of Public Expenditure', in J. Jowell and D. Oliver (eds.), *The Changing Constitution*, 4th edn. (Oxford: Oxford University Press).

McHale, J., Hughes, D., and Griffiths, L. (1997), 'Conceptualizing Contractual Disputes in the National Health Service Internal Market', in Deakin and Michie (1997).

Macneil, I. R. (1974), 'The Many Futures of Contracts', *Southern California Law Review*, 47: 691–816.

—— (1978), 'Contracts: Adjustment of Long-Term Economic Relations under Classical, Neoclassical, and Relational Contract Law', *Northwestern University Law Review*, 72: 854–905.

Madison, J., Hamilton, A., and Jay, J. (1788), *The Federalist Papers*, ed. I. Kramnick (London: Penguin, 1987).

Marshall, G. (1986), *Constitutional Conventions: the Rules and Forms of Political Accountability* (Oxford: Clarendon Press).

Martin, J. E. (and Hanbury, H. G.) (1997), *Modern Equity*, 15th edn. (London: Sweet & Maxwell).

Miller, F. (1992), 'Competition Law and Anticompetitive Professional Behaviour Affecting Health Care', *Modern Law Review*, 55: 453–81.

Montgomery, J. (1997a), *Health Care Law* (Oxford: Oxford University Press).

—— (1997b), 'Control and Restraint in National Health Service Contracting', in Deakin and Michie (1997).

Morgan, P., and Potter, C. (1995), 'Professional Cultures and Paradigms of Quality in Health Care', in Kirkpatrick and Martinez Lucio (1995).

Morgan, R. (1993), 'Prisons Accountability Revisited', *Public Law*: 314–32.

National Audit Office (2000a), *The Cancellation of the Benefits Payment Card Project* (Session 1999–2000, HC 857; London: TSO).

—— (2000b), *Ministry of Defence Major Projects Report 2000* (Session 1999–2000, HC 970; London: TSO).

National Health Service Executive (1994), *Developing NHS Purchasing and GP Fundholding: Towards a Primary Care-Led NHS* (Leeds: NHSE).

—— (1995a), *An Accountability Framework for GP Fundholding* (Leeds: NHSE).

—— (1995b), *Priorities and Planning Guidance for the NHS: 1996–97* (Leeds: NHSE).

—— (1998), *The NHS Performance National Guide 1996–97* (Leeds: NHSE).

—— (1999a), *Regulating Private and Voluntary Healthcare: A Consultation Document* (Leeds: NHSE).

—— (1999*b*), *Regulating Private and Voluntary Healthcare: the Way Forward* (Leeds: NHSE).

NATIONAL HEALTH SERVICE MANAGEMENT EXECUTIVE (1989), *Contracts for Health Services: Operational Principles* (London: HMSO).

—— (1990), *Contracts for Health Services: Operating Contracts* (London: HMSO).

NELKEN, D. (1987), 'The Use of Contracts as a Social Work Technique', *Current Legal Problems*, 40: 207–32.

NISKANEN, W. A. (1971), *Bureaucracy and Representative Government* (Chicago, Il.: Aldine-Atherton).

NORMANTON, E. L. (1971), 'Public Accountability and Audit: a Reconnaissance', in Smith and Hague (1971).

OFFICE OF PUBLIC SERVICE AND SCIENCE (1993), *The Government's Guide to Market Testing* (London: HMSO).

OGUS, A. I. (1994), *Regulation: Legal Form and Economic Theory* (Oxford: Clarendon Press).

OLIVER, D. (1991), *Government in the United Kingdom: the Search for Accountability, Effectiveness and Citizenship* (Milton Keynes: Open University Press).

—— (1994), 'Law, Politics and Public Accountability: the Search for a New Equilibrium', *Public Law*: 238–53.

—— (1999), *Common Values and the Public-Private Divide* (London: Butterworths).

OSBORNE, D., and GAEBLER, T. (1992), *Reinventing Government* (Reading, Mass.: Addison Wesley).

O'TOOLE, B. J., and JORDAN, G. (eds.) (1995), *Next Steps: Improving Management in Government?* (Aldershot: Dartmouth).

ØVRETVEIT, J. (1995), *Purchasing for Health: a Multidisciplinary Introduction to the Theory and Practice of Health Purchasing* (Buckingham: Open University Press).

PITT, G. (1993), 'Justice in Dismissal: a Reply to Hugh Collins', *Industrial Law Journal*, 22: 251–68.

POWER, M. (1997), *The Audit Society: Rituals of Verification* (Oxford: Oxford University Press).

PRIME MINISTER (1994), *The Civil Service: Continuity and Change* (Cm 2627; London: HMSO).

—— (1995), *The Civil Service: Taking Forward Continuity and Change* (Cm 2748; London: HMSO).

PROPPER, C., and BARTLETT, W. (1997), 'The Impact of Competition on the Behaviour of National Health Service Trusts', in Flynn and Williams (1997).

PROSSER, T. (1986), *Nationalised Industries and Public Control: Legal, Constitutional and Political Issues* (Oxford: Basil Blackwell).

RADFORD, M. (1991), 'Auditing for Change: Local Government and the Audit Commission', *Modern Law Review*, 54: 912–32.

RANADE, W. (ed.) (1998), *Markets and Health Care: a Comparative Analysis* (London: Longman).

RAZ, J. (1977), 'The Rule of Law and its Virtue', *Law Quarterly Review*, 93: 195–211.

RHODES, R. A. W. (1997), *Understanding Governance: Policy Networks, Governance, Reflexivity and Accountability* (Buckingham: Open University Press).

RICHARDSON, G., OGUS, A., and BURROWS, P. (1983), *Policing Pollution: A Study of Regulation and Enforcement* (Oxford: Clarendon Press).

RICHARDSON, T., and TAYLOR, B. (1995), 'Contracts', in S. Henry and D. Pickersgill (eds.), *Making Sense of Fundholding* (Abingdon: Radcliffe Medical Press).

ROSS, S. (1973), 'The Economic Theory of Agency: The Principal's Problem', *American Economic Review*, 63: 134–9.

ROWAN-ROBINSON, J., WATCHMAN, P., and BARKER, C. (1990), *Crime and Regulation: A Study of the Enforcement of Regulatory Codes* (Edinburgh: T. & T. Clark).

SAKO, M. (1992), *Prices, Quality and Trust: Inter-Firm Relations in Britain and Japan* (Cambridge: Cambridge University Press).

SHAPIRO, M. (1981), *Courts—a Comparative and Political Analysis* (Chicago, Il.: University of Chicago Press).

SIMON, H. A. (1947), *Administrative Behavior* (New York: Macmillan).

SIMPSON, E. (1996), 'Ministerial Responsibility—a Legal View of the Policy/ Operational Distinction', in House of Commons Public Service Committee (1996).

SIMPSON, J. A., and WEINER, E. S. C. (eds.) (1989), *The Oxford English Dictionary*, 2nd edn. (Oxford: Clarendon Press).

SMITH, B. L. R., and HAGUE, D. C. (eds.) (1971), *The Dilemma of Accountability in Modern Government: Independence versus Control* (London: Macmillan).

SMITH, R. (1996), *Achieving Civil Justice: Appropriate Dispute Resolution for the 1990s* (London: Legal Action Group).

SMITH, R. G. (1994), *Medical Discipline: the Professional Conduct Jurisdiction of the General Medical Council, 1858–1990* (Oxford: Clarendon Press).

SOCIAL SERVICES INSPECTORATE (1999), *That's the Way the Money Goes: Inspection of Commissioning Arrangements for Community Care Services* (London: Department of Health).

SOCIO-LEGAL STUDIES ASSOCIATION (1993), *Statement of Ethical Practice.*

SPURGEON, P. (ed.) (1993), *The New Face of the NHS* (Harlow: Longman).

—— SMITH, P., STRAKER, M., DEAKIN, N., THOMAS, N., and WALSH, K. (1997), 'The Experience of Contracting in Health Care', in Flynn and Williams (1997).

STACEY, M. (1992), *Regulating British Medicine: the General Medical Council* (Chichester: Wylie).

STEWART, J. (1995), 'Appointed Boards and Local Government', *Parliamentary Affairs*, 48: 226–41.

STEWART, J. D. (1984), 'The Role of Information in Public Accountability', in A. Hopwood and C. Tomkins (eds.), *Issues in Public Sector Accounting* (Deddington: Philip Allan).

STINCHCOMBE, A. L. (1985), 'Contracts as Hierarchical Documents', in A. L. Stinchcombe and C. A. Heimer (eds.), *Organization Theory and Project Management: Administering Uncertainty in Norwegian Offshore Oil* (Oslo: Norwegian University Press).

THYNNE, I., and GOLDRING, J. (1987), *Accountability and Control: Government Officials and the Exercise of Power* (Sydney: Law Book Company).

Treasury Taskforce (undated), *How to Manage the Delivery of Long-Term PFI Contracts (Technical Note No. 6)* (London: HM Treasury).
Treitel, G. H. (1999), *The Law of Contract*, 10th edn. (London: Sweet & Maxwell).
Tullock, G. (1965), *The Politics of Bureaucracy* (Washington: Public Affairs Press).
Turpin, C. (1972), *Government Contracts* (Harmondsworth: Penguin).
—— (1989), *Government Procurement and Contracts* (Harlow: Longman).
—— (1999), *British Government and the Constitution: Text, Cases and Materials*, 4th edn. (London: Butterworths).
Vile, M. J. C. (1967), *Constitutionalism and the Separation of Powers* (Oxford: Clarendon Press).
Vincent-Jones, P. (1994a), 'The Limits of Contractual Order in Public Sector Transacting', *Legal Studies*, 14: 364–92.
—— (1994b), 'The Limits of Near-Contractual Governance: Local Authority Internal Trading Under CCT', *Journal of Law and Society*, 21: 214–37.
—— (1997), 'Hybrid Organization, Contractual Governance, and Compulsory Competitive Tendering in the Provision of Local Authority Services', in Deakin and Michie (1997).
—— (2000), 'Central-Local Relations under the Local Government Act 1999: a New Consensus?', *Modern Law Review*, 63: 84–103.
Wade, H. W. R. (1985), 'Procedure and Prerogative in Public Law', *Law Quarterly Review*, 101: 180–99.
—— and Forsyth, C. F. (2000), *Administrative Law*, 8th edn. (Oxford: Oxford University Press).
Walsh, K., and Davis, H. (1993), *Competition and Service: the Impact of the Local Government Act 1988* (London: HMSO).
—— Deakin, N., Smith, P., Spurgeon, P., and Thomas, N. (1997), *Contracting for Change: Contracts in Health, Social Care, and Other Local Government Services* (Oxford: Oxford University Press).
Webster, C. (1988), *The Health Services since the War, i. Problems of Health Care: the National Health Service before 1957* (London: HMSO).
—— (1996), *The Health Services since the War, ii. Government and Health Care: the British National Health Service 1958–1979* (London: TSO).
—— (1998), *The National Health Service: a Political History* (Oxford: Oxford University Press).
Weir, S. (1995), 'Quangos: Questions of Democratic Accountability', *Parliamentary Affairs*, 48: 306–22.
West, P. A. (1997), *Understanding the National Health Service Reforms: the Creation of Incentives?* (Buckingham: Open University Press).
Whittaker, S. (2000), 'Unfair Contract Terms, Public Services and the Construction of a European Conception of Contract', *Law Quarterly Review*, 116: 95–120.
Willett, C. (ed.) (1996), *Public Sector Reform and the Citizen's Charter* (London: Blackstone Press).

WILLIAMSON, O. E. (1979), 'Transaction-Cost Economics: the Governance of Contractual Relations', *The Journal of Law and Economics*, XXII: 233–61.

WISTOW, G., and BARNES, M. (1993), 'User Involvement in Community Care: Origins, Purposes and Applications', *Public Administration*, 71: 279–99.

—— KNAPP, M., HARDY, B., FORDER, J., KENDALL, J., and MANNING, R. (1996), *Social Care Markets: Progress and Prospects* (Buckingham: Open University Press).

WOODHOUSE, D. (1994), *Ministers and Parliament: Accountability in Theory and Practice* (Oxford: Clarendon Press).

ZIFCAK, S. (1994), *New Managerialism: Administrative Reform in Whitehall and Canberra* (Buckingham: Open University Press).

Index

Printed in the United Kingdom
by Lightning Source UK Ltd.
130099UK00001B/111/A